TIDINGS

THE ABSOLUTELY TRUE
STORY OF CHRISTMAS
(AS FAR AS I KNOW)

DJ O'TOOLE

Hibernia Progeny – Indianapolis

ISBN: 978-1-7377011-1-8 (paperback)
ISBN: 978-1-7377011-2-5 (ebook)

Library of Congress Control Number: 2021917839

Any references to historical events, real people, or real places are used fictitiously. Other names, characters, and places are the products of the author's imagination, and any resemblances to actual events or places or persons, living or dead, is entirely coincidental.

Cover art by RL Sather
Edited by Krystyl A Garrett

Printed in the United States of America, or at a POD site in your country.

First printing edition 2021.

Hibernia Progeny Publishing Company
Indianapolis, Indiana
hiberniaprogeny@email.com

www.djotoole.com

For Sheila

and

For all who ever listened to a Christmas song and wondered,
"How did *that* conversation go?"

Two things are infinite: the universe and human stupidity;
and I'm not sure about the universe.
Albert Einstein

A Note from the Author:

When you mix humor and religion, people sometimes get their panties in a bunch. Please remember this is a work of fiction. I am not challenging belief systems or making a religious statement. It's a story. I made it up. Some of the people and events in the story were real. I likely got the facts wrong here or there. Again, it's a story. It's fiction. It was written to entertain and nothing more. I hope you enjoy it.

TIDINGS

1

THE SHEPHERD

Extreme boredom interspersed with periods of mind-numbing monotony. That was how Simon would write his job description if ever given the chance. Simon had just turned fifteen. He nearly had a beard coming in. He was a man now, yet his father seemed to believe his only useful purpose was to tend the sheep. Simon had been tending sheep since he was old enough to pee standing up, or at least it seemed that way. It was so boring. There were never any predators, there were never any vagabonds, and worst of all, there were never pretty girls needing a heroic rescue. There were only hills, sheep, and sheep shit, and more hills, and more sheep, and more sheep shit. This was life in Marisa, located between Gaza and Hebron, more or less. Hours felt like days, every day was the same, every evening was the same.

On rare occasions a platoon of Romans would be marching across the fields in the distance. Simon would watch them warily. They could be cruel for no apparent reason whatsoever. They slaughtered and cooked eight or nine of his cousin's sheep a few years earlier. Claimed it was their right, by order of Herod or Augustus or some other governor. They beat his cousin when he objected but didn't kill him. At least there was that. They went on about their business afterward and never returned. Because of that, and similar stories both real and exaggerated from friends and relatives, Simon would hide when he saw the soldiers. It was a little tougher to hide the sheep, but there were ways if you saw them coming early enough. Knowing every nook and cranny for miles had its advantages.

Tonight, there was nothing. Silence. Even the sheep seemed quiet. The sun had gone down a few minutes earlier, and he could see a few stars as twilight approached. One of the ways he passed the time was counting the stars in the evening as they appeared. It was a game. Each evening he would see how many he could count before there were too many to count. They appeared slowly as dusk settled. Because of the repetition of doing this night after night, he knew where to look for the first twenty or thirty. He had to be quick. Before he knew it, the stars were all out, and the game would be over. The brightest ones were obviously first, then the dimmer ones came quick as rabbits. He made it to eighty-two once; that was his record. He stopped when he saw more stars than he could tally in his head.

Simon started counting, spinning left, then right, then left again. Seventeen, eighteen, spin and point. Turn left, twenty-six, turn around, twenty-seven. Those he had memorized, now he had to scan. And they were coming quicker. Thirty-five, thirty-six, and there was another, thirty-seven. He counted and turned, turned and counted.

Then he stopped.

Where did that one come from? There was a very bright star to the northeast, not one he had memorized, yet it was brighter than the others.

He assumed he was just dizzy and had confused his directions. He rubbed his eyes and looked at the fields to get his bearings.

Then he stopped again.

All the sheep were lying down, as if resting. They weren't asleep— they had their heads up. He scanned the fields. It wasn't just some of the sheep, it was all of them. Simon may have coined the phrase "WTF" that night, we will never know for sure. He certainly understood the sentiment. Let's just assume he did, in fact, invent the phrase.

This is just weird, he thought. *What's going on?* Then he looked around quickly, perhaps there *was* a predator. No wait— they wouldn't lay down for a predator.

"I just don't get it," he said aloud to no one. Then he remembered the bright star. There it was, to the northeast. *That's just weird too. I swear it wasn't there last night.* Simon was confused. Granted, he was fifteen, and fifteen-year-old Judaean "men" with "almost a real beard" were easy to confuse. However, this was his element. He had tended sheep for as long as he could remember, and never had he seen anything like this.

A trumpet sounded, followed by several more, then harps and a chorus. The sound was so abrupt and loud, he fell over backward in fright.

"What the fuck?" he yelled (We agreed that was his line, did we not?).

Simon saw a light growing brighter just above the hill to his left. It wasn't the star; it was more of a... glow. Terrified, he crawled backward like a crab. The floating glow began to take the shape of a man. Simon started crying. He had never been so frightened. He tried to get to his feet to run. He stumbled, lost his sandals, and fell. Then he was up and running faster than he ever thought he could, barefoot across the rocky terrain.

"Simon."

The voice came from behind him, but also from everywhere. Terror filled him. Even though he ran, the music from the trumpets seemed to be all around him. His heart was pounding, and he was breathing too hard.

"Simon... stop running," said the voice. Simon hesitated and slowed his pace. He looked over his shoulder, and he stopped running. He also stopped crying.

"Wait a minute...how'd you know my name?" Simon turned and asked the floating, glowing man.

"Behold, I bring great news from the Lord our God!" the glow proclaimed. The man-features were becoming clearer, but the glow was extremely bright, causing Simon to squint. "Fear not, for I have been sent from Heaven to bring news of hope. I bring tidings of comfort and joy. I have been sent to...Hey, you little shit! Did you just throw a rock at me?"

"I don't like Romans!" Simon shouted.

"I'm not a Roman. Stop it!"

Simon threw another rock. The rock passed through the middle of the glowing, floating man.

"Stop it. I'm trying to tell you something important so you can spread the word."

"Are you a ghost? Why are you floating? Where is the music coming from? What kind of Roman are you?" Simon's mind was searching for answers. His mouth kept spitting questions.

"If you stop asking questions, I'll tell..."

"Why are you glowing? Good Lord! Are those wings? Can you really fly? Are you going to eat my sheep? Why are you so bright?" Simon continued, shielding his eyes with his hand.

"SILENCE!" the angel commanded loudly. Very loudly.

Simon stopped asking... stopped thinking... began trembling... and wet himself a little. He sat on the grass and began to cry again.

"Oh perfect," the angel muttered. "I get the crybaby with the weak bladder.

"Cut it, guys," the angel said much louder as he glanced upward, making the knife-hand back-and-forth at the neck gesture. The music trailed off awkwardly. The angel looked at Simon and shook his head. He sighed, and then sat cross-legged in front of Simon.

"Hey, kid, it will be okay. I'm not here to hurt you or take your stuff. I'm not a Roman. I don't care for that lot either. The Boss sent me to give you a message." The angel's voice was gentle.

"The Boss?" Simon asked. He was still sobbing.

"Yeah, God. The one you read about all the time. The one you pray to. The one you go to Synagogue for. The one that does shit you can't understand but you roll with it because He probably has a reason. God."

Simon stopped crying and looked at the angel. "God? Has a message? For me? Shit! Am I in trouble?"

The angel smiled. "No, kid, you're fine. He likes you, thinks your star game is pretty cool. He told me He moves stars now and then to mess with you. Trust me, He doesn't pay that kind of attention to most kids. He likes you. That's why He sent me. He'd like you to do something for Him."

Simon's eyes got bigger as he began to understand. "God wants a favor?" He beamed.

The angel smiled too. "Something like that."

"What do I get out of it?"

The angel's smile faded. "Seriously? You're talking face-to-face with a fucking angel. God chose you out of millions of others, and you want to know what you get out of it? Un-fucking-believable." The angel threw up his hands and shook his head.

Simon fell to his knees. "I'm sorry, I didn't really mean it. I love God. I can't believe any of this is really happening. Please forgive me."

The angel held up his hands to stop Simon. "It's okay. This must be a strange day for you. And I already gave you the answer to your question. What you get is the knowledge that God likes you. That has to be pretty comforting, I would think. He *loves* everyone, we all know that. But *like* is a different matter. I know some angels that assume God likes them, but they don't *know* He likes them. You get to *know*. How cool is that?"

Simon felt warm as a grin broke out across his face.

"So, here's the deal, kid. Pay attention. God wants you to listen carefully to what I'm about to tell you. Then He wants you to spread the word. He knows other people like you, too, and that they'll listen to you." The angel winked at Simon with a nod and a smile. "God has decided to have a son. A human son. And His son will grow to spread the Word of God and save the world. Between you and me, this is going to change everything. Not everyone is going to be happy about it, either. Anyway, His son will be born in the City of David."

Excited, Simon shouted, "Like the prophecy in the Torah!"

"Yes! That's it exactly! I'm glad you understand." The angel was smiling. "Now, do you remember that star you saw? The one you didn't recognize? God just threw that one up. It's bright now so you can find it. Soon it will get even brighter. It will point the way to where the Little Boss will be born. While you and I are talking, hundreds of other angels are talking to hundreds of other shepherds. You will not be alone sharing this wonderful news. Soon everyone will have the chance to go and see for themselves."

God likes me, Simon thought. He couldn't stop grinning.

"Will I get to meet God's son?" Simon asked.

"That's up to the Boss, little man. I really don't know."

Simon didn't care. *God likes me*. Simon spent the rest of his days with a slight smile on his face.

***

Simon told his father what happened. His father examined Simon's head to make sure he hadn't fallen and cracked his skull. His father was skeptical, but who wouldn't be? He tried to gauge whether Simon was messing with his old man. Simon persisted in telling the story. His father noticed that with each retelling, the story stayed exactly the same. Simon told anyone who would listen. Strangers at the market, close friends at synagogue, his Rabbi, the neighbors, his cousins... it didn't matter. Simon was following orders. And God liked him.

The people, like Simon's father, were skeptical at first. Simon held his ground and told the truth. The people started talking. Some were curious while others just mocked the boy. But Simon wasn't the only voice telling the tale. Other shepherds from nearby villages were soon telling similar stories. They told of angels visiting them in the fields, of glorious music from Heaven, of angels proclaiming the coming of the Son of God. As weeks passed, more and more stories were told of shepherds being visited by angels. The people who heard the stories noticed the bright star that they could see with their own eyes. Skepticism gave way to curiosity. Curiosity gave way to optimism. Optimism gave way to hope. The word spread across Judaea. It spread across Samaria. It spread across Galilee. It even spread into Decapolis and Nabataeans. The people were talking. And they believed.

2

JOSEPH

"Joseph!... JOSEPH!" Asher was angry. Again.

Joseph heard Asher calling his name in the distance. He paused for a moment and closed his eyes. *Perfect, this is exactly what I need,* he thought sardonically. He opened his eyes and looked down at the board he was planing. *I probably spend more time than I should making things perfect, perhaps I should settle for good enough.* He knew it would never happen. His father had taught him at an early age to make the most out of every opportunity to impress people. If you're going to craft things for paying customers, his father had told him, make sure they know it was your hand that crafted it, and that it is the best they would ever see. Joseph assumed all sons find themselves at odds with their fathers sooner or later, his teenage years were proof enough for him; however, for the most part, he and his father got along well now.

"Joseph!" Asher's voice was getting closer. It was loud with sharp edges. Asher must be in one of his moods.

But then, when is he not? Joseph smirked at the thought.

Joseph often wondered how his relationship with his father would have grown had he stayed in the Jerusalem area. The two were finally beginning to have friendly conversations when Joseph decided to move to Nazareth. Joseph was experienced enough as a carpenter to suggest things his father had not tried or considered. His father was always eager to share his woodworking wisdom with his son. They were beginning to understand one another. So, when the chance to work in Nazareth presented itself, Joseph was torn. His father convinced him to seize the opportunity. Ultimately, he was glad he did, but that did little to keep his mind from wondering how it would have been. There were times, especially early on, when he had missed his family terribly. It was difficult being in a strange new place, not knowing many people. Work kept his mind focused and clear during the day, but the nights alone were very long. The loneliness was unbearable at times. However, as weeks turned to months, he met more and more people, and the loneliness eased. Within a few months, he had a strong group of friends and things were much better. *It's funny how quickly time passes.* He had been in Nazareth nearly four years now.

"Joseph!" Asher called again. Asher was technically his boss. In reality he was more of a supervisor with family connections, but Joseph always tried to show the man the respect his position deserved. Joseph knew what Asher wanted to discuss. Asher was about two-thirds the size of a normal man. This was an important fact to note considering the pending "discussion." It was not the first time the two had had words on this very topic.

"How many times are we going to do this, Joseph? Seriously, I'd really like to know. It seems to me that we have this issue on every single job." Asher had his hands on his hips with his head tilted slightly. Joseph rolled his eyes.

"Yes, Asher, we do have this conversation every time," Joseph responded, "which means one of us is not listening to the other."

"Well at least you're willing to admit you don't listen!"

Joseph sighed and closed his eyes. *How does this man still have a job? Oh yes, an uncle who owns the company.*

"That's not exactly what I said," Joseph replied.

"I don't care what you said. What I care about is the fact that you keep wasting materials on these projects. You make everything too big! Your entire team makes everything too big. I sometimes wonder if you do this just to piss me off. Is that it?" Asher was literally spitting as he spoke. The evidence was resting on his beard.

Joseph decided it was time for some brutal honesty. He had danced around the obvious in past conversations about this topic. The little man was not getting it.

"Asher, look at my arm." Joseph's right arm was extended with his elbow bent at a 90-degree angle. "THIS..." Joseph pointed to his elbow then his hand, "...IS A CUBIT! This is how we measure things. It's a fairly standard unit of measure for most people. My cousin is a very large man. He knows that the distance between his hand and elbow are a little longer than most, so he adjusts to compensate."

Asher looked agitated and tapped his foot impatiently. "What's your point?"

"My point? You must be kidding. My point, miniature human, is that measuring with *your* tiny arms is going to make *everything* seem too big!" Joseph said the words too quickly, they were out of his mouth before he could filter. Asher's face was becoming pomegranate red. Joseph knew his honesty would come back to bite him.

"How dare you! I am every bit as big as any of you!"

Joseph figured he might as well go all in. He stepped up to within a foot of Asher and looked down at his face. He was easily an entire head taller.

"Really? Are we sure we're not deluding ourselves? Maybe just a little?" Joseph could not hold back the smile as he said the words.

Asher's eyes narrowed, and his hands turned to fists. "I would fire you this instant if there were any decent carpenters in this God-forsaken town.

Fine, you don't like me much, you feel like you have to rebel against me and make little jokes."

Joseph smiled at the unintentional pun.

"Why? Because you're jealous of me. I get it. It makes sense. I only hope you can come to grips with the fact that I have my position because of my skill and experience. Someday you'll be in a similar position. I hope you'll have to deal with some upstart shit that thinks he is better than he really is!"

***

"The king's going a bit mad," Martin said to Joseph and Roger as they wrapped up their workday. "The man was a brilliant leader, he built fabulous palaces, churches, and ports. But let's be honest, Herod's been king for what?... thirty years? I think time is catching up with him. He may be going senile or just crazy."

"He's a foreigner and shouldn't be king. My dad said it from the time I was a wee shit and I agree with him," Roger interjected. It did not fit with the current conversation, but the other guys on the crew barely noticed. Roger was Roger. He could be a little dark cloud at times. The xenophobia was a new twist though.

Joseph gave a quick head tilt but ignored Roger's new-found prejudice and continued with Martin. "You keep saying that he's mad, but what evidence do you have? I mean, other than killing two of his sons... and his wife?"

"Other than killing his own family? Are you serious?"

"Kings *always* do shit like that, they're kings! Spoiled jealous little twats that spend their lives having servants wipe their asses," Joseph replied. "Someone pisses on their manna, and they wipe out an entire village! That doesn't make them crazy. It just makes them spiteful little bitches."

"I hear he's not even Jewish. His mother isn't a Jew so he can't be. She's an Arab. His father 'converted' or some nonsense." Roger made finger quotes.

The others paused briefly, giving Roger a blank and somewhat confused look.

Martin pushed on. "I have a perfect example for you: did you hear what happened at the new temple last week? A couple teachers convinced some students to take down the golden eagle above the entrance, the one Herod put there for the Romans. After all, we Jews are not fans of golden idols. Herod had the teachers and students involved dragged into the street where he had them burned alive! Who does that? Sane people don't do that. Sick bastard."

"Okay," Joseph conceded, "that's messed up. I hadn't heard about that."

"He's crazy," Martin said, "and so is his sister. They say she whispers poison thoughts in his ear to get him to do her dirty work, but I digress. His health is deteriorating. He looks like he's in pain and seems angry all the time."

This was true. The others nodded in agreement.

"I'd be angry, too. Remember how years ago Herod was buddies with Marc Antony? Then Antony hooked up with the Egyptian chick? Next thing you know, she gets nearly half of Judaea, and Herod loses half his kingdom!" Joseph said, his hands in the air for emphasis.

"Don't much like the Romans either," Roger again.

"Seriously?" Joseph looked at Roger. "None of us do, but they run the entire world. I wouldn't throw that bit around too much if I were you."

Martin shook his head and smiled. "He got the kingdom back after that shit-storm passed. The point is, he was a good king and did good things for our parents and for us, but the last several years he's been losing his shit. He's making bad decisions and killing way more people than he ever has in the past."

"Joe, he's got a point. Things have gotten strange. The cheese might be sliding off Herod the Great's cracker," Roger said.

Joseph smiled because it was the first thing Roger said that had anything to do with the current conversation, and because Roger had such a unique way to phrase things.

"You're probably on to something," Joseph said as he laid down his saw, "but you probably shouldn't say it when the Romans are around."

Joseph wandered to the door of the public building. It was nearly complete; his crew was finishing up the trim work and building a few benches for the meeting hall.

Despite being a carpenter himself, Joseph's father was less than thrilled that Joseph had chosen the same path. His father was coming to grips with it the last few years but would have preferred Joseph were more like his brothers. His brothers were doctors and accountants, except for Maury who was an actor. His father hated that even more. "Joseph, be a doctor." "Joseph, be an accountant." "Joseph, be a lawyer." *Sorry Dad, this is Israel... we're all Jewish. We can't all be doctors and lawyers and accountants.* He ran his hand over his beard and considered this line of thought. *Still, we live in a world of brick and stone, and I work with wood. Good career move, maybe Dad was right.*

Joseph walked back to the other two. "You guys will be there, right?"

"By 'there', you mean your next confrontation with Asher, right? Or are you still obsessed with this crazy wedding idea? Wedding feasts are so dreadfully boring," Roger said, suppressing a smile. "Of course, we'll be there. We wouldn't miss this for anything. In fact, it's all Maggie can talk about these days."

"Same with my wife," Martin said. "Yes, we'll be there, too, as long as you'll be serving wine or mead or beer. Not sure I can stomach a whole evening with you sober. It's bad enough working with you day in and day out."

"You guys are both idiots." Joseph threw a rag at them. "Thank you."

Joseph was to make his marriage official in two days. He was looking forward to it, too. He was in love, the big stupid kind, the kind that makes you forget how hard things are. He and Mary were good together. No, they were great together. Everyone could see how perfect they were for each other.

"Let's wrap this up and go grab a drink before we head home for the night. I'm buying," Joseph said. These were his two best friends in the world.

"Ooh, Caesar is breaking into the vault to grace the peasants. Yes, my liege, at your service," Martin laughed. "It's about time you bought a drink!"

"Shut up before I change my mind, dumbass," Joseph replied, smiling. "You know I've been saving silver for nearly a year."

They wrapped up their work for the day and secured their tools. It was early evening and Nazareth had many fine eating establishments. These three were not interested in fine restaurants - they were interested in Micah's.

Micah had taken over his father's eatery about the time Joseph, Roger, and Martin were becoming carpenters. Micah may have been the smart one when it came to choosing careers. The tavern was not a sophisticated place; it rarely saw rich patrons or government officials. It was a local dive where everyone knew everyone else. It was home. Joseph and his friends would often enjoy wine and beer, olives and figs, fish and goat, and more wine and more beer. Micah was a natural at running the business. In all honesty, he was better than his father before him.

They walked through the dirt streets for several blocks until they could see Micah's just ahead. They entered and sat themselves at a table in the corner.

"No! ... No! ... Out, you bastards! We don't serve your kind." Micah, always with a smile, had greeted them the same way for years. "I suppose you're not leaving without a drink? Fine, I'll get the wine. But you'll be paying me this time! I'm not a charity!" Micah loved to pretend to be inconvenienced by his friends.

"JOSEPH IS BUYING!" Martin yelled to Micah.

Micah stopped and turned. "Which of you two morons hit him with a shovel? He's clearly not himself. First, he promises to marry the little waif girl, now he's throwing money around like he has some? Is he ill?" Micah asked with a wry grin.

"Bite me, asshole!" Joseph laughed. "Waif girl? That's funny, I can't wait to tell her you said so."

"Now hold on a sec... I was just playing. The last thing I need is to deal with an angry Mary. I'd rather get questioned by the fucking Romans."

"Go get some wine, and pull up a chair. Let's get down to some serious business." Joseph was happy. Life was good. He had fabulous friends, a good job, and he was going to marry the girl of his dreams. *Thanks, God. Not sure what I did to deserve all of this, but thank You.*

The men stayed a little longer than they intended. It was getting dark out. They laughed and drank. They drank and laughed. The exchanges were mostly juvenile. The women reading this know exactly what I'm talking about... men still think crotch trauma is funny.

"Martin, is it true that when your first girlfriend had to the chance to see you naked, she chose to be stoned to death instead?" Roger asked laughing.

Joseph laughed in mid-sip, and his drink came out his nose.

Micah chimed in. "I heard she even picked out the stones and passed them out to the crowd."

"Fuck you both," Martin grinned. "And it wasn't my girlfriend, it was when I was shagging Roger's mum. And they didn't stone her, they all felt sorry for her. She had suffered enough raising such a stupid ugly little monkey."

They all laughed.

Roger shook his head. "A long, long time ago, when Martin's mom was simply old..."

"How long ago was that?" Martin was determined to head this one off.

"Hundreds of years ago, days of yore. Now stop interrupting me," Roger replied.

"Days of my what?" Martin had him.

"Not your anything, days of yore."

"Days of my what?"

"Not *your*, yore. Days of yore."

"I heard you, your what?"

"No, days of YORE!"

"Days of my what?"

"YOOOOOORRRRE!"

"You're obviously fucking with me."

"I give up," Roger said.

Martin stood with his arms raised above his head and took a theatrical bow.

"Well," Roger said, "I'd better get home to Maggie. She misses me when I'm not there."

The other three laughed uncontrollably.

"Yes, I'm sure she just sits in the corner and weeps until you get home," Martin said laughing. Roger's wife was a strong-willed woman with a wonderful sense of humor. They all liked her a great deal. She was not the type to worry or fret if Roger was a few hours late. It was quite clear to all of them that Roger could only stay away from his wife for so long. He was a bit whipped, as it were, but in the very best way possible.

"I should head home too. Thanks for another fun evening." Joseph jabbed at his friend. "Martin, you're a dick. Just saying. Micah, what do I owe you?" Joseph settled his bill with Micah and headed out the door with Roger.

3

DIVINE INTERVENTION

Nazareth, much like most of the larger cities, could be dangerous at night. There were always a certain number of misguided souls who liked to prey on the weak and helpless, or in this case, the drunk. Three such shady characters were assessing their prospects in an alley. Shaking down a couple of friends out relaxing after work would be an easy way to get some silver. They had done so countless times before. Anyone foolish enough to fight back would get their throats slit.

None of their actions go unnoticed. God sees everything. Sometimes He allows things to play out as they will. Other times, like now, He does not.

God called for Michael, the head of God's army. You might ask why God needs an army and that would be an excellent question, but not one I would attempt to answer. Nonetheless, God has an army of angels and Michael is their leader. The reason he is their leader is fairly easy to understand: He is one hundred percent bad-ass. Mike Tyson with Cus D'Amato bad-ass. The Wayne Gretzky and Michael Jordan of bad-asses. This is the same Michael that made Lucifer whine and cry like a little bitch. Michael is good at his job, and he likes it. He still holds the position today. Ask Jordan or Gretzky how hard *that* is. Being the best for ten or fifteen years is impressive. Being the best for millennia? That's Michael.

"Yes, my Lord. You called?" Michael looked God in the eye. God really liked that, so few were willing to look Him in the eye.

"Thanks for coming, Mike. I have a special assignment for you. As we've discussed, I have plans for Mary and Joseph. They're important to Me and I would like to keep them safe. Some morons down in Nazareth are going to try to mess with Joseph tonight. I would greatly appreciate it if you could make sure that didn't happen."

"No problem, Sir, I'd be happy to help. Would You like to welcome them home?" Michael asked.

"No, you don't need to kill them, I just need them to back off Joseph tonight. Feel free to break some bones, though. These shit heads have been pissing Me off lately."

Michael smiled. "My pleasure, Sir."

***

Joseph and Roger walked down the quiet side streets of Nazareth. They were not stupid drunk. They had that happy glow buzz that you get with a few drinks with your friends. Both were young and strong, but neither were particularly gifted as fighters. Martin was a decent fighter, but he stayed back with Micah. The two were deep in conversation about work, women, Rome, that weird bright star to the south. They were not paying attention to their surroundings. They did not notice the three shadows approaching them from behind.

The shadows moved silently. The drunk morons were just ahead. They likely did not have much silver, but anything was better than nothing. The three slipped through the dark, unseen by anyone but the alley cats. They had been working together long enough that they did not need to speak. Each knew what to do with just a glance from the others. They drew their knives. It made the convincing much easier. Their targets were large enough that they may actually have to use them. Killing was never a first choice but it was better than getting caught or killed yourself. At this point it was just another part of their business. They were getting close now. It was nearly time to strike.

Michael enjoyed being underestimated. It made the game that much more fun. He would often appear as the meek and frail. The reactions were much more entertaining. He had once appeared as a toddler. That was a special occasion for a particularly horrible human being who was to be brought home. He watched the shadow men approach. They were louder than they thought they were, but for the most part they appeared to be good at their chosen profession.

A small beggar stepped out of the darkness between the shadow men and their prey. The beggar looked at all three of them. He seemed to have no trouble seeing them in the shadows. He was small and frail, dressed in rags. He appeared to be very old. There was something about his eyes, though. They were sharp and alive. Menacing.

"Please change your minds," the beggar asked the approaching thugs in a very small, frail voice. "This will end badly for you." The beggar grinned. He knew they would keep coming. They always did. He could ask them one hundred times to just leave, and one hundred times it would play out the same. Good decisions never go hand-in-hand with a life of crime.

The thieves' targets walked around a corner a block ahead and disappeared out of sight. One thug glanced at each of his partners, signaling he would deal with the little man in front of them. He quickly stepped up to the old man and clamped a strong hand over the beggar's mouth. He raised the blade to cut the little annoyance's throat before their prey became wise to them. No one would think twice about finding a dead beggar in an alley.

A lightning quick hand came up and grabbed the thief's wrist, twisting it while applying pressure with the thumb. The pain was excruciating.

Another hand shot up and struck his throat hard before he could make a sound. His eyes were wide, and he could not breathe nor make a sound. His throat was swelling. His wrist twisted until it snapped. He was struck three times in the face and twice in the ribs. He could taste blood and feel his broken teeth with his tongue. He was completely disoriented and confused. He felt himself airborne until he hit the wall. Then he felt nothing. He was out cold.

The other two stopped and stared. Their comrade was just tossed about like a rag doll by a tiny, frail, old man. The little man just stood staring at them with those intense, piercing eyes. They forgot about the two drunks they had been following, who went on about their business, chatting like school girls, unaware that anything was happening behind them.

They rushed the little man with blades ready to strike. Instead of fear, they saw him smile. That was difficult to compute, that was just wrong. Their momentum carried them forward, but both had a split-second realization that things were not as they appeared. The old man moved faster than they could follow with their eyes. The hands holding the knives were bent at impossible angles with surprising strength. Both cried out as their wrists shattered. Then the beatings began. Neither could remember a time in their lives when they were hit as hard or as violently. Losing consciousness was a gift.

Before the last one passed out from pain and shock, Michael brought his face nose to nose with the would-be attacker. "I tried to warn you. Pay attention to your elders, you little shit. You should really consider another line of work. Don't make me come back here for you." Michael struck him once more. He stood and assessed his work. The three were collapsed in awkward piles of broken flesh that would heal in time, though probably not completely. *That was fun. Maybe next time I'll be an old woman.* He chuckled to himself as he transformed back to his normal form. The rags turned into a flowing white robe and his face turned from old to ageless. He stretched his wings wide and took one last look around before ascending.

Joseph and Roger continued walking and talking. At one point they thought they heard some yelling, but this was Nazareth, people were always yelling. They worked their way back to their homes. Tomorrow would be another day of work. The day after would be Joseph's wedding day.

4

MARY

Mary lay in bed on her side and stared at the wall. She had been awake for what seemed like hours. It was dark when she first woke but it was well past sunrise now. So many thoughts were running through her mind. Her marriage was to become official today. It started nearly a year ago when her father and Joseph signed the marriage contract. Among other things, the contract spelled out the Bride Price that Joseph must pay her father for her hand in marriage to offset the loss of someone who helps around the house. Joseph had been working hard since then to raise the silver for the Bride Price. He contacted her father last week. Joseph was ready to fulfill the contract, and her father scheduled today to finalize the wedding.

The signing of the contract made them officially "betrothed", but the marriage wasn't considered official until the Chuppah. The Chuppah was a slightly stranger custom where Joseph would pay her father the Bride Price, then Mary and Joseph would go to a room and consummate the marriage with specifically chosen friends waiting outside as witnesses. Awkward. Once they have done the deed, there's the more embarrassing step of presenting the bloody "proof of virginity" cloth to the friends waiting outside. Even more awkward. Mary thought this was a silly tradition. She had never personally known of anyone who was not a virgin on her wedding day. Those were always rumors and hearsay. It must be one of those old man rules that no longer made sense. Some grandpa man must have made up a story that his cousin's son "nearly married a harlot! We need to make a new rule to protect these upstanding young men." She mimicked an old man voice in her head as she had the thought. It made her smile.

Once the stupid cloth business was taken care of, they would be off to the wedding feast, with a procession of family and friends parading the streets to Joseph's house. The food and drink would likely last late into the night, that would be the real party. From that point on, she would live with Joseph. That also made her smile.

There was much to do beforehand. She could hear her mother trying to be quiet in the next room as she readied for the day. Her father was probably up and in the fields with the livestock. He would pass his duties to a neighbor or friend as it got closer to the chuppah and wedding feast. Her parents genuinely liked Joseph, as did everyone else, even her sisters. She felt warm as she thought about him. She was happy to her soul.

Mary was in her late teens but in many ways acted much older. Unlike some of her bolder friends, she had very little experience with boys. She had always been fascinated by them but terrified as well. She was not shy, per se. She was open and gregarious when with her friends or people at synagogue but had great difficulty speaking to boys. Get her face-to-face with a boy and all words would escape her. Joseph was different. Something in his eyes just set her at ease. He was a few years older and seemed like nothing ever bothered him. He had lived in Nazareth for several years now, although he and his family were originally from some small town near Jerusalem. Mary and Joseph attended the same synagogue. He was easy to talk to, and it was easy to spend hours and hours together. They had similar interests and shared many of the same friends. In fact, Mary's best friend Maggie was married to Joseph's friend Roger.

Maggie and Roger had been officially married for over a year now. Maggie had explained in great detail what was expected from a wife. Mary giggled a lot and blushed often, but she wanted to know everything. At first sex was incredibly awkward, Maggie had told Mary. It was somewhat uncomfortable the first few times, and she was afraid she was doing it wrong. Mary was not sure she wanted to ever get married after hearing Maggie explain it.

Maggie had confessed these concerns to Roger, and he seemed relieved. It turned out he thought he might be doing it wrong as well. Once the two were open about it with each other, it started to get really good. Stupid good. Could-not-keep-their-hands-off-each-other good, to the point where Maggie could barely think about anything else, let alone talk about anything else. Now Mary was intrigued by the thought, although very nervous as well. *Joseph is going to see me naked. What if he doesn't like me that way. I will have to see him naked too. I've never seen a man naked. What if I laugh? No wonder I can't sleep.*

So many random thoughts racing through her mind. She rolled from her side to her back and stared at the ceiling. Change of scenery. She ran her hand across her belly. There was a bit of a bump. *Food baby*, she thought smiling. She closed her eyes and thought about the day ahead. Maggie was probably on her way over to help with food and other arrangements. Maggie would help carry food, flowers, and whatnot over to Joseph's house for the party. Joseph's house that was soon going to be hers as well. She wondered what Joseph was doing. She was looking forward to seeing him.

Her mother was probably preparing food already. Mary couldn't smell it yet, but that was just a matter of time. Her sisters would be helping. Typically, the grooms' family would be helping as well. In fact, they would be leading the efforts to prepare the feast. Most weddings occurred between people from the same village or town. This wedding was a little unconventional in that respect, as Joseph's family lived far away. He had moved to Nazareth about four years earlier to work with his friend Martin. It was a good opportunity, and he could not let it pass. She was glad he moved; she never would have met him otherwise. He sometimes traveled to see his family, but not very often. It was a three-day journey if the weather was good, four days if it was not. His family was made aware of the wedding feast but were unable to make the journey to participate. That left the burden of preparing everything to her family and Mary and Joseph's friends.

Food baby? She touched her stomach again. There was a definite bump. She had barely eaten anything yesterday; she had been too nervous. *Am I bloated? Gas perhaps?* It wasn't painful or uncomfortable. Very odd indeed.

Mary, we should talk.

She heard the words as if spoken aloud, but it seemed more like something in her head. The voice was familiar, but also not. *Maybe I should eat something*, she thought.

You can eat later.

She sat up in bed. "Mom," she yelled, "did you say something?"

A small voice came from the next room. "It's about time you woke up. Think you could find your way out of bed long enough to help us prepare for tonight? Or are you having second thoughts and decided to hide in bed?"

No, her mother wasn't the voice she heard, maybe it was all in her head.

Getting warmer... the voice in her head said playfully.

She wondered if she was having some kind of breakdown from the stress of planning and the anticipation of the wedding activities. Perhaps this was a normal reaction. That seemed thin even to herself, a very weak argument.

"Would you prefer I speak aloud?" the voice inquired.

Her eyes were wide open as she gazed around the perimeter of her room. She was frightened and confused. The voice seemed to be coming from everywhere and nowhere. Moments before, she thought it was something innocent and worthy of mocking herself. Now she seriously wondered if she was losing her mind. She was trembling. She was a coiled spring ready to release at the slightest "boo."

"I was really hoping this would go better. I don't often interact with My people and when I do, it always starts with fear, confusion, and disbelief. Oh, and there is always the groveling. So help Me, Me, I could really do without the groveling." The voice paused briefly, then pressed on. "Please take a deep breath. Relax. You know Me. You have loved Me your entire life. Relax. We need to have a chat, it's important. I am going to take a physical form so we can have a conversation. Please keep it together. You know Me. It's all good."

A soft light appeared at the end of Mary's bed. It slowly intensified, shifting and swirling into the shape of a man. The bright white morphed into a head, torso, arms, and legs of light. The man-form began to take on colors as the brightness slowly faded. The colors and light converged to reveal a kindly old man in simple robes sitting at the end of her bed. He had shoulder length white hair and a close white beard. He smiled at her. His eyes were bright, full of light, and took on a greenish-brown color. Mary inexplicably had the thought that she had always preferred blue eyes, although rare in this part of the world. The old man smiled a little wider and his greenish-brown eyes changed to blue.

Mary's eyes were wider than they had ever been. Her lips parted slightly. She licked them. She paused for several seconds that felt like a lifetime to her. She took a deep breath. She took another. She licked her lips a second time. And then her hands grabbed the hair above her ears, and she began to scream.

"There's the fear..." the old man said.

She continued to scream, clenching her eyes with her hands gripping the hair at the side of her head. The man raised his right arm into the air, palm out, fingers slightly curled. Time stopped for everyone except Mary. He sighed and let her get it out of her system.

"Are we done?" the man asked.

Mary stopped screaming and looked at her new guest. She looked like a wild animal backed into a corner. "I don't understand. Who are you? Why are you here? How did you get here? Did you drug me?"

"... and the confusion," He muttered.

She truly did not understand what was happening. More questions flooded her mind. Why was there an old man at the end of her bed? Why was he smiling? What did he want? Why did he say, "so help me, me?"

We've all seen the cartoons where someone gets an idea and they show a lightbulb above their head. It's been used for decades, and we all understand the point without thinking too much about it. Illuminated lightbulb equals idea. It is basic, simple, and clean. They do not have the same blatant imagery for when someone finally realizes the truth. There is no clichéd symbol for the moment someone finally 'gets it'. Okay, that is not entirely true. In the Warner Brothers Roadrunner cartoons, when Wile E. Coyote finds himself several feet off the edge of a cliff and just hovers there for a moment, right before he plummets to the ground, he holds up a little sign that says "Yikes". That would be an example of someone 'getting it'. That does not, however, apply to every moment when someone finally 'gets it'. The idea lightbulb imagery is universal. It does not matter whether it was a good idea, great idea, sketchy idea, or horrible idea. It applies across the board. The "Yikes" sign only applies to when the realization is that something ominous is about to happen. My point, patient and forgiving reader, is that we need a universal image for when someone finally 'gets it'. If we had one, we could put it over Mary's head as she realizes God is sitting on the end of her bed. I cannot speak for you, but I might wet my pants a little. Just saying. Anyway, I digress.

"Oh shit," Mary said. "This can't be happening. I must be dreaming. I must have bumped my head and I'm hallucinating. Or I have totally lost my shit. I've gone crazy. I'm seeing things and have voices in my head. Fuck! I really wanted to do good things. Now my Mom is listening in the next room as I argue with phantoms. I honestly never thought I would lose my shit. Seriously. I thought I was more together than that."

"... and the disbelief. He called it! The Kid called it early on! Fear, confusion, disbelief... Just like He said! It's like He's omniscient! It's in the hole! It's in the hole!" Quoting Caddyshack 2000 years before it was filmed may not make sense to you, but sometimes God quotes these things for Himself. Good comedy is timeless.

Mary stared at the old man at the end of her bed. He was perfect. He was beautiful. He was God. Her eyes teared up as she realized she was completely unworthy to be in the same room with Him. She looked into His eyes and saw no judgement or criticism. He simply smiled at her, and it filled her with calm joy. She wanted to accept this odd situation with grace, but her rational mind made her remember her inadequacies. She slipped off the bed and onto her knees. She began to weep softly as she bowed her head. "I'm so very sorry I haven't been a better person," she began. "I'm so sorry I haven't been a better student, a better daughter, a better friend. Please forgive me."

"Oh, crap." God rolled his eyes. "The groveling too? I guess I'm batting 1000. I really hate the groveling. Trust Me, child, I would not be here if I did not believe you a good soul and a worthy person. Please get up and sit with Me. I very much would like to have a little chat with you." He patted the bed next to Him.

She glanced up at Him with tear-streaked eyes. She was calm and happy, yet still did not feel like she belonged in His presence. "I'm sorry to... who is that?" Mary pointed at an angel standing next to God. The angel was magnificent. His wings were snowy white and his eyes were like fire. He was everything one would imagine an angel to look like.

"That's Gabriel. He's one of my most trusted angels."

"Gabriel? The Gabriel from the Torah? The one that's the Herald of God? The one that proclaims God's intent? The one that trumpets God's will?" Mary asked. "Why isn't he saying anything?"

God smiled at her. "You continue to illustrate why I chose you, Mary. Yes, Gabe is my Herald. He usually does the talking for me. He's exceptionally good at it. It's his true purpose. However, we, meaning he and I, went through some tough times a few years back with some of our colleagues. It was an internal issue that had nothing to do with people. Consider it some work-related unpleasantness. Anyway, as a result, he's decided not to speak anymore."

"Please forgive me... I'm not sure I understand... your herald has decided not to herald?"

"It's a little more complicated than that, but yes, Gabriel has decided not to speak."

Mary giggled. "The Voice of God clammed up?"

"It really is more complicated than that. Gabe helped with the little internal issue we had. Nothing you guys, meaning humans in general, need to worry about. At least not until the Boy is born. But when it was said and done, Gabe vowed not to speak again. I'll explain it to all of you someday."

"Please, I may have bumped my head. I must have died without realizing. I'm absolutely sure I don't understand what is happening," Mary said.

She raised up and sat next to Him on the bed. He smiled. "You probably didn't need the added stress on a day like today, huh?"

She smirked at His remark.

"Sadly," He continued, "it's not going to get any easier for you. I've included you in My plans, and they will change everything you think you know.

"The world has reached the point where it needs a new direction. I've been pleased by much of what has transpired, but I've also been disgusted by a few things as well. I can be a bit of a perfectionist. I try things to see how they play out. If I don't like the results, I try something new. Humans, for example, are a good illustration of that. Before I made humans, I dabbled in animals. Some were perfect, like sharks and alligators, so I keep them around. Others, like dinosaurs and mammoths, not so much." God was looking straight ahead as He spoke.

Mary had no idea what God was talking about but could not take her eyes off Him. She slid a little closer and let the sound of His voice engulf her.

"And you made everything over a few days?" she asked.

"The answer to that is yes... and no," God responded. "Time is a funny thing; it works differently for you than Me. Yours is measured by the movement and rotation of planets. It's very linear. It doesn't work that way for Me. I could give you the technical explanation, but I already lost you by mentioning dinosaurs. Let me put it this way, for you time is a river, and you ride on top in a boat. You go where the river takes you. You can look behind you, but you cannot get back to areas you've already passed. You move only forward down the river through time.

"For me, time is the same river, except I am a fish beneath the water. I can swim alongside you, moving forward through time. But I can also swim side to side, or up to the surface, or down to the bottom. Or... I can swim back upstream. The tougher part for you to understand is that I do all those things at the same time. I have options; you don't. Well, not when it comes to time. So yes, I created everything in mere days, but they were My days, not your days," God stroked His beard. "Good question.

Most people don't think to ask that one. They just assume they understand. *That* is an excellent segue into my point about why the world needs
a new direction. Before your question, I was explaining the shift from
animals to humans.

"Humans were one of My better ideas, they are far more interesting
than animals. Giving you free will makes it so. Although I may think I
know how you will react to things, you, or people in general, often surprise
Me in ways I never expected. Not gonna lie, it can make things fun for Me.
It also allows for creativity. As mankind has progressed, they moved from
creating simple tools from wood and bone, to building fabulous palaces
and temples from wood and stone. Mankind has grown to create music,
poetry, and artwork. You should see what they do in the future with the
arts and architecture. Some of it is fairly impressive. Not always, however.
Disco is annoying, and rap can be offensive. I'm still not certain how I feel
about grunge. I guess I'm more Pearl Jam than Nirvana. And I've never
cared much for the harpsichord." God's brow was furrowed.

Mary stared blankly. "Am I supposed to understand any of this?
Because I don't."

God smiled. "You, my dear, will have the distinct pleasure of experi-
encing all of these things from Heaven someday. For now, though, you're
correct to reel me in a little. I mentioned earlier that I don't often interact
with My people. I suppose I need a little practice. However, none of that
matters. Let's get back to people. I really like people. You are special to
Me. That's why I gave you souls and allow you into My kingdom once
your work here is done. Well, some of you anyway.

"Over time people get complacent or downright lazy. I occasionally
give you reminders of the things I expect from you. I kept things simple
with Moses. As you know, I gave him a list of ten things that are important to Me. He did a great job delivering the message. For the most part,
people took things to heart and behaviors got better. Earlier on I got a

little frustrated by what I considered a lack of respect. So, I asked Noah to build the ark, and I wiped the rest of the slate clean. It was kind of a dick move on My part, but this is My party, at the end of the day I call the shots. I keep seeing people go through a similar progression. Most of them are great but over time they drift away. People lose sight of the important things. So, I step in and give you all a push in a different direction." God paused and looked at Mary.

"You mentioned that earlier, that the world needs a new direction. You also mentioned that You have included me in Your plans. I'm honored and humbled that You would consider me for anything. Truly, I am. However, I'm also frightened." Mary spoke honestly. It was easy to forget the kind old man at the end of her bed had been known to wipe out cities and bring plagues to get the attention of kings and pharaohs.

"Indeed, you are in My plans. You have a very important role to play, that's why I chose to speak to you in person. I'm sorry, Mary, but I'm not offering you a choice. I need your help. It must be you. I have decided to give the world a jumpstart. This will be a major game-changer, and you are key to making it happen. I've decided to teach the world what I want and how you, meaning all My people, can join me in the Kingdom of Heaven. I love you all, even the sick twisted bastards among you. People are losing focus, and it's time to mix things up." God seemed to stare right through Mary.

"Are you sure you mean me? I'm not very good at much. Mother gets frustrated by my attempts to cook. I don't understand how I could possibly help you with anything." Mary was wringing her hands.

"You're going to give birth to My son. You will be mother to the Son of God," God said blankly, then smiled a little.

"Oh, fuck no! I am not having sex with you, old man!" Mary's hands shot to her mouth, and her eyes got as wide as saucers when she realized what she had just said. "I'm so sorry! I can't believe I just said that to you! I'm so very sorry!"

God laughed out loud and shook his head. "Free will... I love it. Your reaction is understandable. No worries, and if it makes you feel any better, I have no intention of having sex with you." God grinned wide.

"I'm so confused. How am I to have Your child? I'm a virgin! Honest!" She placed her right hand over her heart and raised the other in the air. "Swear to ..." She trailed off, looking more confused. "You know I am! I can't have Your child. I'm marrying Joseph! Tonight! No, I'm sorry, I can't do this. And how am I supposed to get pregnant without having sex?"

God smirked. "First, I'm God, I can do shit, being all powerful and whatnot. Second, you're already pregnant. That's not a food baby." He pointed toward her belly.

Her eyes got even wider and filled with tears. "NO! Oh, please God, no. Please tell me you're joking. Joseph!" She looked down at her feet, then around the room as if she was looking for an exit. "JOSEPH!" she yelled. "He won't understand! Please, no. I LOVE HIM! Don't make me lose him. PLEASE!" She dropped to her knees and grabbed God's robes, crying uncontrollably. "Please no! He's the only thing I want. Please don't do this! PLEASE!" she pleaded.

"Joseph will be with you. Talk to him." God tried to reassure her.

Mary did not hear, or the words did not register. She continued pleading through a steady stream of tears. "Please don't make me do this. He'll hate me! He'll think I slept with someone else! Please don't do this! He could have me stoned to death! Or worse, he'll never speak to me again!" she sobbed. She could barely catch her breath.

"Mary." God placed His hand upon her head. He slid it down the side of her face and moved His fingers under her chin, raising her face to His. "I'm asking a lot of you. I chose you over all others, and I have a reason for that. This is not a punishment. Talk to Joseph, it will be okay. He won't abandon you, and you won't be stoned to death.

"You must be strong for Me, Mary, and for My son. This will be difficult. It's unfair of me to expect this of you, but I do. And you won't disappoint Me." God wrapped His arm around her.

"You should choose someone stronger, someone wiser. I don't think I can handle this. Please choose someone else. Please don't let me lose Joseph." She had stopped crying, but her face was still streaked with tears.

"Please have faith, child. I do the things I do for a reason. I chose you for a reason." God's fingers were still under her chin. He released it and stood. He paced to her door and then turned back toward her. "This is important, Mary. This child will change everything from this point forward. His birth will divide Judaism. It will spawn multiple religions. It will be the source of great joy and happiness, yet also the source of great pain and despair," God said. The smile was no longer on His face.

"And You're okay with that? I don't understand," she said, her brow furrowed.

"It has to be. It must happen. It fills Me with great joy and great sorrow. I can't explain the reasons to you. You'll have to place your faith in Me that this is necessary. You'll give birth to My child, and you'll name him Immanuel. You and Joseph will raise..."

"NO!" Mary interrupted.

"Excuse me?" God looked annoyed.

"Absolutely not!" Mary stood and placed her hands on her hips. She stared at Him strong and stern-faced.

God tilted his head slightly and raised one eyebrow. "I'm sorry, what are we talking about?"

"We are NOT naming him Immanuel!" she demanded.

God smiled a little. "Yes, we are. You have read your Torah. You know the prophesies. His name will be Immanuel."

"No! Not going to happen. I don't care what the Torah says, we are NOT naming him Immanuel!" Mary insisted.

God sighed. "Why are you digging your heels in on this? I've already decided."

"No. I'm sorry, but no. I can't allow you to make a stupid naming decision. It happens far too often that parents give children stupid names. I won't allow you to do this. No, you're not going to name him Immanuel." Mary said. The fists on her hips were so tight, her fingers were turning white.

God paused. He was taken aback just a little. "What's wrong with the name Immanuel? How is that stupid?"

"Are you serious?" She tilted her head and furrowed her brow. "Immanuel?... You must be kidding me? You want to have a son, a son whom You claim is going to spawn multiple religions. A son who is going to teach the world about You. And You want to call him Immanuel?"

"Yes," God said, but was strangely losing His confidence on the issue.

"No. Absolutely not. I won't allow it. Immanuel? Seriously? You want people to pray to Manny, the Son of God? You know they'll call him Manny. No fucking way, it's a mistake. I can't allow You to make it. No one will take him seriously. I'm sorry, no. It's not going to happen." She held firm.

"Not Manny, Immanuel," God said with less conviction. She might have a point here.

"No. You know I'm right. Kids will call him Manny when he is younger. The name will stick. And then he has no credibility. You might as well call him Percy. Sorry, pick a different name," she insisted.

"I think you're over-reacting," God responded.

"No," she demanded. "Pick another name."

God began to understand some of the prayers He had received over the years regarding headstrong wives. He sighed. "Fine. It's possible you have a point. What name do you suggest?"

"Jack. That's a good strong name. Or Jesus, that's another strong name."

"Jesus?" God tried out the name on his tongue.

"Yes. I like it. How about you?" She looked hopeful.

"Okay, Jesus it is." God shook his head, clearly humored by the exchange. "That's a great example of why I chose you, Mary."

Mary smiled, though it faded nearly as quickly as it appeared. Her thoughts returned to Joseph. "Please," she asked, "Please explain all this to Joseph. He won't understand. He'll hate me, and I can't bear that."

God looked her in the eye. "Having faith is the most difficult thing I ask of everyone, and the most important. You must trust in Me. This will be a strange journey, but it will work out."

Mary knew this was big, bigger than anything she could possibly compare it to. Yet she also knew, in her heart, that God would do His best to have her back on this.

God and Gabriel looked around as if preparing to leave. God stopped suddenly and looked at Mary. "I have a strange request, but I hope you'll honor it. It's important to Me."

Mary nodded and said, "Of course I will, whatever you ask."

"When you eventually tell people the story of how we met, of everything we spoke of tonight," God continued, "please tell them it was Gabriel, not Me, who told you of all this. I don't mean when you speak to Maggie or your immediate friends. When raising the boy, and especially as he becomes a man, you'll tell the story. Please tell them it was Gabriel. After all, he is the Herald of God."

Gabriel rolled his eyes.

"Will Gabriel speak again?" she asked.

God looked at Gabe. "That is entirely up to him."

Gabriel narrowed his eyes at God with a stern look on his face. God raised his hand, twisted his wrist, and ambient sound returned. Mary hadn't realized it was missing until it was back. Time resumed for the rest of the world.

Both turned to bright, bright light, and then were gone.

5

FRIENDS

"Are you okay, dear?" her mother called from the other room, "It sounded like you screamed for a second."

"I'm fine," Mary called back. "I'll be out in a few minutes."

But Mary was not fine. She wasn't close to fine. She was processing what had just occurred, or at least she was trying to. She was a ball of contradiction. She was consumed with confusion, fear, joy, awe, contentment, and terror. *Did that just happen?*

It did.

The voice inside her head said with calm confidence.

Her eyes were wide, and she stared straight ahead. She was sitting on the bed with her elbows on her knees as she dropped her face into her hands. Her mind was racing with thoughts of the conversation in which she had just participated. With God. *The* God. The God that wants her to have a baby. *His* baby. *Oh, fucking hell.* Mary shook her head and laid back onto the bed. *What's happening?* She opened her eyes and stared at the ceiling, bringing her right hand to her forehead. Her left hand unconsciously went to her belly.

Just outside, Maggie knocked lightly on Mary's bedroom door. There was no answer, so she turned and looked at Mary's mother. Her mother made the universal hand gesture to go in anyway, the back of the hand, fingers down, sweeping motion that says 'go on, go on'. Maggie opened the door and went in. When she saw Mary lying on the bed staring at the ceiling, she closed the door behind her. She walked to the bed and sat down next to Mary.

"You okay?" Maggie asked.

Mary was startled by the sound of another voice in the room. When she saw Maggie, she brought her left hand to her face and began to weep.

"Oh, sweetie..." Maggie leaned in and hugged her friend. She laid next to Mary and moved the hair from Mary's eyes with her finger. "I know it's a scary day. You'll be alright. Marriage is a good thing."

Mary turned to look her friend in the eye. "You don't understand. You don't know..." she trailed off. She wasn't sure what to say. She wasn't sure how to explain any of what had just happened. It was so incredibly frustrating. She knew she would sound bat-shit crazy. She closed her eyes again and said, "God was just here."

Maggie paused a moment and tilted her head. "Of course, He was... He's everywhere."

"No," Mary insisted, "God. Was just here. With me."

Maggie looked even more confused. "I'm sorry, what?"

"God. God was just here. God. The Great I Am," Mary replied. "We had a conversation. He asked me to help Him."

Maggie's head tilted to the other side, eyes narrowing. "I'm sorry, what?"

"I'm being serious, Mags." Mary looked at her, eyes pleading. "I'm not losing my shit. Something crazy and huge and wonderful and terrifying just happened here. I'm supposed to have God's baby. I'm pregnant."

Maggie looked at her friend. She wanted to ask, "I'm sorry, what?" one more time but thought she might get punched. Understandably punched. She thought better of it. Mary was visibly shaken, she was trembling and appeared to be close to throwing up. She had a crazy look in her eye, not the look of a lunatic, more the look of a cornered animal sizing up its options. A cornered animal that appeared to be close to throwing up. Her eyes darted back and forth as she appeared to be looking for the right words to say. Maggie was concerned.

Mary grabbed Maggie's hand and placed it on her belly. "I'm fucking PREGNANT!" she said louder than she needed to. Maggie's eyes got wide. *That must be why Mary is losing it, she's pregnant. But wait,* she thought, *Mary tells me everything. How is it she didn't tell me about having sex? And Joseph... oh, damn, was it Joseph?* Had Mary met someone without telling her? Unlikely. Mary is the best, most honest person she knew. She let the panicked thought pass. But something had shaken Mary. *What the hell is going on?*

"So.... You and Joseph... had sex?" Maggie asked.

"No."

"So... it wasn't Joseph?" Maggie hoped her friend didn't answer.

"No. Not Joseph, not anyone, I'm still a virgin," Mary replied.

The corners of Maggie's mouth curled up. She tried to suppress her smile. "You haven't had sex? With anyone? No one at all?"

"No."

"Well, thank God. Hon, there's no way you're pregnant if you didn't have sex." Maggie released her smile.

"Mags... you're not listening. Shut up and listen." Mary sat up and looked her friend in the eye. "God, our God, *The God*, creator of every-thing, was just here. HERE! With Gabriel! We spoke for a long time. He wants me to have His baby. God's baby! ME! I DON'T KNOW WHAT TO DO!!! I'M FUCKING LOSING MY SHIT! It's a *huge* honor, but I'm terrified! And He already put it in here." Mary grabbed her belly with both hands. "Why me? Why now? What is Joseph going to say? He's going to hate me! How will he believe any of this? It's obvious you don't. What am I going to do? I can't do this. I can't..." Mary trailed off and began to weep again as she collapsed back onto the bed.

Maggie stared blankly at her friend as a thousand different thoughts ricocheted through her head. *She's crazy. Maybe she hit her head. Maybe it's stress. Maybe I should get her mother. She's losing her shit. What did God look like? Did God speak? Did Gabriel? What did they wear? Does God wear sandals? Why does she think she's pregnant? Shit, we need to get ready for the ceremony!*

"Okay, slow down and start from the beginning. What are you talking about? You said a lot... about being pregnant... and God. Help me understand," Maggie said while she stroked Mary's face. "I'm here to help you." She wondered if she was too late to help. Whatever happened, Mary was a train wreck.

Mary propped herself up again and looked at Maggie. She shuddered a little, trying to catch her breath. She wondered how she would have responded to Maggie if the tables were turned and Mary was the one trying to understand. The thought made her smile, which probably made her seem even more crazy in her friend's eyes. "I'm sorry to unload on you like this. I really am. I need you; I need my best friend. I'm not crazy. Please just listen until I'm done."

"Of course, Mary," Maggie replied. "I'll always be here for you. Okay, shutting up. Tell me what happened."

Mary replayed everything, in great detail. She skipped the parts where God mentioned strange words like dinosaurs and Pearl Jam. She explained that God wanted to make a change. She relayed that she was to have God's son. She even included that God wanted to name the child Immanuel.

"Hold on," Maggie interjected, "I know I promised to listen to you all the way through, but seriously, did you actually tell God 'no'? That He couldn't name His child Immanuel?"

"C'mon, Maggie," Mary replied. "You know I'm right! They would've called him Manny!"

"Agreed! But know your audience!" Maggie insisted, "It's not like you were talking to a woman down the street. It was fucking God!" Maggie's eye got wide. The crazy kind of wide. Her heart skipped a beat, and she felt a dread terror inside. She immediately dropped to her knees and put her hands together in prayer. "I'm so sorry I just said that. Please forgive me Lord, I didn't mean to swear... or take Your name in vain... or whatever it was I just did. I'm so sorry."

Mary beamed. Maggie was awesome, what would she do without her, she thought. Maggie had been her rock since they were old enough to need a rock. In all fairness, Mary thought, she had been Maggie's rock as well. There had been many times Maggie had needed and used Mary's shoulder as well. Mary loved her friend dearly and knew in her heart the feeling was mutual.

"Mags..." Mary paused. She had tears welling up in her eyes. "What am I going to do?"

Maggie got up from her knees and sat next to Mary on the bed. She placed her hand gently on Mary's cheek. "Girl..." Maggie paused. "You're screwed! No, seriously... *You're screwed*!" Maggie laughed.

Mary grabbed a pillow and swung it straight at Maggie's face, connecting exactly where she aimed. They both fell to the bed laughing. When their giggling fit ended, they were both lying sideways on the bed facing up with their feet on the floor.

"Seriously, Mags, what do I do? I need to tell Joseph."

Maggie stared at the ceiling. She thought about what Mary had just said. It was far more complicated than those last five words conveyed without the context of the moment. "Yes, Mary, you do. I have no idea how, and I have no idea how he'll respond, but you need to tell him. I can come with you. I should come with you. When do you want to tell him? After the wedding seems a little shady, what do you think?"

"Crap, I'm getting married today!" Mary sat up. "I totally forgot that part with everything that has happened. Ooh... I have to tell him now, don't I?"

Maggie just nodded. *There's no way this is going to go well.* Joseph was a great guy, but how many guys are going to believe their fiancé got knocked up by God Himself? Granted, guys can be pretty stupid, but this was a bit much. Maggie wasn't sure she believed it either. She loved Mary and trusted her to her soul, but this was... difficult... to wrap her head around. *No, this may not go well at all. Not liking the odds here.*

6

HEROD THE GREAT

Time for a quick history lesson. We are going to use current time convention references, specifically BC, to help with understanding, yours and mine. The people of this age used the convention of their time. I could look it up, and it would even be accurate, but you and I would have no idea what timeframe it referred to and what good would that do? Let's agree that they are using whatever year they referred to and we are reading the translated version. I appreciate your willingness to compromise on this.

At this point in history, most of the known world was ruled by Rome. The Roman Empire stretched from Britain to Egypt. For the sake of scale, this was an area approximately equal to the size of the continental United States from the state of Washington to Florida. The Empire was massive. The army that fought for this impressive expansion was also massive. The Roman Empire was most of the entire known world. Many of the soldiers who fought in the Roman army had never actually seen Rome... or Italy for that matter.

The empire essentially encircled the Mediterranean Sea. Although overall rule of these vast territorial holdings was by Emperor Augustus in Rome, there were many client kings throughout the empire. On the far east end of the Empire was the small kingdom of Judaea. Judaea was ruled by the client king Herod the Great, and included Judaea, Samaria, and Galilee. For 32 years of his rule, which started in 37 BC, Herod had proven himself time and time again to be a true ally to Augustus. The two had formed a friendship and trust. It was 5 BC.

***

Herod the Great sat in the garden plaza of his Jerusalem palace. He stared at his feet. His sandals were dirty. The King of all Judaea, Samaria, and Galilee apparently cannot keep his feet clean. Oh sure, it was easy to do if he stayed in the palace, but sometimes he preferred to walk rather than ride to the Temple, and the streets were dirty. As were the people. He never feared for his safety walking as he was always well protected. The Celtic Guard that had once served Cleopatra made sure he was safe. He wondered how she ended up with them in the first place. The Celts were big and fought like mad men. Their reddish-brown hair and pale skin made them stand out more than most foreigners. Many had freckles on their arms and noses, probably under their beards as well. *What a crazy bunch of ginger bastards that lot is, can't understand a damn word they say either.* They were a gift from Octavian (who was called Augustus now that he was Emperor). The Germanic guard, also a gift from Octavian, protected the palace. Like the Celts, the Germanic guardsmen were also big and fought well, better than most of the Romans, if Herod were to be honest. So, no, he never feared for his physical safety from the people.

His reputation was another matter. The people had been talking. They were unhappy. They thought taxes were too high. *They think I don't appreciate and respect our religion.* Herod had placed a large golden eagle at the entrance to the New Temple. The people just did not understand. Herod had been appointed King of Judaea by the Roman Senate. He had to throw the Romans a bone now and then. They picked Herod because he was loyal and would keep the Jewish people in line. That was over thirty years ago. Rome mostly did not care what religion they practiced in the outlands, provided they paid taxes and supplied soldiers. The Romans had ridiculous gods that made no sense to Herod, yet the Romans ruled most of the world. Maybe they were on to something with their pantheon of ridiculous gods. Regardless, Herod placated the Romans because it kept him in power and they mostly let him be, but Herod's people did not understand. His secret police reported to him daily. They infiltrated the population and monitored the mood of the people. They were his ears and eyes. Discontent was bubbling up. It was a toxic situation and must be dealt with. The people were scheming, he could feel it.

The truth was Herod was sick, a cancer or disease of some kind was eating him inside out. He knew he was sick; he was in pain every day. He did not realize, however, that it was taking his sanity bit by bit. Paranoia was eating away at him. His physicians gave him ointments and medicines that were foul to taste and mostly did nothing. Some of the medicines eased his pain a bit, but wine did that as well. He took a sip from his goblet and placed it back on the side table next to the stone bench upon which he sat. He continued to stare at his feet, but no longer considered them. His mind was elsewhere now.

The people were speaking regularly of the prophecies lately. There are several passages in the Torah that referenced the coming of a messiah, a savior to deliver the people of Israel. The writings prophesized the birth of a new king of Israel. One even referenced the child king would be born in the City of David. King David lived in Jerusalem, mere miles from where Herod was sitting. The people believed this so-called Son of God would be coming soon and this angered Herod. Herod was raised in Judaism. He knew the passages well, but prophesies didn't actually come true, did they? Certainly not in his lifetime. Besides, the passages did not make sense when considered side by side. How could the child be born in Jerusalem yet be referred to as the Nazarene? Nazareth was nowhere near Jerusalem. It did not make sense. There may be something to these prophesies, but mostly he felt they were veiled references to something else. Herod did not believe that the true child of God was coming anytime soon. He did believe that some charlatan may try to deceive his good but stupid people into believing it was so. They may even try to pass themselves off as this new King of the Jews. This would not be tolerated. Not in any way. Not at all.

Herod looked up at the sky. It was a sunny, cloudless day. He glanced at his surroundings. The sun cast shadows throughout the garden plaza. The trees and greenery were bold and vibrant in the sun. The statues stared blankly at nothing. Arbors, porticos, and trellised archways were sprinkled about in all directions. Flowers, trees, shrubs, and ponds with fountains were perfectly spaced. It was an impressive plaza, to be sure. However, the beauty did little to ease his mind.

Someone was obviously planting these rumors of a messiah, trying to build on the discontent. *It must be a scheme to undermine my authority, or perhaps a grand deception to trick the people into supporting a usurper.* He had no intention of allowing anything of the sort.

Herod rarely got time to himself these days. There were always pressing matters of state to deal with, or he was receiving foreign dignitaries or conferring with the Romans. Always too much to do and no time to do it. Sitting alone in the plaza was a rare treat. However, he knew this solitude would not last today. He received word that Octavian was sending a messenger with important news. Why the pre-messenger did not impart the news was beyond him, it seemed like a ridiculous waste of time to Herod. Sending a messenger to tell you that a messenger was coming, who does that? Octavian, of course. *Perhaps this one will only inform part of the news, requiring yet another messenger.* Herod shook his head. *These children should not be rulers, something I should never say out loud,* he smiled to himself.

While he waited, he closed his eyes and enjoyed the warmth of the sun on his face. *Might as well make the most of this solitude while I have it.* There was a slight breeze that brought the smell of flowers. Herod was content. It had been a long time since he felt this way. He knew it was fleeting but vowed to milk every last drop until some fool had the misfortune to interrupt him.

Herod sat alone, enjoying the plaza, for nearly another hour. He heard the patter of footsteps approaching. He took a deep breath and then opened his eyes. A servant approached with what was obviously an emissary from Rome. A young one. *Oh, fucking hell, why do they insist on sending these mind-numbed children?*

The servant approached cautiously, making sure Herod was aware of their presence. "I beg your pardon, Your Majesty. Lucius Magonus brings word from Augustus."

Lucius Magonus stepped forward and bowed to Herod. "It is a true honor to meet you, Your Grace."

Herod stood. "You are dismissed," he said to the servant. The servant bowed, turned quickly, and retreated the way he and the Roman had come. Herod turned his attention to the young messenger. He said nothing for a while, he simply looked at the man. He knew he was making Lucius extremely uncomfortable. It was more fun messing with dignitaries and rulers of foreign lands—messsengers were too easy to intimidate. Still, he enjoyed the little game. He waited an unnecessary amount of time before extending his hand toward an adjacent bench. "Sit. I'm sure you've had a long journey."

Lucius hesitated, then nodded and sat. A bead of sweat rolled down the side of his face.

Herod resumed his position on his bench. "What news do you bring from Octavian?"

"Augustus," Lucius corrected.

Herod ignored the flash of anger at being corrected. The boy was right. Octavian was emperor now and the Roman senate decided to rename him Augustus Caesar. "Yes, Augustus. The Princeps and I have been friends so long now, I sometimes forget they changed his name."

Lucius nodded. "Augustus has declared that all of Rome and all of Rome's territories are to conduct a census of the entire population. Caesar wishes to know exactly how many citizens comprise the Roman empire."

"A census?" Herod asked, "of Rome? All of Rome?"

"Yes. All of Rome." A monotone reply.

"You're serious?" Herod asked, not quite believing his own ears.

"Indeed," Lucious said, raising an eyebrow.

"The entire Roman empire... incredible. I'm not certain I could provide an accurate estimate of the population of Jerusalem, let alone Judaea," Herod replied, more thinking out loud than responding.

"That will change, Your Majesty. Caesar would like for you to determine how many people make up Judaea. Not just the number, but who they are, where they live, what they do for a living, and their ages. Family lineage would be helpful too. He would even like to know about the women and children. Everyone." Lucius Magonus spoke as though he had delivered this speech more than once. He looked blankly at Herod. "The plan is to set up census stations in every village and town across your kingdom. Heralds will be dispatched to spread the news across the country. Proclamations will be posted. Those not appearing at the polling stations will be punished. Caesar asked me to convey that this is not a request. The population is to be informed of the consequences of refusing to be counted as well. This is an order directly from Augustus Caesar. There will be a census of the entire population of Rome."

Rome made up nearly half of the known world. The scope and magnitude of this task was beyond anything Herod had ever considered. Octavian wanted to tally every citizen. More specifically, he wanted to tally every tax-payer. Caesar would have the entire population cataloged. He would be able to correctly assess the amount of gold collected. Skimming from the tax collections would no longer be possible. He would have a listing of every professional, tradesman, and farmer. As crazy as the scope of the project may seem, it was absolute genius. It had never been done before. It had never been considered before. True genius.

Herod considered the messenger. He was obviously well educated, probably in Rome. That meant he was from a wealthy family, likely the son of a senator. His youth belied his intelligence. Herod had to caution himself from making assumptions without doing his due diligence. He too easily assumed youth to equal ignorance. In this case, he was wrong. The young man understood exactly what he was conveying. Moreover, he understood why he was conveying it.

"Will the individual kingdoms be allowed to maintain a list of their citizens for their own use?" Herod asked.

"Of course. Caesar suggested you would be the first to ask me that question, he knows you well, and yes, you were the first to ask. You may maintain the records for your own use. This is a large undertaking, and Augustus wants you to benefit as he will from the information the census will provide." Lucius looked at his fingernails.

"So then, you are one of many spreading Caesar's intent to catalog all of the empire. Does Caesar have a timetable in mind to complete such a monumental task?" Herod asked.

"Indeed, he does." The messenger scraped under his fingernail with his thumbnail. "Augustus would like the raw data from the census collected and delivered to Rome before year's end."

Herod was surprised by the answer, and he was rarely surprised by anything. "By the end of the year? I must insist, young emissary of Rome, that Octavian be reminded of the huge burden he is asking of his true supporters. This is not a thing that can be completed in mere days. This will take months at a minimum. The number of personnel required to collect the data he is requesting is ... it is unprecedented. Nothing of this magnitude has ever been attempted."

"No, Your Grace, it has never been attempted, but I already recognize that you see the value of the endeavor, as Augustus said you would. Caesar has made it clear to me who his true favorites are. You, sir, are at the top of that list. He has every faith that you will deliver on this. He has every faith that you will understand the haste, appreciate the magnitude, and will embrace the need as if it were your own."

Herod stared at the young messenger. *Fuck. A census of the entire population of Judaea? By the end of the year? Fuck!* Herod's face remained blank. *This is all I fucking need. On top of everything else I have going on, now I have to count every head in the fucking kingdom.* Herod knew there were at least a hundred other kings or senators or leaders having the same thoughts about now. *I get the need. I recognize the genius of the idea, truly brilliant. But by the end of the year? Fuck me.*

7

TIDINGS

Herod assembled his small council and advisors in a meeting room in the palace. He explained Caesar's request for a census and laid out the timeframe. There was complaining and bickering and whining about the impossible nature of the task and the unreasonable timeframe expected. One councilman appeared to not be paying attention at all. He was picking grapes and figs from a silver platter and stuffing them into his mouth. He was doughy and soft. *Hopefully his mind makes up for his gluttonous nature.* The disgruntled murmurings began to change shape, and ideas with merit began to emerge.

"It seems to me," one offered, "that this needs to be conducted by the military. The council is too small to cover the entire kingdom. The military has the human capital required to be in each city. The military will also command the respect of the people and, by their very presence, convey the weight and seriousness that you are giving this task."

"Agreed," Herod said. "At the conclusion of this meeting, I will summon my generals. The foreign guards will remain here, however. The presence of the foreigners at the census stations would not play well with the people. It's simple optics. They mostly despise my relationship with Rome as it is. Other suggestions?"

"We will need to provide the military with the forms and information they will need to collect the required data," another offered. "Allow the council to prepare a brief questionnaire for each citizen to complete. You will, of course, have final say regarding the content of the questionnaire. It should include only the information deemed necessary. It should be brief in nature due to the number of citizens involved. As it is, this endeavor will take considerable time."

"What of the ones that cannot read or write?" another interjected. "We are dealing with the entire population. Most have not received any education at all. I suggest including advisors to read the questionnaire to the citizens and record the data. I have faith there are many within the military to take on this role. Forgive me, Your Grace, but my knowledge of our military is not a keen as it could be. Do enough of our soldiers possess the literary ability to conduct the surveys?"

Herod frowned. It was a valid question, one that he was not entirely sure of the answer. "Prepare a questionnaire for the census, and bring it to me for my approval. I will confer with the generals to determine the number of literate soldiers available for the task. It is entirely possible that we may be required to supplement their number with others. Please prepare of list of potential advisors to accompany the military for this task.

"We will also need a complete list of the cities and towns that will host the census stations." Herod noticed a solitary figure lurking in the back corner of the room next to a pillar. Tobias. The man said nothing, he only stared off into the distance while standing in the shadows, appearing not to be paying attention to any of the proceedings before him. Tobias was the head of Herod's secret police. He was given access to places few others were allowed to tread. Tobias was one of the most useful people in Herod's service, and he was paid handsomely for the information he provided. But there was more to it than that- Herod genuinely liked the man. Tobias was cold, brutal, honest. He was not burdened with sympathy or empathy. Tobias provided information and results. And secrets. Herod was not sure how Tobias obtained the information he provided, things your best friends would not know or guess. Herod had decided early on not to question the man's methods as long as the information stream kept flowing. Tobias kept track of the mood of the general populace, and occasionally of Herod's very own family. He was invaluable. Having him appear uninvited to meetings or gatherings did not bother Herod in the least. He looked forward to the updates that Tobias would provide.

"We will need a preliminary schedule that includes document preparation, distribution and posting of proclamations, census team deployment estimates, and an estimated completion date. We must deliver the results to Rome by the end of the year. Work backward from that to prepare the schedule." Herod wiped his forehead with the back of his hand. "I would like the draft proclamations brought to me for approval as soon as possible. Make that happen before the census questionnaires.

"Are there any questions before we adjourn?"

The council and advisors stared blankly back at Herod.

"Very well, get to work."

Herod stood. The group followed suit and started leaving, engaging in private conversations as they departed. Herod wandered over to the plate of fruit where the pig-man had been stuffing his face. He began to reach for some grapes but stopped as he heard Tobias speak.

"I wouldn't eat those. The squishy one was scratching his ass between bites. That fucker is disgusting."

"Yes, he is. Thanks for the warning." Herod had a pained expression on his face. "Did you catch any of the meeting?"

"A little. I'm not sure I understand the purpose, but you intend to interview people. I may have missed the number, but it sounded like you wanted to interview everyone? Can that even be done?"

"Yes," Herod answered. "Octavian has a bug up his ass and wants to catalog the entire empire. It's a logistical cluster-fuck."

"Wow. Seriously? The entire empire? That is incredible. Good luck with that." Tobias smiled.

"What? You're not going to offer to take the lead on this?" Herod smiled back.

"Oh no, you're the king, you deal with it. I'm just here to enlighten you on the state of your world." Tobias pushed the plate of fruit further away.

"Fair enough, I'll take care of keeping the Romans happy. But since you brought it up, what is the state of my world?" Herod asked.

"In general, the people are pissed about the taxes."

"You've mentioned that before," Herod said. "In fact, that seems to be your favorite thing to report. I am aware the people are displeased, but with time it may get better."

"It hasn't changed to this point, and it may even be getting worse. They aren't exactly optimistic. These are the rumblings from your people." Tobias shrugged.

Herod frowned. His head felt as though it were splitting open. It was difficult to focus when the headaches got this bad.

Tobias looked at the floor. "There is something else. There is more and more talk about the coming of a messiah."

Herod shrugged, "What else is new? There is always talk of the coming of a messiah."

"This is different," Tobias said. "It's troubling because the stories are very similar. Shepherds are claiming to have been visited in the fields by angels."

"Angels? Shepherds are being visited by angels?" Herod's eyebrows raised.

"Yes, angels," Tobias replied.

"Angels. Fine, they say they are being visited by angels. What are the angels doing with these shepherds?"

"They..." Tobias paused. "The angels are bringing tidings."

"Tidings?" Herod asked.

"Yes, tidings."

"Tidings?" Herod repeated.

Tobias nodded.

"Tidings. What does that even mean? Tidings of what?" Herod watched Tobias squirm and hesitate. This was uncommon, he was normally forthright and confident.

"The direct quote... tidings of comfort and joy."

"Comfort and joy?" Herod's brow furrowed.

"Yes, comfort and joy."

"Comfort and joy?" Herod repeated, incredulous.

"Yes, tidings of comfort and joy." Tobias pursed his lips.

"You're fucking with me, aren't you?"

"Not at all. That's the quote from the shepherds. And it's coming from more than one, many leagues apart from one another. It's such an odd thing to say." Tobias trailed off.

"Shepherds are morons. Forget the comfort and joy, what's the rest?" Herod was still not convinced Tobias wasn't pulling his leg. But there was something ominous about this news, it felt like trouble.

"The shepherds report that angels are telling them that God is planning to have a Son, a human Son. This Son of God will be the new King of the Jews and will save them all from... I'm not exactly sure from what, but they refer to Him as a savior. I assume they think He will save them from Rome... or you, Your Grace."

Herod rolled his eyes. "They *always* talk about a coming messiah. They've been prophesizing that crap for as long as I can remember. The Son of God thing is a new angle, but it's the same hollow crap they always hang their hope on."

Tobias was flustered, searching for the right words. "No, this is different. It's the same story hundreds of leagues apart. I've never seen or heard anything like it. Whether *we* believe it or not is inconsequential. *They* believe it. It's unifying them. This kind of fanatical hope is dangerous."

Something was brewing, and Herod did not like it. He had always been observant. He had always picked up subtle clues and could read between the lines. He had an instinct that he could count on. Something was different with these new prophesies. Tobias claimed they were consistent across the land. The secret police had made multiple reports to confirm it. Something was happening.

"I don't feel this is an immediate threat to you, but I believe to my core that there is something going on," Tobias said.

"Do you believe these prophesies?" Herod's eyes narrowed as he asked the question.

"I didn't say *I* believed them. I do believe *something* is going on though. These shepherds won't back down from their stories, even when being strongly persuaded to do so." Tobias was referring to the less-than-gentle techniques employed by the secret police once they had a suspect in custody. It often got messy and usually led to the need to dispose of a body.

The point was not lost on Herod. "And you say this news is unifying the people?"

Tobias merely nodded.

"Fanatical hope..." Herod trailed off leaving the rest of this thought unspoken. He looked up at the ceiling, his arms dangling loosely at his sides. He trusted Tobias and accepted that this news was something. What it meant was unclear, but he would have Tobias investigate the matter.

In the meantime, Herod would work it over in his mind. He liked to dissect problems and tried to see them from multiple angles. He could usually divine motivation, causation, origin, and consequence if he let himself contemplate the information fully. He was determined to find whoever was behind these malicious rumors. Someone was playing a dangerous game, and Herod was going to make sure they knew the game was lost before snuffing the light from their eyes.

"Bring one of these shepherds to me. I would like to speak to one in person. Perhaps I can convince him to explain what all of this is really about and who is behind it all." Herod's mind was churning now. He was determined to eliminate this sickness before it spread further. He brought his hand to his brow and placed his palm to his forehead. His headache was raging, and he needed to rest. Without saying another word, he turned and walked away.

8

TELLING JOSEPH

"It might be better to go see Joseph at his house where you two can have a conversation without your family hearing," Maggie suggested. "I'm sure he will be reasonable. Or ... I don't know, Mare, I just don't know. This may be hard for him to take. Let's grab some things for the feast and take them to Joseph's. Your mom won't think that's weird. But on the way, I'd like to find Roger. I think it would be better if he came with us. It might be good for Joseph to have a calm friend there." Maggie also thought it might be good to have Roger there on the off chance that Joseph totally lost it. She wouldn't say this to Mary, though. Joseph was a level-headed guy, and she couldn't recall a time, ever, that he had lost his cool. But just in case, having Roger there would be good for both Joseph and the girls.

Mary nodded but said nothing. She was still dealing with a thousand thoughts in her head. The biggest of those was Joseph. She was genuinely afraid that he would leave her. The thought made tears well up in her eyes. *This is all so crazy, is any of this really happening?* She slowly stood and faced her friend.

"Okay... Let's get this over with." She began to cry.

"Pull it together until we get outside," Maggie said. "We still need to make it past your family."

The girls made it outside without trouble. They grabbed several items and said they were taking them to Joseph's house. Mary's mother did not look up from what she was doing. She merely said, "At least you're out of your room. I wasn't sure you would leave it today."

Once clear of the house, Maggie said, "Follow me, let's go find Roger."

Mary looked at her friend as they walked. "You know Roger isn't going to believe any of this either, don't you?"

Maggie hadn't thought that far ahead. She liked the idea of having Roger there as they broke the news to Joseph, but she hadn't once considered how they were going to tell Roger what was happening. *Crap, this just keeps getting better. Roger will think we are both nuts. Fantastic.*

"You're right," Maggie replied, "I'm not sure how any of this will work. I just know it has to. If the story you told me is true, and I believe that it is from seeing your eyes as you told it, then we have to find a way to convince our men. They have to believe."

"Thank you, Mags," Mary said. They continued walking with arms full of food for the feast later that day. Mary hoped there would still be a feast. She really was trying to be strong, but the tears kept sneaking up on her. What should be the greatest, most glorious news ever told, was going to be received with skepticism, denial, and ridicule. How could any rational human believe any of this?

Faith.

Mary looked around as they walked. She was sure she heard the word, but Maggie made no reaction, as if it was inaudible. *God*, she thought (it may have been more of a prayer), *I'm trying to have faith, please help Joseph have faith too.*

They continued down the side streets toward Joseph's house. Roger and Maggie lived close to Joseph, a few doors down the same lane. Maggie let herself in to her home to find Roger sitting at the table eating some dates and beans. Mary followed her in.

Roger looked up as they entered. "Hey, babe. Hi, Mary." He looked at the food they were carrying. "Shouldn't you be taking that to Joe's?" he asked as he took another bite of beans.

Maggie's eyes got a little wider. She had an idea. "Yes, we need to take this to Joseph's. Can you help us carry it?"

Mary saw where she was going with this. "Yes, Rog, we would definitely appreciate some help with all of this."

Roger looked at them skeptically. They each had an armful, but it appeared to be more than manageable.

Maggie saw his look and acted on it immediately. "If you can grab this stuff, I'll get a few other things, and we can all run them down to J's house."

She frantically scanned the room for something she could take that would make sense. She was not finding anything, and she was taking too long. Her eyes darted back and forth as she tried to think of something. Anything. Her mind went blank.

"Dates," Mary said, seeing that her friend had blanked. "Can you bring some dates, too?"

Roger stared at his wife and her friend. Something was not quite right, these two were up to something. He took the items from his wife's arms and continued to watch as she ran off and grabbed a small bag of dates.

Maggie turned and saw his doubting face. She was never good at deceiving her husband and, more importantly, she did not *want* to be good at it.

"Oh, stop it," Maggie said to her husband with half a smile. "Just follow us to Joseph's. You'll find out what's going on when we get there."

"Dates?" Roger asked. "Seriously?"

"Shut up," Maggie said with a grin. "It's the best we could come up with. We need you to come with us. It's kind of serious."

"Kind of?" Mary asked with her eyebrows raised. Maggie just looked at her. She had that "just work with me" look in her eye. Mary said nothing else, she only nodded and turned toward the door.

The trio walked the few doors down to Joseph's place. Mary raised her hand to knock but froze with her hand suspended in a fist. She simply stared at the door. Terror overcame her, and she was having trouble breathing. Maggie hugged her from behind, then tapped on the door. Joseph called from inside for them to enter.

Joseph was cleaning for the party that night. He smiled when he saw Mary and his friends enter. He took the items from Mary's arms and placed them on a table. Then he turned and gave her a big hug. She wrapped her arms around him and closed her eyes, burying her face into his shoulder. When Joseph tried to release, she held on tight.

"Hey beautiful, what's with the death grip?" He asked with a smile.

Mary said nothing. She merely held on to him, concentrating on the moment, trying to will it to last. Forever would be good. Joseph glanced up at Maggie and Roger with a quizzical look.

"Don't ask me," Roger shrugged, "I have no idea what is going on."

Maggie looked worried. "Mary... hon... you need to tell him."

"No," was the only muffled reply from Joseph's chest.

"Mare," Maggie prodded.

"What's going on?" Joseph asked.

Mary released her grip and took a couple steps back. She motioned for him to sit. When he did, she sat next to him.

"I need you to let me tell you about my day. It has been a very strange day. In many ways, it has been a glorious, magical day. In other ways, it frightens me to my very soul." Mary was looking off into a non-seeable distance as she spoke. "I beg that you listen with an open heart, because God wants you to."

Joseph raised an eyebrow. "You know what God wants?"

"As it turns out, yes, I do." Mary looked Joseph in the eye. "God came to see me this morning. We had a long conversation."

Roger laughed and started to get up. "I thought this was going to be something serious. You had me worried. I really don't have time for this right now."

"Sit!" Maggie cut him off, "sit and listen. This *is* serious." Roger looked at Maggie. He didn't seem convinced this was not some sort of ruse. Still, he waited. Momentarily at least...

"So, you prayed this morning? Is that what you mean about speaking to God?" Joseph asked, trying to be patient.

"No." Mary replied. "God came to see me. In person. Sat on my bed with me and we spoke eye to eye."

Joseph's eyes narrowed. "You're not making sense."

"Please just listen, it's a long story. It changes everything for us, for you and me. God wants us to do something." Mary looked at Joseph, eyes pleading. "He wants us to have His baby. God's baby."

"What are you talking about? You're starting to sound crazy. Are you trying to sound crazy because you're having second thoughts about getting married? Is it nerves? I've never seen you like this." Joseph looked at her critically.

"Joseph, I love you. All I want is to be your wife. I'm excited and happy about that. But God wants me to carry His son." Mary looked down at her belly and placed her hands there. "His son is already inside of me."

Joseph tilted his head, eyes wide. "Are you trying to tell me you're pregnant? What the fuck, Mary? Why would you say something like that? It's sick. And on our wedding day? What's wrong with your head? This better be some kind of joke." Joseph scowled.

Roger glanced quickly at Mary, then at Joseph, then back to Mary. He was thoroughly confused. This was entirely too weird for words. Maggie placed her hand on top of his own.

"Please just listen to what happened," Mary asked, calmer than she thought possible, given the circumstances. She told the story of her morning, much like she had explained it to Maggie. Only this time she could tell her audience wasn't listening. She could see a rage building inside of Joseph. He sat staring at the floor with a pained grimace on his face. Tears welled in her eyes, then slid down her cheeks as she continued. His eyes were dark and brooding, and she could sense how tense he was. She continued explaining the events with God, even the part about Gabriel. And then she was finished. She looked at Joseph, waiting for his response, but his eyes were still focused on the floor.

Silence.

Roger shook his head. "Amazing. That is absolutely amazing." He looked at Mary in awe. Maggie smiled at her husband; she knew he would believe.

More silence.

Joseph sat still, staring at the floor. He was silent for what felt like an eternity to Mary. She could still see the rage building. His breath was slow and methodical. *Had he listened at all?* she wondered. *To any of it?*

Slowly, much too slowly, Joseph began to stand. He clapped his hands together once. Then once again. He began clapping his hands together, very slowly and very deliberately. His eyes were on fire with rage and anger, and they were pointed directly at Mary. He continued clapping, much too slowly, and he even tried to smile. The smile came off as a pained scowl, nearly the look of a madman, the kind of face that would frighten children.

"That... was an incredible pile of ox shit. Well done."

Mary's heart sank.

"You're pregnant?" Joseph asked.

"Yes." Mary began to cry.

"And you expect me to believe God, OUR GOD, got you pregnant by waving His hand? Are you fucking kidding me?"

Mary dropped to her knees. "Please God, you promised you would talk to him. You promised to make him understand. I cannot bear this. I cannot do this. Please pick someone else. I just can't..." She trailed off crying uncontrollably.

Maggie ran to her friend and hugged her tightly. She shot Joseph a glance that could melt stone.

Joseph rolled his eyes and turned away.

"Dude!" Roger yelled at his friend. "Why are you being such a dick? Why would she make something like this up?"

Joseph glared at Roger. "I don't know Roger, why would she? I'm not entirely sure what the fuck is going on here."

He was about to say more when there was a knock at the door.

"Fuck," Joseph said, hesitated for a second but couldn't think of a smartass reply, so he walked to the door. The others looked toward the door as well. Joseph opened it, but there was no one there. He looked to the left and to the right, but there was no sign of anyone. *Well fuck, why the hell not? Why would anything make sense today?*

As he turned back to the others, he froze. Standing behind them was an old man (as it turns out, it was the same one who talked to Mary earlier that day) and a very tall, very bright angel. Joseph stumbled backwards and fell onto his bottom. He immediately regained his feet and put himself between Mary and the intruders. He lifted his fists in the air and yelled, "Get out before I hurt you!"

Roger was next to his friend in half a second, also ready to fight. Maggie plopped to the floor, sitting v-legged with her mouth open. Her mind was having difficulty making sense of what she was seeing.

The old man smiled. "The fear..."

Gabriel nodded.

Mary smiled too. *I guess He knows His people,* she thought, remembering her own reaction hours earlier.

Joseph and Roger shared a quick glance. The old man seemed to be glowing. He seemed old and young at the same time. And that there was something... different... comforting... something about him that defied description. That observation entirely ignored the fact that an angel was standing next to him. The angel glowed brightly and was adorned in jewels and stones the likes of which they had never seen before. He had long, flowing hair and a strong chiseled face. He had wings, big white wings, just as they had always been told.

"Wait... what?... I don't... who?..." Both men tried to articulate something, anything. Bits and fragments were all that came out.

"The confusion..." God said with a slight smile. Gabriel merely nodded. He had heard it too many times to be surprised by it, but God seemed entertained.

The reactions happened in the span of seconds, but it seemed to take much longer. It hit Joseph, just as it did Roger and Maggie, that the old man, the him, wasn't a him, but was a Him, or more specifically THE Him. Eyes got a little bigger, there was back-pedaling, there were confused looks. Gabriel just waited patiently for this part of the little game to play out. It was like a ritual. God rarely showed Himself to His people. When He did, He enjoyed the recognition progression that nearly always played out the same way. God mentioned often to Gabriel that His people could be so predictable one minute, and completely unpredictable the next, and He genuinely enjoy that.

"This can't be happening," Joseph said.

"Am I dead? Was there an accident? What a weird dream..." Roger was dazed.

"And the disbelief. Every time!" God proclaimed, showing his teeth as he smiled. "Okay, I'm going to ask you to refrain from the groveling... Stop!" God pointed at Roger who appeared to be heading to his knees.

"Mary, Maggie, Roger... have a seat. Joseph, I need you to stand for a moment."

Joseph stood before God. The anger from earlier was gone. It was completely forgotten, to be honest. He was awed and amazed, and he had the strong urge to grovel.

"Son, I'm not going to lie, I'm disappointed. I expected a stronger reaction from you. Jealousy? Really?" God walked over to Mary and placed His hand upon her cheek. "This young lady loves you more than life itself. She came to you with something important, something significant to both of you. Something that will change your lives forever. She came to you immediately. She didn't wait for a convenient time.

"She even told me that you wouldn't understand. She was terrified to tell you this news, but she did. She came right away, with your truest friends, because it was the right thing to do. She knows you well. Sadly, her gut feeling was that you would not believe the truth. And you did not. Granted, you nearly did at first, but you let doubt and jealousy win your mind," God paused for effect.

Shamed by God. Now let's just take a step back and think about that for a moment. Of all of the humiliations one can endure, of all of the humbling situations we can put ourselves in, of all of the regretful, foot-in-mouth moments we find ourselves having to own up to, can you think of anything worse than meeting God in person, disappointing Him, and then have Him call you on it? Wow. You would have to be strong indeed to recover from that Heavenly kick to the jewels.

Joseph had tears of shame running down his face. "I am so sorry..."

God shook his head and wagged his finger. "Not Me, son. Not Me."

Joseph looked at God for a moment, not quite understanding. When it hit him, he turned to look at Mary. How could he have ever doubted her? She had been the best thing in his life since the moment they met. She had always been honest, to the point of being too honest. Tears flowed freely from his eyes. He loved her so very much, yet he let her down. He believed the worst when he had no reason to do so. He felt small. Worse than that, he felt as though he failed her. The truth, he realized at that moment, was that was exactly what he did. He failed her.

You have a choice. Let it consume you... or use this lesson to make yourself stronger, better.

Joseph was not sure if those were his own words in his head, but he *was* sure he would never fail Mary again. He wiped tears from his eyes, though they were immediately replaced with new ones. He walked to where Mary sat and knelt before her. He took her hands in his and looked her in the eyes.

"I failed you. You deserve a stronger man. I never should have doubted your words, because they're *your* words. You have never told a lie that I am aware of. And yet I didn't believe you. I doubted because I could not process that any of this could be real. I am so very, very sorry."

Joseph stood and turned toward God. "...and You are wrong, Sir. I do owe You an apology. I did not keep my faith in the face of difficult news. I assumed since I've never seen You myself that no one else has either. I let logic and common sense displace faith in the unseen. Please believe, even though I had a moment of weakness, my faith is strong. As is my love for You and all You do." Joseph bowed his head.

Mary spoke from behind Joseph. "I understand that this is a difficult thing to wrap your head around. Believe me I do. I'm still working through some of that myself. I'm also still having trouble believing any of this is real. It's a lot to take in."

"Did you notice before Joseph recognized Me, he immediately put himself between you and the perceived danger?" God said to Mary. "*That* is his true heart. That is the reason I chose you, Joseph. I have no second thoughts about you. I know you are a good man. I know your faith is strong. I know how much you love Mary. I also know you will be an excellent father as I know Mary will be an excellent mother. I chose you both very carefully. I made sure you are both strong enough to bear this burden and wise enough to make it work."

Joseph partially raised his hand to ask a question. "I'm not exactly clear on how to make this work. I'm still not entirely sure what all of this means. Can you help me with some of the logistics here?"

Gabriel smiled at the question.

"Fair enough," God said. "What would you like to know?"

"If this is Your child, how do I fit in?" Joseph asked.

"Yes," Roger interjected, trying to be helpful, "what are the logistics? What is the process? How does Joseph get from here to there?"

Joseph, Maggie, and God silently stared at Roger (as did Gabriel, but he was always silent). He smiled back at them for a moment before realizing they had entered into an awkward silence. He looked about for a moment, but they continued to stare. He thought back to what he had just asked, not quite understanding what had just happened.

"What?" Roger asked.

"Seriously?" Maggie groaned.

"Seriously. What?" Roger asked again.

"You just man-splained logistics... to God no less," Maggie rolled her eyes.

"Did I?" Roger asked. Joseph, God, and Gabriel nodded. "Oh crap, I did. Wow, sorry about that. I'll just sit down now." And he did.

God smiled at him and shook His head.

"Yes, I guess I skipped some of the finer points. Okay, let's talk details. This is My child, but I can't be a father to Him, not in the sense that you are thinking. I won't be doing the day-to-day parenting. I won't be doing *any* of the parenting. I won't be on the sidelines cheering Him on at His soccer games or helping with His homework." God looked at Mary and Joseph. "That will be you two. In fact, I'll have very little interaction with Him at all.

"The bulk of your task is to raise Him. You are to teach Him to know who He is and to know who I am. You'll teach Him to pray as if He is just another boy. You'll let Him know He is my son, but in all other ways He is to be raised as a normal human. I will counsel Him in other ways. Some ways He will see clearly, others He will not. With your guidance and love, He will grow to be the leader I need Him to be." God paused.

"I would love to be able to tell you this will be an easy task. However, that is not the case. Problem number one is that He will be born a human boy child. You've all seen what *they* can be like. They have no fear of heights, no common sense, no understanding of danger, a love of farting and burping. They are constantly moving, they get into everything, and they have horrible aim while peeing. And they are so needy. This will test your parenting skills, let alone your patience.

"Problem number two is that as He gets older, not everyone is going to like Him. He is going to piss people off because He will know things that others think He can't possibly know. He may also be a tad bit arrogant at first. He will learn humility eventually, but one typically needs a few life-lessons before that kicks in.

"Problem number three, and this is the most immediate concern, sooner or later King Herod will find out about Him. How do you suppose the fine king will react to news of a messiah born in his own kingdom? Herod is dangerous and unpredictable. He is also losing his mind slowly due to an illness." God smiled and winked. "Being God lets you in on all sorts of good secrets."

Roger hit Joseph in the shoulder with the back of his hand. "Martin and I told you he was mad."

"Yes, you did, here's a cookie," Joseph replied, patting Roger on the head. Roger shrugged away from him.

"Herod will be a problem. He has been in charge around these parts for a long time and he likes it. He has spies throughout the kingdom that report to him regularly. He knows what is happening in his kingdom. I mentioned he is ill, but that does not make him dumb. He has remained in power because he is intelligent and because he is ruthless. My angels have been telling shepherds what is coming. That news has made its way to Herod. When he hears these reports repeated enough times, you won't be safe."

"Won't be safe?" Joseph asked, obviously confused. "How could we not be safe? Are we not under Your protection?"

The others looked to God for an answer.

God grimaced. "It's not that simple. The way I do things, because I encourage free will, I mostly let things play out as they do. I occasionally step in, but as a rule I tend to stay out of human affairs."

"That explains a lot," Maggie said, "like all the pain and suffering that happens daily. Horrible people treating weaker people badly. Rape, murder, assault, robbery… and You're okay letting it just play out?"

Gabriel looked up and raised an eyebrow at her brash question.

God looked Maggie in the eye, His face all seriousness. "Yes, I am. It has to be this way, for reasons I cannot explain to you right now. But it's the same reason I let all the good in the world happen too."

"That's a bit of a cop out, don't you think?" Maggie asked sharply.

God looked at Maggie and smiled. "There are reasons for everything I do. That will have to suffice."

Maggie looked down, *that's just another cop out.*

It's not a cop out. You must have faith.

Maggie's eyes got a little bigger. Her eyes shot to God's. *You heard that?*

Yes. God smiled.

Maggie's eyes got bigger still. *Please get out of my head.*

I can't, I'm everywhere all the time.

Oh crap, I'm never touching myself again.

I tend to look away at times like that.

Maggie's eyes were wide as saucers, and she began to blush. "Oh, God..." She mumbled as she turned away from the others and buried her face in her hands. She was mortified. The others did not notice.

"Wouldn't this be a case where You would intervene if we were in trouble?" Joseph asked.

"Yes, probably," God said honestly. "I've stepped in and helped all of you before on occasion. If I do step in, it will be in ways you do not see, or I may ask others to intervene. My point, though, is that there may be times when I will not intervene. You are on your own in those moments. Herod will be a danger to all of you. He has eyes everywhere. Be wary of strangers. You have some time, but eventually you will need to leave Nazareth."

"Where are we to go?" Mary asked.

"Make your way to Bethlehem, the City of David. You will have the baby there. Make a few stops before then and do not stay in any one place too long. Try not to be noticed. Do not draw attention to yourselves,"

"I don't understand," Joseph said. "If Herod is a danger to us, why would we go to Bethlehem? It's at Jerusalem's doorstep."

"Yes, it is," God smirked. "Many people will be tested on the day My Son, our Son, is born. It will be quite the spectacle. It is to happen in Bethlehem. Get there in six months."

"Six months?" Mary asked. "Am I already three months pregnant? You just put Him there this morning!"

God, still smirking, said, "Yes, but look on the bright side, you got to skip the morning sickness."

***

God and Gabriel disappeared at some point. They didn't make a big deal of it, one moment they were there, the next moment they were gone. It was during a lull in the conversation. None of the four actually witnessed them leave, they just ... left. That seems as good a way as any to suggest the conversation is over.

Mary, Joseph, Maggie, and Roger sat for a while without speaking. Each was lost in his or her own thoughts, trying to make sense of what they had just experienced. Each was staring at their own feet, mostly unaware of anything else happening around them. This was not difficult because absolutely nothing was happening around them. The room was silent and still. Except for the breathing, there would be no sign of life there at all. They were savoring the encounter. They tried to memorize every word.

Eventually, Mary spoke. "That is a lot to take in, don't you think?"

"I'm very sorry I didn't believe you," Joseph said to her. "And yes, it is."

Mary looked at him and smiled. There was a touch of sadness in the smile.

"What happens now?" Roger asked.

Joseph tilted his head a bit. "I'm not entirely sure. I suppose we go on with our lives. We do what we would normally do. It might be best not to mention any of this to anyone."

The others nodded in agreement.

Joseph looked at Mary. "We are supposed to get married today. I was a complete ass. Will you still have me?"

Mary smiled. "You're lucky the Old Guy liked you. I trust His judgement. Anyway, it seems we are truly a match made in heaven. I'm not sure our choice matters much at this point, but if things were different, I would still want to be with you ...even though you are an ass."

Joseph smiled at her.

"Such a romantic," Maggie said laughing.

"Screw you, shrew," Mary replied smiling.

"We should probably get some sort of plan together for the wedding and feast. We need to be on the same page today while we have so many friends and family around. This may be a difficult day to keep our shit together, considering the day we've had to this point," Joseph suggested.

"Should we tell the Rabbi?" Maggie asked. "This is new ground for me. On the one hand, it seems like he would be the one person who could help us with all of this. On the other hand, I'm not convinced he would believe us. Let's be honest, *we* are having trouble believing all of this, and *we* lived it."

The others just looked at her without saying anything. No one knew what to say. She had two valid points.

9

THE WISE MEN

The headaches were acceptable, as were the dry-mouth and overwhelming urge to pee. The nasty taste in the mouth and vague recollections of saying idiotic things were also bearable. As for the other hazy memories of dancing on tables, knives thrown at walls, and uncontrollable laughter, these were all normal pieces of the lives they lived. *Not normal for most people*, Melchior conceded to himself, *but normal for us*. No, all of these things were bearable. It was the bright morning light that he could not tolerate. Melchior tried to pry one of his eyes open, but the stabbing brightness slammed it shut. He sighed and pushed his face into the pillow. *It's far too early to get up anyway. The caravan can wait. Again.* His head was pounding. Surely the others were still asleep as well. The previous night was their best party yet.

They had been traveling for what felt like months, always heading west. Gaspar had a vision in a dream, though he claimed it wasn't a dream at all, that it really happened. Melchior and Balthazar were privately skeptical. Gaspar claimed that the three of them were "invited" by God himself to come west to witness the birth of God's son. Much wine had been ingested while discussing the implications and consequences of following Gaspar's dream... vision... occurrence. Normal people would consider Gaspar mad for thinking, let alone admitting, that he had a conversation with God, but Melchior and Balthazar were only intrigued. They were skeptical that it was an actual conversation, but not at all skeptical that it was a dream that had much significance.

The three of them had met many years earlier and had become fast friends. Minds like theirs needed other minds like theirs to challenge and keep each other sharp. Hours and hours of philosophical and technical conversations had been shared between them, exploring every subject imaginable. Kings, emperors, and senators consulted with them regularly. They were sought out because they were the very brightest minds the world had ever known. Though they did not always agree, they were always respectful of each other's opinions and convictions. Melchior and Balthazar immediately agreed to join Gaspar on this adventure west. Whether because of a dream or miracle, the three agreed this was important.

They were given the moniker Wise Men by one of their clients, and the nickname stuck. They were requested by royalty and governments, and as such they were paid handsomely. The fact was, they each had more wealth than they could squander in a lifetime. Because they did not want for anything, they were often bored and looked for entertainment in various alternative venues. Many of these venues fell outside the lines of good taste. Allow me to be blunt: they drank far too much, gambled far too much, and truly enjoyed the company of women. Lots of women. Those who sought their counsel were always pleased they did but were equally pleased when the three of them were finally gone.

The Wise Men recognized the value of blowing off steam. As they traveled westward, they would periodically throw fabulous parties in the evenings once they had stopped for the night. They spaced the parties to two or three per fortnight, though sometimes more often if some event had caused stress or concern to their entourage. Their servants and guards loved them for it. Everyone was invited. Everyone had value and was important. The caravan was often late leaving the morning after one of these events. Sometimes they would not leave until early afternoon. This day was shaping up to be such a day.

***

The night of Gaspar's conversation with God, be it dream or otherwise, was very much like the party of the previous night. They had been requested by some leader in Parthia to consult about the ongoing but tenuous peace with Rome. After several days of counsel, they blew it out partying with the locals. Gaspar explained the events this way to his two friends:

They stumbled back to their suite of rooms with the lovely escorts provided by the good Parthian rulers. Balthazar and Melchior passed out cold in the parlor, as did their dates. Gaspar's new friend had also passed out. He could not remember her name, but she was fun and a good drinker. He sat on a chaise trying to maintain his balance. Someone was trying to get his attention, repeating his name. It wasn't a voice he recognized, and yet it was. He tried to focus on the room around him. It was spinning a bit.

"Gaspar. You with me pal?" The voice asked.

"Wassis ... who... is talking... where?"

"I'm right here. In front of you. Probably the one in the middle," the voice replied playfully.

Gaspar tried to focus. "Oh, there you are. Hi." Gaspar saw three small pleasant-looking old men gazing back at him. Or one or two. Seeing was hard.

"Hi, Gaspar. I would prefer to speak to all three of you, but this will do. I was going to speak to you three earlier, but to be honest, watching you morons drink is far too entertaining to interrupt," the old man said with a smile.

"You were at the party? Awesome. Sorry we didn't speak earlier. Have you seen my other sandal?" Gasper was looking at one bare foot.

"Okay... going to need your attention for this, so I'm going to sober you up a little." The old man reached forward with his finger extended and lightly touched Gaspar on the forehead.

The instant the finger landed on his forehead, Gaspar was totally awake, totally sober, and totally aware of who had touched him. He dropped to his knees and placed his forehead on the floor. "Forgive me, Father, for I have sinned."

"Okay, that's funny. Not something you will ever say to your Rabbi, I think. You often surprise Me, Gaspar, you are always a couple steps ahead of your time," God told him with a smile, "Yes, you have sinned. A lot. But we can deal with that later."

"I don't understand," Gaspar said quietly as he considered what God had just said.

"That's funny too. The last time you didn't understand something, you were nine. Get up, Gaspar, and have a seat next to me. I'd like to speak with you for a bit." God patted the seat of the chaise Gaspar had occupied earlier.

Gasper looked at what he thought had been a kind old man. His mind was clear now—he was looking at God. God had taken the form of an old man, but light emanated from His entire being. He nearly looked human. The eyes gave him away. They were light. No pupils, no irises, just light. Gaspar moved to the chaise and looked upon God as He sat on a chair in humble robes. Gaspar kept looking at His eyes, they were bright white light, but you could stare without looking away.

"The light..." Gaspar began to say before trailing off, still staring intently at His eyes.

"Yes, that's a good place to start, and is something you and your friends might actually understand," God considered before continuing, "I am the light. You have heard that before, 'God is the light'. It's actually true, it's not a metaphor. I truly am the light. I am everywhere and everything because I am the light. A few years from now, a fun, smart kid like yourself decides to figure out the mathematical equation for energy. He dances around the answer for a while, nearly getting it. He keeps coming up with a constant that he recognizes but doesn't quite understand why. He understands the mass component but just cannot place the constant. Then it hits him. The constant is the speed of light. You should have seen his eyes when he figured it out. Or, I guess I should say when he *figures* it out, since he hasn't been born yet. Time is a tricky concept, even for me and I invented it. But it doesn't apply to me, which makes things a little confusing. Anyway, Albert figures out that energy is a function of light. He also understands at that moment that I am, in fact, light. He will be the closest as a mortal to understanding who and what I am. I'll fill you all in later when you join Me in Heaven.

"The reason I'm telling you about Albert is because Melchior and Balthazar will think our chat was just a dream you had. Once you tell them about Albert, they may not admit it to you, but they will believe. They will believe because, of the three of you, you are not the numbers guy. Balthazar is the mathematician. They will not think you could create Albert in your subconscious without some external input."

"I'm still not sure I understand," Gaspar said honestly.

"No, but you will come close. Let's get to the nut of why I am speaking with you today. I am planning to shake things up a little. I have decided to have a son, a human child born of a human mother. It's going to happen relatively soon in a town called Bethlehem. It's a nice little spot just down the road from Jerusalem. I would like you and your friends to come witness it."

"A son? Why on earth would you want a son? Kids are horrible. They are an enormous headache. Screaming, pooping, running about, getting into everything," Gaspar said sourly.

"Do I need to touch your forehead again? I thought I sobered you up! I'm not looking for your permission. I'm also not looking for a little sprout to bounce on my knee. It's for you! And for them!" God pointed in no particular direction. "The world needs a push in another direction. The Noah thing, in hindsight, was a bit heavy-handed, so I thought I'd try something different. My Son will teach you about Me, and love, and forgiveness. He will show you what you need to do to join Us in Heaven. He will be tasked with convincing the enlightened souls of this world that a change of heart is being requested by Me. By requested, I rather mean commanded. I don't mean to be a diva here, but it's kind of My party, and this is the way I would like to see things go. I swear the very best and very worst thing I ever did was giving you people free will."

God paused for a moment, smiled, then continued, "He will actually succeed, too. Not the way you or He would expect, but He will. And as a great big thank you, the benevolent ruling class will mock and torture Him, and then they will kill Him. Such is the way of My free-willed children."

Gaspar was appalled. "You know this? You know all of this will happen and yet You continue? Why would You do such a thing? *How* could You do such a thing?"

God smiled. "If you only knew the half of it. It goes far beyond anything I've told you thus far. Hundreds of thousands will die in His name. Hundreds of thousands will be killed for merely believing in Him. You and your friends have been blessed with a keen intellect far beyond that of most of the population. Yet even you, my irresponsible but brilliant friends, cannot understand My motives and My objectives. Let Me leave you with this: I do this because I have to. He will die to absolve you of your sins. Yours, and everyone else's. He is being sent to save the world. He is being sent to show you the way to save yourselves. He is being sent by Me to hand you the keys to the Kingdom of Heaven. Sadly, most of you will be too thick to see this opportunity for what it is.

"That's enough for now. I would really like you boys to come to the birth of My Son, it should be quite a spectacle. There are a few things I would like to request, if I may. I'm trying to be nice and not pull rank here. My child will be raised by His mother, Mary, a virgin, and a carpenter, Joseph, who loves her. They are both really great young people. I chose them carefully. It will be a rough start for them. Not everyone is going to be pleased about this. In fact, some people will be outright pissed. That will continue for centuries, by the way. I would like to ask if you three could escort them to Bethlehem. It's a long journey from Nazareth, and it would be good for all of you." God winked with a slight smirk.

"Before that, though, I would like you three and your caravan to stop in Jerusalem and let King Herod know why you are there. Tell him you heard the birth of the King of Kings was happening somewhere in the area, an event you wanted to witness. Don't mention Mary and Joseph by name, and don't mention that they will be traveling with you." God removed a bit of lint from His robe. "Herod is a little tortured of late, and I think this news may push him over the edge. Get a read on the situation and warn Mary and Joseph if the good king is losing his shit over this.

"Lastly, when you get to the birth, I would ask that you three chip in and give them a little something to help them on their way. They will need all the help they can get. Things may get interesting afterward, and dangerous." God searched for more lint on his robes.

"We are honored, Lord, to be of service to you." Gaspar was on the verge of tears. He felt happy and content and fulfilled. He felt excited, awed, humbled.

"Thanks, kid," God said. He pointed to Gaspar's passed-out associates. "And thank them for Me too.

"After you get a read on Herod, head to Nazareth. Once there, ask around for a carpenter named Joseph. I'll make sure you ask the right person." God nodded. "Once you convince Mary and Joseph to accompany you, head to Bethlehem. Look to the sky, I'll point the way. I'll make it easy for you to find. It will be a long and dangerous trip. I want you there, so I'll have your back if you find yourselves in serious trouble. That does not mean I will bail you out if you get overly stupid. Stay on task and you should be alright.

"By the way, the little forehead touch saved you from one big-ass hangover." God smiled, and then was gone.

Gaspar had to repeat the conversation he had with God at least four times before Melchior and Balthazar would speak of anything else. Even then, the three of them spent hours and hours exploring what it could mean. Gaspar knew exactly what it meant. He was there. The other two had to examine it logically for a bit, whether it was a dream or vision or something else entirely. In the end, they all knew they would be heading west to Judaea. Although not entirely sure how all of this would play out, they were fairly certain that God would throw a pretty fabulous birthday party for the kid.

The Wise Men knew the journey would take them many weeks. They made preparations, collected the necessary provisions, and assembled a crew for the caravan. Altogether they numbered twenty-seven and they were prepared to set out within a week. God had indeed pointed the way quite clearly. They only need follow the bright star in the western sky, and that is exactly what they did.

***

Melchior was awake but kept his aching head buried in his pillow. He slowly let in light to try to adjust his eyes. He had to pee and desperately needed some water. *I'm glad we only have these parties occasionally.*

"You awake?" Balthazar asked from the other side of the tent. Tent is somewhat of an understatement, as this one had multiple rooms and easily covered a thousand square feet. It was a long journey, but not one without luxury.

"Yes," Melchior replied.

"Me too," came Gaspar's voice from underneath a pile of blankets.

"We're about three weeks out from Nazareth. So far, the weather has been agreeable. I think we could skip a day of travel and not throw us too far off schedule," Balthazar said. His voice was somewhat gravelly.

A muffled laugh came from under the pile of blankets. "You were on fire last night, Balthazar," Gaspar said, still laughing. "I haven't seen you drink like that in months. Feeling a little low this morning?"

"It's not morning, it's already afternoon. And yes, I feel like shit, it hurts when I blink. Let's just skip travelling today and head out all the earlier tomorrow," Balthazar grumbled.

"No argument here," Melchior chimed in.

"Fine with me," Gaspar added.

Melchior pulled his pillow back tightly over his eyes. He was asleep in minutes. Balthazar was also asleep before long. Gaspar was having trouble getting back to sleep, though. He tossed and turned, adjusting his pillow, adjusting his blanket, adjusting his body position. Nothing seemed to help. He turned to his side and opened his eyes. They were not quite focusing, but he could make out the form of a person moving about on the far side of the tent, and a smaller form moving as well. As his eyes began to focus, he could see it was Ella. She appeared to be cleaning up. Even from his position on the floor, he could see the tent was a disaster from the party the night before. Ella was collecting goblets, picking up half-eaten pieces of some form of food items, and bits of trash. She straightened pillows and put random items back in their proper places.

While she worked, a small shadow followed her every move. It was Ella's son, Aaron. In all honesty, Gaspar wasn't sure how old the child was. He had a vague memory that age five was correct. He seemed smallish for five, but five felt right. Gaspar realized that in his fragile state, he was rambling in his own mind. *Brilliant.*

In the weeks they had travelled together, Gaspar had never heard the child speak. They had a cordial relationship, Gaspar and Ella. They were not exactly friends, but he liked her well enough. She was hired to help with the caravan. He never questioned her about the boy's father. He had a sinking feeling the father was out of the picture, probably permanently.

Gaspar found he couldn't take his eyes off the boy, he was so fidgety, always moving. Aaron was constantly tapping on things, shuffling his feet, swaying. Gaspar realized the boy was reacting to some sort of music in his head. That made sense. He was dancing... well, maybe not dancing. He was moving like someone who was enjoying a good song. It was fascinating to watch.

10

PREPARATION

The small council reported to Herod as instructed. Herod studied the draft proclamation they had delivered at a table in his study. Much of the work required to run a kingdom was done from this very chair. The room was not large and was furnished with only a couple tables and some comfortable chairs. There was a window that let in natural light in the daytime. The main attraction of this room for Herod was the quiet. Herod liked silence when he was concentrating on tasks or signing orders.

He took his quill and dipped it into the stone jar holding the ink. He made a few notes on the proclamation, crossed out a line, and wrote an alternative. He reread from the beginning, adding only one more note before nodding to himself. This would do. He set the proclamation aside and reached for a blank parchment. He began scribing additional notes, including several questions to be included with the census. He paused with quill in hand as he reviewed what he had written. He added several more thoughts and completed the page with instructions for the council on what he expected next. He laid the quill next to the stone jar and pushed the parchment away from him.

He enjoyed the quiet while working, yet it always made him pensive. His mind would wander back in time to mistakes made or missed opportunities. He would replay events in his mind, cringing at the things he could have done better, should have done better. Or he would cringe at the things he should not have done at all. In his youth, his temper would get out of hand, and he would act instead of reason. Over the years he learned to control the anger, manage it, but the past could not be undone. These memories would eventually lead him back to Miriam. They always did.

Miriam. The one true regret of his life. He missed her. He missed the way she moved, the way she spoke, the way she smiled. She never loved him the way he loved her. She resented him, and it made him crazy. He had never really wanted anyone the way he wanted her. He had always wanted her to feel the same for him, but she never did.

Herod's sister planted the seed in his head that Miriam was being unfaithful. His sister liked planting little seeds. He supposed it was his own fault for letting his sister manipulate him the way she did. It always led to bad things. People would end up beaten, jailed, or dead from the seeds planted by his sister. She was not a nice person in her youth, and it turns out, her demeanor did not improve with time. There was very little redeeming about her now. Yet Herod let her be her. He wasn't always as forgiving to his family members, but he had a soft spot in his heart for his sister. That was unfortunate, because she instigated the events leading to the death of his true love, Miriam.

Could he truly blame his sister for his own actions? The more he considered the thought, the more he believed he could. Partially, at least. She had planted the seed. But in the end, it was Herod who made the order. It was Herod, whose rage was so great, that he ordered the death of his beloved. The only real regret in his life.

So, tell me why? Why did you kill me?

"You know," Herod responded aloud, though he was alone in the room.

Because you are a moron?

Herod paused, "Yes, partly."

You thought I was fucking someone else?

"I did."

You know I wasn't.

"I do."

You even knew it then, didn't you?

"I did."

Stop giving me bullshit two-word answers. You fucking had me killed! Why would you do that? You are such a fuck stick! If you thought I hated you before, you have no idea what you'll be dealing with now.

"I think I may have an idea."

Do you? You may think so, but I am going to haunt your ass to the grave and beyond. Fuck head!

Herod sighed. Miriam was an angry misguided soul when she was alive. He could only imagine how she would be now. She never loved him the way he wanted. She never loved him the way he thought she should. And he had her killed. Not because of evidence of a wrong-doing, but because he was angry and wanted her to love him the way he loved her. Loving a stranger forced upon her was not Miriam's modus operandi. Miriam was never a fan of being married to Herod. He was old to her eyes, and fat and boring besides. She was force-fed a marriage of inconvenience because her parents "thought that was best." Seriously? Fuck that!

And the bastard fucking killed her! Let's not lose sight of that precious nugget.

The lines of reality were blurred for Herod. He assumed it was grief, but he was wrong. The sickness inside him was eating away at his sanity. That's the funny part. Funny in a "wow, I didn't see that coming" way. The sickness was not eating away at his sanity, per se (even though I said it was in the previous sentence... thanks for not keeping score), it was eating away at his judgement. It was attacking his right and wrong. It was attacking his ability to distinguish reality from fantasy. It had blurred the lines between life and death, which is why he continued to answer Miriam. There was a small, microscopic part of him that knew she was dead. Dead dead. The kind of dead you never come back from. Yet, the illness erased some of that reason and replaced it with "of course she's dead, but she's speaking to you and expects an answer. Don't be that dick, the one who doesn't answer. Hello? We're waiting!"

With each day, Herod embraced the task of ignoring reality and simply accepting the things in his mind without question. He knew his body was sick, he could feel that. He could feel the pain in his stomach that felt as if someone was clenching his innards with an iron grasp. He could feel the lack of energy. He could sense his vision and hearing diminishing with each passing day. But he did not sense his grip loosening on logic. He did not sense the paranoia. He did not recognize that his judgement and decision making were becoming noticeably baffling. The people around him noticed, but Herod the Great did not.

Herod looked at his notes on the table and the edited proclamation beneath them. They would be sufficient. He called for a servant to have them delivered to his council. He stared silently at nothing for several minutes after the servant left. He needed to get his mind off Miriam. He decided to walk to the garden plaza, hoping the sunshine would lift his mood. He was expecting a visit from a Roman emissary. They could meet in the plaza as easily as in a council room.

11

INTERROGATION

Two soldiers were marching down the expansive hallways of Herodium, King Herod's most spectacular palace. They were dragging a man in tattered robes, who sometimes stumbled along with them during his brief periods of consciousness. The man was bloodied and bruised, obviously beaten. He appeared to be in his late thirties or early forties. The soldiers were less than gentle as they escorted or dragged the man along the smooth polished floors of the hallway. The man would occasionally open one eye, sometimes even both, as he tried to establish where he was as he regained consciousness. He had the look of one completely disoriented. The hallways were silent except for the soldier's sandals tapping on the marble and the sound of feet dragging. Blood would periodically drip from the corner of the man's mouth.

"You there!" One of the soldiers called ahead to a servant crossing the hallway into another corridor. "Where is the king?"

The woman paused and regarded the soldiers and their companion. Her shoulders drooped a little as she saw the man's condition. *These heartless bastards. What did this one do? Get caught petting a puppy?* She scowled. "The last I saw of our good king, he was in the garden plaza."

The soldiers marched ahead with their captive, turning down the hallway the servant had just vacated. They continued down the corridor toward the daylight of the plaza at the end of the hall. They stepped through to the plaza, momentarily allowing their eyes to adjust to the bright light. They spotted Herod about a hundred paces ahead. He was speaking to what appeared to be a Roman dignitary. The soldiers approached to within several feet of the king and kneeled, allowing their captive to collapse to the marble. Their eyes were cast down to the ground.

"My king," one of the soldiers spoke as a greeting.

Herod gave them a disgusted look. "Silence. Do not interrupt while I treat with my Roman friends."

He turned back to his guest. They spoke in hushed tones for several minutes. The Roman nodded, bowed to Herod, then turned and walked away in the opposite direction.

Herod watched his guest walk away, then turned back to the soldiers. "Stand," he commanded.

They both stood, leaving their captive face down on the floor.

"If you interrupt me again, I'll feed your balls to the jackals." Herod leaned a little closer to their faces, "while they are still attached."

Both soldiers had their eyes to their feet. "Yes, My Lord. It will not happen again."

Herod looked to the man lying face down on his plaza.

"What's this?" the King asked.

The soldier who spoke looked at his king. "Tobias brought him to the front gate and bade us deliver him to you in all haste. He said this one is a shepherd and has been telling of a messiah. That the angels of heaven have been telling people to expect Him soon. That the Messiah will be the true King of Israel."

Herod frowned. He had forgotten he had asked Tobias to bring him one of these shepherds. Herod had wanted to question one face-to-face, to try to get to the bottom of these rumors.

"Stand him up," Herod commanded.

The soldiers lifted the man to his feet. The man had regained consciousness and had a very good idea where he was now. He was frightened. He shook off the soldier's grips so he could stand on his own, although not steadily. He looked the king in the eye.

"What is your name, and what do you do?" the King asked.

"I am John. I am a shepherd," the man replied, pretending to be more stable on his feet than he actually was.

"Why were you brought to me, John the shepherd?" The King smiled. There was no mirth or kindness in the smile. *I swear, half of these morons are named John.*

"For telling the truth," John the shepherd responded, still looking the king in the eye.

Herod was openly annoyed by the man's response. "And what truth is this, John the shepherd? Please, enlighten me of your truth." The King's ominous leer remained.

John was fairly certain he would not be leaving the palace upright. In fact, he was quite certain he was going to die here and now. He looked around the courtyard and noted it was a beautiful sunny day. *Is it better to die on a sunny day or a rainy day? I'm about to die, and I'm thinking about the weather.* His mind was racing. Terror gripped him briefly, until he felt an unseen hand grip his shoulder. Calmness flooded over him. He heard a voice in his head whisper, *Tell him the truth, John. It will be okay. The Kingdom of Heaven awaits you. I promise you nothing that happens here will cause you pain. The worst that can happen is meeting Me sooner than we had planned, and that's not such a bad thing, is it?*

John wiped at the dried blood on his lip and smiled. Tears welled in his eyes. "An angel of the Lord appeared to me as I tended my flock. He said, 'Fear not, for I bring tidings of comfort and joy.' He told me of the coming birth of the Son of God. That God is sending His very own flesh for the salvation of the world."

Herod smirked. He leaned over to the silent soldier and drew his longsword from its scabbard. He stood, the sword tip down in front of him, and rested both hands on the pommel. "Been drinking, John the shepherd? Maybe found some fun mushrooms to chew on? Bump your head along the way at some point? Because that sounds a lot like crazy talk to me."

"I speak the truth," John responded.

"Truth?" Herod's eyebrow raised. "Does that sound like truth to you, John the shepherd? It sounds to me like the babbling of a madman. Or worse, the bile of a discontent trying to poison the will of the people against me! Tell me, John the shepherd, will it still be the truth as I have these fine gentlemen slowly cut your fingers off and shove them down your throat? Or perhaps were you mistaken? Perhaps you were drinking after all? Perhaps you would prefer to stop spreading lies, live out your miserable existence, and be forever grateful that you have a merciful and forgiving king? Who put you up to this? Tell me the name of the would-be usurper who is having you spread these lies! Tell me, and you walk out of here a free man!"

John hesitated. He was frightened. His eyes darted side to side, looking for an escape. He felt the invisible grasp on his shoulder again, and it steadied him. He took a deep breath and slowly looked Herod in the eye again. "I am a simple man, My Lord, but that does not make me a stupid man. We both know you have no intention of allowing me to leave this place." John paused as he continued to steady himself. "Truth is truth, be it sunshine or rain. An angel of the Lord came to me with news to share with my people. As long as I continue to draw breath, I will spread this news."

Herod stared blankly at John for a moment. *Why are people so stupid? And why do I despise them so much of late?* He felt the sickness eating away at his insides. He wanted to sit down. His head was pounding, and he was breathing too rapidly. He moved both hands from the pommel to the grip. He slowly lifted the sword and raised the point to the base of the shepherd's throat.

Do not do this, Herod. This man is nothing to you. Let him go.

The words were clear in Herod's head, but it was not Miriam's voice. His eyes grew wide as he turned to one of the soldiers. "What did you say to me?"

The soldier hesitated and looked back at his king. It took him a moment to realize Herod was speaking to him. "Excuse me, My Lord, but I said nothing."

Herod's head snapped to the other soldier. "You dare question me? Who the fuck do you think you are?"

The second soldier's eyes grew wide. He took a half step backward.

"Please sir, my brother is a mute. He has never spoken, never in his life," the first soldier interjected. He had heard the king was going mad. This was the first he had seen it up close.

John the shepherd was also confused. What was the King talking about? Tobias' soldiers had beaten him for hours, though. It might be fun to see someone else get smacked about a bit.

It wasn't them, Herod. This is your Lord God Almighty. The God of Abraham and Moses. The God you've pretended to worship all these years. The God you nearly believe in. It's that or you are going bat-shit crazy. Either way you need to stand—the—fuck—down.

Herod hesitated and the sword tip dropped to the marble floor. He turned his back to the soldiers and the shepherd, keeping his right hand on the sword hilt.

"Are you a shepherd or a sorcerer?" Herod asked with his back to the three. This new voice in his head was disturbing. He did not believe it was actually God. It was more likely a trick by one of these three, or Miriam being spiteful somehow.

The soldiers looked at each other and then at John, who gave a confused look back. Suddenly they were all in the same boat, not one was sure what was happening and not one was very comfortable with that. The trio looked back at Herod, waiting to see what was coming next. The tension was thick.

"Fuck it." Herod spun to his right bringing the sword up as he turned. It neatly took the head off the speaking soldier. John crouched in place covering his head with his arms. Herod spun the other direction and planted the sword into the mute soldier's ribcage. It lodged there as he fell, taking the sword with him as he collapsed to the ground.

Wow, you truly are one crazy fuck. Was that really necessary? Let the shepherd go. You've killed enough for one day, don't you think?

Herod's head was pounding. For the first time he wondered if there was more to his illness than he originally suspected. This new voice in his head was a very unwelcome development, one that had him questioning his own sanity. Fortunately for Herod, his narcissism wouldn't allow such questions for long.

"Fuck off," the king said.

John, still crouched, looked up at the crazed king. Herod stood staring straight ahead. He was covered in blood. John and the floor around him were also covered in red splatter. Herod's arms hung loosely at his sides. He said nothing, staring blankly ahead for what seemed like minutes. John stood slowly, keeping his eyes on Herod, whose eyes then fixed on him.

"Do you see what your little sorcerer's game has made me do?" Herod said as he gestured to the bodies on the floor.

"It might have been the crazy that made you do that," John replied. At this point he had accepted his inevitable death. He was horrified by what had just happened. He hoped the God-voice in his head earlier would hold true to the promise of a painless death. He could hear feet running into the garden plaza and assumed correctly it was more of Herod's soldiers. He was quickly subdued by several of them.

A large, pale-skinned soldier with reddish hair addressed Herod. "Are you harmed, My King? Have you been injured?"

"I'm fine. Please kill this man. Then find someone to clean up this mess." Herod turned and walked away.

***

The servant woman was watching from just inside the palace. She was in the dark shadows of the entryway and went unnoticed by those in the bright light of the plaza. The acoustics of the plaza were such that sound traveled easily toward this entrance. She had watched the bizarre and horrible scene play out before her eyes. She had heard every word. She resisted the urge to throw up and instead slid down the cold wall until she was seated. She wept silently for the poor shepherd. She wept uncontrollably for what seemed like hours. She decided she no longer wished to serve this king.

Once she regained her composure, she walked slowly to her chamber and gathered her things. She wrapped her belongings in a large bundle and carried them to the main entrance of the palace. As some merchants were leaving the palace after delivering their wares inside, she walked as if she belonged with them out the front gate. She had decided to go back to her hometown. Her sisters were still there—perhaps she could find work there somewhere.

Once outside, she ducked down an alleyway and scurried along as fast as she could. She spoke to no one. She never made eye contact. She simply pressed on. No one would notice her absence today. It may take days before they noticed she was not there. Hers was not an essential role, even though she had played her part in the palace operations for many years. She was merely an accessory, another nameless servant to the king. She continued onward for hours, heading toward the outskirts of town.

She arranged passage with a caravan going to Amathus. From the time she left the palace and the grisly scene she had witnessed to the time she knocked on her sister's door, three days had passed.

"Isbel? Isbel, is that you?" her sister asked. It had been nearly five years since they had seen each other. Isbel grabbed her sister and hugged her tightly. Overcome with emotion, she cried and could not stop. Her sobs were heavy and inconsolable. Her sister was confused but simply held her and let her cry.

Isbel never returned to Jerusalem, but she spoke of it often, especially about her horrible last day at the palace and the things she had witnessed. And about how the king had gone mad. She had seen it with her own eyes.

12

FIONN

Fionn, the leader of the Celtic Guard, walked down the corridor of Herodium with Tuathal at his side. He was walking briskly, quicker than normal. He had a serious expression on his face. There was no joy in his eyes today. Some days his eyes shown like the sun. On those days, he would have a hint of a smile and his eyes would be bright. On those days he was jovial and approachable, but not today. Today he looked tired, serious, and intent on getting somewhere.

"What's on your mind?" Tuathal ran his fingers through his beard as he asked.

"Not here," Fionn replied curtly as they continued down the hallway. Herod had too many ears throughout the palace.

Tuathal regarded his friend for a moment with a quizzical look on his face. His gaze drifted back down the corridor, and he said nothing else. He followed along at the same brisk pace. The sound of their sandals on the floor echoed off the walls.

They were headed to the barracks that they currently called home. There had been many places they had called home over the years. Some were in lavish palaces like this one, some were in cities, some were encampments, some were basic tents near battlefields, and some were out in the wilderness wherever they could find a place to sleep. They had travelled so often over so many years that the idea of home had lost its meaning.

Home was where you stayed until you were needed elsewhere. The word no longer held a connection to family. It no longer held a connection to youth or friends or pleasant memories. It no longer was a place longed for or regarded with melancholy. It was just a place. Home was just a word.

They entered the barracks and made their way to Fionn's quarters. Fionn motioned for Tuathal to sit as he grabbed a chair for himself.

Tuathal knew the best way to approach his friend in one of these moods was to reminisce first. "How many leaders have we served together?"

Fionn rested two fingers to his lips. "Seven, that I am certain of, though I may be forgetting one. Or two. We aren't as young as we once were." He grinned.

"That sounds about right. It's been a long time since we met on the shores of Caledonia."

"I still can't believe you made it across the channel on that piece of driftwood you called a boat. Was Hibernia really that bad? That you risked your ass to get to Caledonia?"

"I barely had a beard then. I was a kid, I just needed to get away. You were just a kid then as well. I'm glad you were there when I got to shore, I had swallowed far too much salt water," Tuathal grimaced.

"I never intended to help you, but I just couldn't turn away. I had never seen anyone throw up that much. It still makes me laugh to this day." The sparkle was returning to Fionn's eyes.

"And that started it all. We've seen a lot since then, mostly death and violence, but there were some good things as well."

"That is the world we live in," Fionn replied. "I think I enjoyed Egypt the best. Cleopatra had a mean streak, but she was a solid ruler. I was disappointed when she gave us to the Romans."

"So, what's on your mind? You seemed rather focused in the hallways. You aren't the one who normally gets pissed, that's my shtick. Don't be stealing my act."

"We've all seen that Herod has been losing it lately. What I saw today makes me think it may be far worse than we thought. He killed two guardsmen today."

"Ours? Our men?" Tuathal scowled, releasing a glimpse of his temper.

"No, they were Roman. Still, he was unhinged. I got there after the fact, and I'm not clear how it played out, but there were two dead soldiers on the ground. Herod and a shepherd were covered in blood. Herod was in a daze."

"Maybe the shepherd killed them?"

Fionn raised his eyebrow and grimaced. "Not a chance, you know better. They were Roman soldiers. It was obviously Herod, or they would have fought back. My point is, I am not certain we can trust him to make rational decisions anymore. It was fun to joke about up until now, but this is getting serious."

"What can we do about it? He's the king."

"I'm not sure yet. Just keep an eye on our men, and check in with me if any of his orders seem out of place." Fionn was becoming pensive again.

"Will do. By the way, what happened to the shepherd? Or should I ask?"

Fionn shrugged. "Herod asked me to kill him. I snuck him out the back instead. I'm not really sure why, it just seemed like the right thing to do. I guess there had been enough killing for one day."

13

THE WISE MEN HEAD WEST

The caravan pushed onward, as they had for many days. They were approaching the outskirts of Jerusalem. The plan was to travel a bit further, then make camp for the evening so they could visit King Herod in the morning. The previous day the Wise Men sent a messenger ahead to alert the king of their imminent arrival. It was the Wise Men's opinion that a little forewarning of their approach seemed to work out better for everyone involved. If nothing else, it allowed the hosts time to gather enough wine to make things worthwhile. Should they not be welcome at this time, the messenger would return with that news, and the caravan would just push on to Nazareth as God instructed.

The traveling could be quite boring, not the evenings, but the actual traveling. It involved monotonous days of walking or riding toward the next destination. It was usually too hot or too cold, and it was always dirty. The roads were typically in bad repair, unless they were in Rome. The Romans took the time to build things properly. However, the rest of the world, especially between cities, did not follow suit. There were occasional sandstorms or rainstorms. The wheels of the wagons would sometimes be damaged by rocks or holes along the way. After several days of travel, there was less to speak about with the rest of the caravan. Weeks into the journey, people mostly traveled in silence. There were always exceptions, but that was typically how things played out.

Usually on the last day of travel to a destination, the Wise Men would walk together to discuss the next day's events. It was a ritual they had perfected over the years. It helped prepare them for the meeting ahead. In all their previous travels, they had not yet met the King of Judaea. They had met many other kings and leaders across the known world, but not Herod. Meeting kings was nothing new, but this time things were different. This was an important mission, considering who assigned it.

Melchior began the pre-game ritual as always, with a question about their next meeting. "What do we know about Herod?"

"A lot, as it turns out." Amusement played on Balthazar's lips.

"Fair enough, dick head. I'll be more specific. What are his strengths?"

"He's been leader of Judaea and the surrounding lands for thirty-two years. That kind of longevity only exists for those who are either very smart or very lucky. Though the latter may be true, I am more apt to believe he has ruled so long because he knows what he's doing. No, more than that, he can anticipate what others are doing as well," Balthazar added. "This one is not to be underestimated."

"Strengths..." Gaspar said, "He has a solid army for one. He's favored by Augustus for another. Having the emperor of Rome on your side helps the strength perception. This apparent friendship has helped Herod to convince Rome to let him deal with the people of Judaea directly. What I mean by that is Rome typically forces its will upon their subjects. To my knowledge, Judaea is the only land exempt from the state religion of Rome. That is a direct result of the friendship between Herod and Augustus. It's brilliant if you think about it. History has shown the Jewish people will never accept any other religion. They'll never worship the gold idols of Rome. They would prefer to die one and all in resistance, if necessary. Herod must have convinced Augustus of the futility of strong-arming the Jews into accepting the religion of Rome. The fact that Rome agreed to allow this exception is unprecedented," Gaspar continued. "I'll get into how they screwed it up when we discuss weaknesses."

"I'm looking forward to hearing that," Balthazar said. "Moving on with strengths. Herod was born to be a builder. He is obsessed with massive building projects. The projects he has completed across his kingdom are second to none. The palaces and temples are incredible. For the temple in Jerusalem, he essentially built a small mountain to place it on. The port city of Caesarea is beyond words. His projects rival, and usually surpass, those of the Romans. The projects create work, giving the people focus and purpose. But there is a downside here that will also make the weakness list."

"He is also ruthless," Melchior offered.

"Is ruthlessness a strength or a weakness?" Gaspar asked.

"It can be both," Balthazar said, "but in his case, I would have to say strength. Herod isn't loved by his people. They don't consider him to be a true Jew. Some don't consider him Jewish at all. Herod mostly rules by fear, as many leaders do. His ruthlessness and his intelligence are probably what have kept him in power for so long."

"Very good. Now what are his weaknesses?" Melchior asked.

Balthazar started them off. "As I mentioned, he doesn't have the support of the people. They don't really like him. Partially for his relationship with Rome. I mentioned the port city of Caesarea earlier and the weakness associated with Herod's projects. While the people do love the temple in Jerusalem, they consider Caesarea antithetical to Judaism. It smacks of pagans and Rome, and the people despise him for it."

"As you may be aware, Herod also has a history of killing his own family," Melchior said. "His own sons for example. And wives. Early on, he married Miriam, a Hasmonean princess. It was a calculated move to gain credibility with the Jewish population. He ended up falling for her hard. She hated him, but that's beside the point. He loved her—the crazy, head-over-heels kind of love. The kind of love that makes you do stupid things. Like when Balthazar sees a jug of wine."

The others laughed.

"I partially agree with your earlier assessment about his ruthlessness," Gaspar said. "I can see where it can be a strength for him, but I contend that it's a weakness as well. He killed several of the rabbis from the Sanhedrin, the Jewish court system. The people were not pleased. In fairness, he's avoided additional aggressions toward the Sanhedrin for the last decade or so because of the popularity of Hillel and Shammai, the two who now run it.

Gaspar rested a finger on his lips. "Earlier I touched on Herod and Augustus screwing up the religion compromise, please let me explain."

"We insist," Melchior replied. Balthazar merely nodded.

"Thanks. You guys are just peachy," Gaspar's voice was thick with sarcasm. "Anyway, the agreement to exempt Judaea from the state religion of Rome was an excellent idea. One that could have convinced the Jewish population that this accord with Rome would be a good thing. It was absolutely in line with what the three of us would have suggested had they asked our counsel, but as you know, Rome never asks our opinion on anything. They continue to insist they're the smartest people in the room. Every room. Ultimately, Augustus was troubled for allowing it. It made him uneasy to allow one kingdom a pass that was not allowed in any other kingdom. It was a bothersome toothache that Augustus could not stop agitating with his tongue. He ended up imposing an additional tax on all of the Jews in Herod's kingdom for the privilege of not being force-fed the religion of Rome. It's not a small tax, either.

"As you can imagine, it had a predictable result." Gaspar rubbed his hands together. "While grateful they were free to worship as they always had, the Jews in Herod's kingdom were furious about the new tax. They accepted it, given the alternative, but they hate Herod and Augustus because of it."

"It's a shame they don't ask for a little advice now and then. We could have helped them with this. It wouldn't have even been a difficult fix. They had the answer. They had a happy and productive compromise in the palms of their hands. It's a shame they're so arrogant," Melchior said.

Balthazar laughed. "Said the real smartest guys in the room."

Gaspar pinched his nose. "If it looks like a camel, smells like a camel, spits like a camel... it's a camel."

14

DAY DRINKING

Herod sat on a stone bench in the garden plaza. It was warm for this time of the morning. The sun was bright, with only a few clouds in the sky. There was a slight breeze to help cool the heat of the morning sun. He would move the meeting to the shade should it become oppressive. His guests would be arriving shortly. Herod had heard much about these Wise Men, consultants to kings, hired to provide creative solutions to difficult problems. They were usually effective in resolving issues. He had heard many stories about their successes, but also— stories of the aftermath. If the stories were accurate, these men would have lavish parties to wrap up their services, sponsored by the host, of course.

Herod wasn't sure why the Wise Men had requested an audience with him. They tended to spend their time in the east. Most of their consulting activities occurred outside the limits of Roman Empire, though that was not always the case. Judaea was the eastern limit of Rome's holdings. He had heard they traveled as far east as the Chinese Empire, a place Herod could only imagine. So, what was bringing them to Judaea? He could only speculate on their motives. It could be as simple and benign as they were passing through on their way to another engagement. It could be as complicated as they needed information only Herod possessed. There was no way to be sure. Whatever the case, Herod would find out soon enough.

Are these men spies? Miriam's voice floated into Herod's head.

"No, Miriam, I don't believe they're here to spy," Herod answered aloud. These conversations were so normal to him now, he no longer tried to hide them from anyone who may overhear.

Herod continued to ponder the possibilities. Eventually he could hear footsteps on stone pavers approaching in the distance. He glanced up to see three strangers being led to him by one of the servants. He stood as they were led directly to him.

"Greetings, Great Herod," one of the men spoke. All three bowed to the King of Judaea. "My name is Melchior. These are my associates, Balthazar and Gaspar," He motioned with his right hand as he introduced his colleagues. "We humbly thank you for granting us an audience today."

Herod smiled and bowed his head slightly toward his guests. "It is a pleasure to meet the famous Wise Men. I have heard many stories of your travels. You are welcome here. Our meeting is long overdue. Please sit, let us get to know one another."

Herod motioned to the stone benches adjacent to his and waited as the three men sat. He turned to the servant. "Bring the wine and cheese."

Herod watched briefly as the servant turned and retreated the way he had come. Then he eased himself onto his bench and regarded his visitors. The one called Balthazar was taller than the others, and his skin was a shade darker. Herod assumed he was from the east, possibly Satavahanas or Kalinga. The other two had olive skin, which meant they could be from anywhere. Except, looking closer, Herod noticed Gaspar had a slight slanting to his eyes that indicated he may be from somewhere northeast, like Wusun or Kangju. All three were dressed in expensive robes and had an air of dignity and grace.

"You have obviously traveled far," Herod said. "Is there anything you would like before we get to the business of the meeting? Would you prefer something more substantial than wine and cheese?"

"Your hospitality is legend, Your Grace. Wine and cheese will be more than enough. Thank you for your graciousness." Gaspar placed his hand over his heart.

"We have indeed traveled far, Your Grace," Balthazar said. "We've journeyed from Sagala. We assisted Strato the Second with some unpleasant dealings. We were able to help retrieve his son, who had been kidnapped by nomads. At least, they assumed he had been kidnapped by nomads. We were able to ascertain that the nomads were actually sent by Rajuvula, the King in Mathura. We brokered a deal to get the king's son back. Strato was very pleased, as he and his son are very close."

"I've heard of Strato, yet haven't had the pleasure of meeting him," Herod said. "Perhaps one day."

"You would find him to be a wise and decent man," Balthazar continued. "However, his days may be numbered in Sagala. Rajuvula torments Strato weekly. He sends raiding parties and sabotages supply shipments. Strato is Greek and is very far from Greece. He's isolated that far east. Most of his allies are too far away to bring aid in real time. Rajuvula wants to invade Strato's kingdom and make it part of Mathura. Rajuvula hasn't figured out how isolated Strato really is. Sadly, one day he will."

"That will be a sad day indeed," Herod replied. "Perhaps Greece will come through for Strato before it's too late."

"That would be a true blessing," Balthazar said. He knew no such aid would come from Greece, but these are the niceties of small talk. Herod was polite to express concern, but the Wise Men knew Herod could not care less about a small kingdom in eastern Punjab. These exchanges were just part of the game. Herod was sizing them up just as they were sizing him up. Balthazar knew, as did his associates, that Herod would be curious about why they had wanted to meet with him. He would push to get to the point before long.

The servant returned with a large tray of assorted cheeses, followed by another servant with wine and goblets. They placed the cheese on a table between the seated guests and poured wine, first for Herod, then for his guests. They toasted to health and good fortune, then continued with the small talk. The Wise Men drank the wine more aggressively than most of Herod's previous guests. Herod wondered how long it would take to start affecting their reason. The rumors about the Wise Men suggest they could hold their own when it came to drinking and he was beginning to believe the rumors.

The Wise Men were surprised that Herod didn't push to determine the purpose for their visit. His patience was impressive. They were drinking the wine slightly faster than normal. This started as a joke that Gaspar expressed while the three discussed their approach to the meeting the previous day. They agreed that once they got to their purpose, the meeting would likely be cut short. Gaspar joked that they should drink as much as they could before then because they may never get to drink Herod's wine again. All three of them laughed at the thought, and then laughed harder as they realized that was exactly what they were going to do.

After another thirty minutes of small talk, Herod finally broached the subject, "I am truly entertained by your company. I had also forgotten how fun day drinking can be. I thank you for reminding me, but as you said, Balthazar, you have come a long way to get here. I imagine you had a reason to do so. As charming as I can be, I doubt you came all this way to day drink with an old king."

"Day drinking with a king, young or old, is all the reason we need," Melchior said enthusiastically. The others agreed, laughing.

"It's true we are here for a reason," Balthazar said. Herod did not notice the change in focus of the other two Wise Men as they refined their gazes to assess Herod's reaction. "As you know, our travels take us far and wide. We get the great pleasure of meeting fascinating people and hearing wonderful tales. Some of the tales are obvious fancy while others are too somber and heartbreaking to be fiction. It's a glorious world, yet a tragic one as well.

"Lately, we've been hearing a tale." Balthazar tilted his head. "A tale that's being repeated thousands of leagues apart by people who don't travel. We've heard this tale enough over the past several months that we don't believe it to be fancy."

Herod's eyes narrowed reflexively, and his body stiffened slightly. It was an unconscious reaction and an acknowledgement that he knew where this story was going. Melchior and Gaspar, watching Herod closely, missed nothing.

"The tale we're hearing is that of a messiah. We're hearing a tale of angels from Heaven appearing to shepherds in their fields. One that tells us God Himself is going to have a son, a son who is to be King of the Jews. And that this child of God is to be born in the City of David. We were skeptical at first. Who wouldn't be? Over time, though, we've come to believe this prophecy. So, to answer your question, we're here to witness the birth of this new king." Balthazar folded his hands in his lap.

Herod's eyes flashed and his jaw clenched. How dare anyone purposefully come face to face with him to discuss a possible usurper! It was insulting they would even mention it. Herod was King of the Jews! He was King of Judaea! These insolent bastards were taunting him with this prophecy. He would have them killed if they did not have such a popular following. Sadly, they would be missed, and it would be too much trouble to deal with.

"I'm afraid you've traveled far for no reason," Herod offered through something resembling a smile. "I have no doubt that you've heard these rumors. The fact is, I've been hearing similar rumors for thirty years. There is no merit to these rumors, I assure you. But you are more than welcome to stay in Jerusalem, or anywhere in Judaea, to seek out the birth of this messiah. It's clearly a waste of time, but it's your time, so do with it as you will."

Melchior stood, then bowed. "As we mentioned previously, your hospitality is legendary, even for a fool's errand such as ours. We've taken enough of your time, Your Majesty. Thank you for allowing us to visit with you today. It's truly been an honor and a privilege."

"The pleasure was all mine, I assure you. I owe each of you a debt of gratitude for reminding me that day drinking is both a pleasure and productive," the king responded, smiling an empty smile. "I will have someone show you out. Thank you again for reaching out." With that, Herod stood and motioned to a servant.

The Wise Men glanced at one another, then stood. They bowed politely, then followed the servant back along the path they had entered on. They did not speak to one another until far outside of the palace. They understood they were being observed closely and that Herod had ears deployed that would report every word to him. The Wise Men had played the game for many years, they knew the rules within the rules.

Herod watched the Wise Men leave. He was fuming. He recognized that the Wise Men were far brighter than most of the people he encountered. He was irritated that they had the arrogance to confront him on a rumor. He was galled that it had been their intent from the beginning. Mostly, he was angry for letting it get to him. *A messiah*, he scoffed to himself, *these men really are fools*. But were they? He mentioned to them that he had heard these rumors for thirty years. That was true, but in all his time in power, he had never heard the rumors repeated to the extent he was hearing them now. It was disturbing. He wanted to laugh it off as he had in the past. But this time was different, and he knew it.

He motioned for a servant, always present just out of sight. "I need Tobias. Bring him to me."

15

GUNDAHAR

Summoning Tobias was a roll of the dice. Herod allowed the head of his secret police to do what he needed to do to provide Herod with answers. That could mean he was no longer in Jerusalem at all. This time he was fortunate, as Tobias arrived within forty minutes of the original call.

"You rang, Your Grace?" Tobias said as he approached the king in the garden plaza.

"Indeed," Herod answered. "The Wise Men were just here. They are camped east of the city. Coordinate with the Germanic Guard, who have eyes on the camp. I want your people to follow them, discreetly, while they are in the kingdom."

"You really don't believe in foreplay, do you?" Tobias smiled. "Straight to the pay off. No wonder you struggle to keep your wives happy."

Herod's eyes narrowed. Tobias realized, too late it seemed, that the king was not in a playful mood. He looked more than angry, he looked genuinely pissed off. Now was not the time for messing with the king.

"Apologies, My King. I will take care of it immediately." Tobias bowed.

"Make the arrangements to have them followed, then report to the council room. We have work to do." Herod turned and walked away without another word.

Tobias watched him leave until the king was out of sight. He dropped his head as he sighed.

Now the fun part, he thought to himself with a good dose of foreboding. *I get to speak to Gundahar.*

Gundahar was the head of the Germanic Guard. Technically, he was one of Herod's generals. Tobias would never admit it to anyone, but he was quietly terrified of Gundahar. He assumed everyone who met him was also terrified of him. The man exuded evil.

Most of the people in the kingdom, at least the ones who knew how things worked, were wary or even fearful of Tobias. He was in charge of the secret police and had Herod's ear whenever he wanted. He was a man to be feared. Yet Tobias considered that merely professional courtesy, more of a self-preservation kind of fear.

Gundahar generated a different kind of fear. He had dead eyes, or perhaps he had death in his eyes. In the many years Tobias had known him, he had never once perceived any amount of compassion, humor, or humanity in the man. Hate? Disdain? Cruelty? Pure cold evil? Yes, those he managed to convey quite clearly. In a normal-sized human, that would be enough to generate fear. Gundahar was nearly a giant. He had to be nearly six feet, eight inches of sinewy rippling muscle wrapped around a core of silent rage. *Yes, fun indeed, always a treat to speak to Gundahar.*

Tobias left the garden plaza and set off down the hallway toward the stairs to the lower level. Though he feared Gundahar to his core, Tobias made a valiant effort to never let it show. He needed to maintain respect, from Gundahar as well as anyone else who may be watching. They were peers, in a way. They were both in key positions as part of the king's most trusted staff.

Tobias noticed the change in temperature as he descended the stone stairs. It was always cooler on the lower level. He made his way down the corridor, made a left, and continued toward the suite of rooms used by the Germanic Guard. The corridors were sparse, with only an occasional tapestry on the wall between the sconces. There was no need for adornment down here. This was a space of function and nothing more. He could hear a nearly silent scraping sound as he approached his destination.

Tobias paused inside the doorway and scanned the room. The room was not large, perhaps twenty feet by thirty feet. There was an unfamiliar banner stuck to the far wall. It was faded red, with what appeared to be a yellow lion fighting a yellow bear at the center, surrounded with black and white scrolling lines and curves. Tobias had heard Gundahar was from Germania Superior somewhere near Mainz, at the very northwest end of the Roman Empire. This man was far from home. The banner was likely his family crest. Beneath the banner was a table with an extremely large man sitting to one side.

Gundahar did not look up, keeping his eyes on the huge sword he was sharpening with a stone. Gundahar repeatedly made large sweeping motions with the stone, from the handle to the tip. Most soldiers did not want an overly sharp sword in battle because it would penetrate bone and become lodged. Gundahar did not suffer this problem as his strokes were so powerful, he would easily cut his opponents in two. The sharper blade helped keep him from tiring; he was nearing his fortieth year and was considered old by some. He had the appearance of a man who had seen many years, but he moved and fought like a man half that age. The people who considered him old never met him in battle.

"Vut do you vant, Tobias?" Gundahar asked without raising his eyes or slowing the stone across the blade. His voice was deep and heavy with the accent of his people.

Tobias did not hesitate. "I just spoke with Herod. He asked that I put my people on tailing the Wise Men while they are in country. He said your men have eyes on them now. The Wise Men likely will not pull up stakes until tomorrow, but you never know. I'd like to get my people there today."

Gundahar stopped sliding the stone across the blade and glanced up at Tobias. He set the stone on the table but did not release the large sword. His dead eyes locked on Tobias. His head was shaven, and his features appeared to be carved from stone. He had an old scar that started at his right eye and crossed his face and nose to the left side of his mouth. Something he undoubtedly picked up in his youth. *Just one of many factors that make up his charming features.*

Gundahar's eyes never left Tobias as he stood from the chair, growing even taller than Tobias remembered, and walked slowly toward him. He stopped about a foot from Tobias and looked down at the smaller man. It was one of the oldest forms of intimidation on the books, one that had little effect on Tobias. He simply stared back unblinking, with a stern look on his face. Gundahar held his gaze a little longer, then turned and walked back to his chair. He placed the sword on the table and turned back to face his uninvited guest.

Instead of speaking to Tobias, he called out a name: "Vilhelm."

Within seconds, the sound of footsteps approached from a room off to the side. A soldier entered and approached Gundahar. They exchanged short sentences in a language Tobias could not discern, one with guttural sounds and rolling syllables. The soldier turned and stood at attention, facing Tobias.

"Vilhelm vill take you to ze Vise Men," Gundahar said as he sat back down in his chair, reclaiming his sword as he did so. He picked up the stone, glanced back down at the blade, and promptly ignored the fact that Tobias was still there.

"Thank you," Tobias said. Gundahar did not seem to hear or care.

Tobias turned to the soldier. "Follow me to the plaza. I have men waiting."

The soldier merely nodded.

16

THE RECAP

The Wise Men did not speak to one another until they had reached their horses in Herod's stables. The servant stood watching them untie the beasts as they prepared to leave.

"The wine was exceptional," Gaspar said. The other two laughed and agreed.

"That was interesting," said Melchior.

They mounted the horses and headed for the gate. Once outside, they glanced around casually to see if they were being followed. They seemed to be alone, and they felt safe to speak openly.

"I don't think our new friend was amused by the reason we're here," Balthazar laughed.

"That's an understatement," Melchior replied. "I'm not going to lie. I like the crazy son of a bitch. He was fun to talk to before we got to the point of it all. He's a smart guy, has some great stories, and is a pretty good day drinker. I nearly forgot I was talking to a nutter."

"It's important not to forget that part. He is also a sadistic fuck who occasionally kills his own family." Gaspar slid an extended finger across his throat. He glanced back over his shoulder, just in case. All was clear. "But I understand what you mean. The man has charm when he wants to. I guess that helps keep him in power."

"Before our meeting he may not have considered the latest rumors much of a threat," Balthazar said. "But it seems he's starting to now. I'm not sure how much more he needs to hear before he starts responding to these rumors. It would be best to head to Nazareth as soon as possible. Those kids probably have no idea who is going to be hunting them."

The others nodded in agreement.

"How do we find them once we get there?" Melchior asked.

"God said to ask around for a carpenter named Joseph." said Gaspar.

"That's a common name and a common profession. Nazareth is a big place."

"Agreed. But what were the first two words of my last sentence?"

"Right, 'God said.'" Melchior pointed at Gaspar. "I'm guessing that's about all the guidance we will need."

"If nothing else, it's a great place to start," Balthazar said.

The three rode in silence for the next several minutes of the journey back to their encampment, each lost in his own thoughts about the meeting and the implications that would follow. There was much to consider, and each had his own way of processing the information. They rode relatively slowly down the streets, barely garnering the attention of the citizens who went about their daily business. A shopkeeper glanced up from a table he was organizing. A woman paused to allow them to pass before crossing the street with two large water jugs. The sun was high in the sky, producing stunted shadows of all things in its reach. The horses eventually began trotting in unison, the hooves tapping the ground as one.

Melchior broke the silence. "He will have us followed. It's his obvious first move. We're likely being followed now."

Gaspar was staring off into the distance. "He has no need to follow us now, he knows where we're camped and likely has eyes there. But I agree, any movement made from this point on will be observed from a distance. He may not even be discreet about it. He knows we know he knows where we are."

Melchior shook his head. "It'll be difficult to protect these kids under the king's scrutiny. We need options. As of now he doesn't know their identities, or, more specifically, her identity. If we follow our current course of action, we lead him straight to her. I believe we need to get creative, my friends."

Balthazar narrowed his eyes to a squint, furrowing his brow. It was his 'tell' that he was deep in thought. This often meant good things were about to come out of his mouth. As a quick aside, when he was about to be clever or funny, his eye got very wide, to the point of being nearly round. Let us agree that for all his intellect and creativity, he would be a horrible poker player. "Normally when we are followed, we break up the caravan and divide our resources. It has always been effective and, with one exception, has always worked to our benefit. But Herod must be expecting this. After all, we've employed it on multiple occasions, and he's no fool. So, I think this requires a little ingenuity. Something he won't expect. What if we do *the Polly* instead?" He smiled as the words came out of his mouth. The others were silent as they stared back at him, processing his proposal.

"*The Polly?*" A grin slowly spread above Melchior's chin. "I love it. We haven't done *the Polly* in years."

"Not *the Polly*. There is no drinking if we do *the Polly*." Gaspar whined. "I agree it's the perfect tactic for this situation, and I applaud you for thinking of it now, but the only time we ever employed it I couldn't drink for a month. I was a much younger man then. As a more mature man, I have greater patience and fewer needs, but those needs are indeed needs. *The Polly* is uncomfortable, it's nerve wracking, and there's NO ALCOHOL."

"My dear friend, we can always modify." Balthazar smirked. "You're correct, there won't be alcohol for a bit. Yet, if we do it correctly, we'll be off Herod's radar in a mere week or two. There's a lot to coordinate before we can pull this off. This one will not be cheap, and there's no cash reward waiting for us in the end, though I do think our new Client will compensate us in ways we've never imagined. Besides, how much fun will this be? It's about time we had an actual challenge.

"Herod is going to want us dead after this. It's only our relative fame and notoriety that has us still breathing at this point. Can you imagine what might have happened at our meeting if we were merely common-ers passing through? We would've never been heard from again. We're playing with fire on this one— the stakes couldn't be higher. We have an ace in our sleeve with our new Client, but He does like to let things play out as they will. When we get back to camp, let's get some food and then sit down and work through the details. I managed to procure a few more jugs of Herod's wine while we were meeting with him. It seems appropri-ate for this particular planning session."

Melchior turned to Gaspar. "What do you think? It sounds like great fun to me. I can abstain for a couple weeks for this. It'll be one of our greatest accomplishments. We've just agreed to escort the mother of God to safety. Someday there'll be books written heralding our part in all of this. Personally, I don't care if we're in them or not, I just want to beat a worthy adversary at a game of wits. This will be our greatest win to date."

Gaspar smiled. "I'm in, of course. But if we pull this shit off, the cel-ebration has to be epic."

"No worries there, my friend."

"Hold on, let's back up a moment." Gaspar narrowed his eyes at Balthazar. "You 'managed to procure' more of Herod's wine? Just how did you 'manage' that?"

Balthazar grinned. "I can't let you in on all my secrets. What fun would that be? It would be like knowing the magician's tricks before the performance. That would spoil the magic."

They were nearly back to camp. Melchior was still smiling as he worked through planning steps in his mind. They would need to find some assistance once they arrived in Nazareth. This posed a challenge because they had never been to this city and their connections were slim to none in this part of the world. Gold was always an effective motivator, but it did not always buy loyalty.

Still, he remained optimistic. He knew that the majority of the populace had no love for Herod. Taking part in this type of ruse would appeal to certain members of the population, despite the danger it brought with it. The trick was finding the right person or people for the job. There were certain qualities required, along with a lack of respect for the law. The Wise Men had often requested assistance from individuals they would not associate with in most circles. However, business is business, and every job required certain tools. "Tools" may be too clinical a term, let's say "assets" instead. Nazareth had the people they would need; Melchior was sure of that. The challenge would be locating them, but it wouldn't be a major challenge.

The encampment came into view. They continued to ride in silence the last few hundred yards. A young man, part of the caravan, was waiting to take the horses. The three stopped just short of him and dismounted. He took the reins of all three horses and led them off.

The Wise Men cleaned up from the relatively short journey. They instructed the staff to prepare dinner as the men gathered in the main tent. Balthazar did, in fact, produce three large jugs of Herod's wine. This was a feat the other two couldn't figure out— he had never left their sight. However, they let it go and began planning for the days ahead. Part of the planning process meant keeping their cups full of Herod's wine. The mystery surrounding its acquisition soon faded to the background as they considered their task ahead. They would be leaving for Nazareth in the morning. There was much to discuss. They drank and planned into the wee hours of the night.

***

The caravan moved out early the next morning. It took the better part of three days to make the journey to Nazareth. Their course took them directly north of Jerusalem. They passed through Ramah and Bethel before setting up camp the first night just outside of Gophna. They continued the next day through the farmlands and hills of Shechem, stopping just south of En-gannum. They made it to the outskirts of Nazareth late the third day. It was overcast and the daylight faded quickly, forcing them to use torchlight to set up camp. The previous two nights, the campsites had been travelling set-ups that required only those tents essential for preparing food and sleeping. This made it more efficient to tear down in the morning, allowing them to move on early. This time, they set up for a longer stay, knowing they would likely be here for many days.

It was not difficult to confirm their assumption that they were being followed. They kept this information to themselves as it would not be productive to let the rest of the caravan in on the danger that followed them. These were honest and hardworking people. The Wise Men had no intention of allowing them to get into trouble. For now, it was best to leave them in the dark. Having the group constantly looking over their shoulder would not be wise. The added stress it would bring them would also be counterproductive.

The Wise Men agreed they would begin their search for the carpenter in the morning. They would also need to make other arrangements as well. The men were going to need assistance to elude Herod's spies. As they settled into their tent, they opened some wine. They invited the entire caravan to join them for drinks, as this was going to be a farewell party for most of them. The caravan would have to disperse in the next few days. It was too large a group and far too easy to track.

They personally thanked each of their staff. The wine flowed late into the night, there was as much laughter as there was food and drink. This night was to appreciate those who helped them on the journey thus far. The difficult work would start tomorrow.

17

MOVE THE PIECES

Herod marched to his small council. He had sent word ahead for them to assemble, he had much to discuss with them. Tobias would be joining them once he had completed the task of arranging to have the Wise Men followed. Herod walked down the corridors of the palace with purpose.

"No, I don't think they're spies, Miriam," Herod said as he walked, "but I agree with you, they're insolent. Punished? I don't know about that. It's easy to punish subjects but these are famous men, men with a history, men with a following. They could cause problems if they spoke of punishment in this kingdom. Don't fret, my dear, I have things under control. I always have things under my control. I'm having them followed. I'll know everything they do and everywhere they go." The Wise Men definitely had an agenda and Herod was determined to find out what it was.

Herod continued down the corridors until he reached the council room. He stood outside for a moment to allow his rage to dissipate. He was still bothered by the tone and unmitigated boldness of the Wise Men's comments. More than that, though, he was bothered that he let the strangers get under his skin. He allowed his anger to show, however briefly.

He entered the council room and quickly scanned the occupants. None were absent, that was good. He was in far too foul a mood to deal with tardiness and lame excuses. Tobias had not yet arrived but given his earlier task, that was expected. He moved to the head of the table but did not sit. That fact alone indicated to all in attendance what to expect from their king on this day. He could almost feel the apprehension radiating back at him. It was satisfying, but not enough to alter his mood.

Herod looked to his right. "Slide down. Tobias will be here shortly, and I will have him sit here."

Without a word the men all slid one place to their right. A goblet was overturned in the process, followed by a fumbling attempt to right the chalice. A servant appeared from the shadows and mopped up the wine with a rag. Another appeared with a full goblet and removed the empty one. Herod slowly shook his head and wondered if the only competent people in the room were his servants. He closed his eyes and sighed audibly.

"Please update me on the status of the census."

A portly advisor, whose name escaped Herod at the moment, stood and looked Herod in the eye. "The census teams have been deployed across your kingdom over the past three weeks. The last few teams left Jerusalem yesterday. Heralds have reported that the actual census tally has begun in about a third of the locations. We're still awaiting word from the farther reaches of the kingdom. So far there hasn't been news of anyone refusing to report."

"If they do refuse?" Herod interrupted.

"They will be forcefully escorted to the census station," the man replied.

"Not good enough. The first soul to refuse in each location is to be stoned to death in the public square. Make certain that the public is made aware of the situation. Also, make sure there is at least one stoning in every location."

The man stared at Herod, confused. "I beg your pardon, Your Majesty, but if none refuse in a given location?"

Herod glared at the man. His earlier thought was proving to be correct. The only competent people in his service were his servants. He placed both palms on the table, leaned toward the man, and said in a slow, menacing tone, "Then find someone, I don't care whom, a beggar or drunk, drag his ass to the public square and *claim* he refused."

The man quickly glanced down at the table. "As you command, My King."

Tobias paused briefly at the door, then took the open seat to the right of Herod. He glanced around the room, noting the obvious apprehension from all at the table. Most of the advisors were staring at some non-existent yet fascinating object directly in front of them on the table. Tobias was not surprised due to his run-in with the king earlier in the day.

"Continue," Herod said.

The man was nervous but did an admirable job of covering it. "As you requested, each location has instruction to catalog all pregnant women who report on a separate form. They also know to inquire of each citizen any knowledge of pregnant women they may be aware of in the area. Each team has designated individuals to covertly track the pregnant women to determine where they live. These individuals will quietly observe until instructed not to do so. While the general census information will remain on site until the task is completed, the lists of the pregnant women will be delivered to Tobias more frequently. It will be weekly from the outskirts of the kingdom, every few days from areas closer to Jerusalem."

Herod nodded his approval. "Continue as planned. However, I want special attention paid to Jerusalem and Nazareth. I want more frequent reports from each. I also want additional teams sent and prepared to escort these women to me should I request it. Get a feel for how many pregnant women we're dealing with, then assign the teams accordingly. The additional teams are only for Jerusalem and Nazareth, at least for now. That may change as we uncover more information."

Herod understood he ran the risk of looking paranoid, not just to his advisors, but to everyone in the kingdom. He had never acted on previous rumors of messiahs or on a prophet's predictions. It was becoming clear to Herod that this time things were different. Tobias had provided him with multiple reports. He had personally interviewed one of the shepherds responsible for spreading these rumors. He still felt a small twinge of guilt for allowing his temper to get the better of him during that unfortunate event. The Wise Men, whatever they may be up to, seemed to think it worth their time to be in this part of the world due to the same rumors.

Of course. Herod's eyes closed and his chin dropped to his chest. It was there all along. The obvious was right before his eyes. The Wise Men were behind it all. That explained their unexpected appearance. *This changes things.*

"Remember, you are at this table because you are trusted advisors to the King of Judaea. The moment I begin to question your loyalty is the day you will no longer be part of this group." *Or breathing*, Herod thought. "These rumors of a messiah involve the City of David, which is obviously Jerusalem. Other prophesies speak of a Nazarene, so we'll focus on Nazareth as well. We'll keep an eye on the pregnant ones because it is an easy task to accomplish while we perform our census. Think of it as a mere precaution. I have complete faith that these rumors were started by some upstarts wanting to unseat me. These would-be usurpers are using prophesies and rumors to gain the support of the people. Whoever is behind these rumors is well organized and apparently well-funded. To be able to plant these rumors across the kingdom took some intelligence and coordination. We are dealing with educated usurpers.

"I had a meeting with the Wise Men. They claimed to be in Judaea to witness the birth of this new messiah. This was my first meeting with these men, though they're known to me. Until now, they've never shown any desire for power or property. They've always provided counsel for monetary gain alone. That and a fair amount of debauchery. When I look at the scope and magnitude of the coup attempt before us, I begin to wonder who is capable of such a thing. I ask myself, 'who is intelligent enough to spread rumors across an entire kingdom without leaving a single fingerprint to identify them?' It occurred to me that the Wise Men are. I ask myself, 'who has the resources to fund such an endeavor?' The Wise Men do. I ask myself, 'who has the arrogance to initiate such an undertaking and think they will be successful?' Again, logic would point to the Wise Men.

"To my knowledge, they haven't assembled an army. However, they may be arrogant enough to believe they can topple my reign with a false messiah, zealotry, and the support of the people." Herod scanned the room. All eyes were upon him as he laid out his theory. Many of the advisors were nodding. The logic was sound.

"Tobias has assigned his best men to track the Wise Men. They'll remain under surveillance until we confirm our suspicions. Because these men are world-renowned, we won't act until we're certain. The moment we prove they are, in fact, behind this coup attempt, we'll be free to execute them. Believe me when I say, after meeting them earlier, I'm looking forward to that."

One of the advisors stood and half raised his hand, like an unsure child at school. "How can you be certain they're the ones behind this messiah scheme? As I understand it, they just showed up at our border days ago. The shepherds' rumors have been going on for months now."

Herod nodded to the man. "Fair question, yet a little naïve. If you were planning to unseat a king, would you show up day one and make your presence known? I think not. You would lay the necessary ground-work to ensure your victory. You would only show up once all the pieces were placed where you wanted them on the chess board. Then you would appear as an innocent witness to the shitshow about to happen. These men are brighter than all of you. I understand you think you're the smartest people in the room... fuck that, in the realm. You're not. These men have become rich by being smarter than everyone else. Everyone. They bring originality of thought that is so far outside the box that it makes you all seem completely ordinary. Don't underestimate them.

"Please don't take these comments as an insult. In all honesty, you are likely the smartest people in the kingdom. You're here because I value and need your counsel. These men are beyond most.

"Yet I daresay no one is cautioning them not to underestimate me. With great intelligence comes great arrogance. That's their weakness: they underestimate everyone else. In their defense, they're right to do so most of the time, but not this time. I can see through their scheme, and they have no idea I've uncovered their true mission."

***

Herod had called another meeting. Gundahar and Tobias were sitting across from one another at the council room table. They had been summoned, along with others, and were the first to arrive. Gundahar stared at Tobias with a blank expression. Tobias shook his head. *There must be freedom in hating everyone.*

Tobias decided to ignore the large foreigner and studied some paperwork that he had brought for the meeting. He went over the notes twice and reread them a third time to be sure he had not missed anything. Being prepared is everything when dealing with Herod. Tobias knew his value to Herod was information. He was Herod's eyes in the dark, the seer of secrets. It was far easier for Herod to find great warriors like Gundahar than it was to find someone to uncover the dark, dangerous thoughts and deeds happening in the shadows. Making sure the information was valid and timely was Tobias' greatest strength.

Two other advisors entered the room. One was not paying attention and began to sit next to Gundahar. He nearly fell backward when he saw the large man glare at him. He quickly stood and moved a couple places down from the large general. Herod entered and sat at the head of the table.

"What is the status of the Wise Men?" Herod asked, looking at Tobias.

"They arrived in Nazareth a few days ago and are camped just outside the city limits. The three of them split up when they entered the city. We were still able to track them. Two spent most of their time visiting drinking establishments. They engaged in multiple conversations with locals, but nothing was exchanged, and they left alone. The third stayed primarily on the streets, occasionally speaking briefly with the citizens. The conversations were quick. He seemed to be looking for something."

"Vhy am I here?" Gundahar interrupted, looking bored.

"Because I called for you." Herod glared at his general.

He turned back to Tobias. "What was he looking for?"

"We weren't able to get close enough to overhear. We didn't want to reveal our presence."

"See if your men can determine what he's looking for. Shake down the people he speaks to."

"Yes, sir."

"I want you and Gundahar to go to Nazareth. You need to oversee this operation. They are obviously up to something, and I need someone there who can act without waiting for orders. Find out what you can, anyway you see fit. Send reports daily at the very least. If you uncover anything, apprehend them immediately. They know they're being followed. They may prove to be elusive when the time comes to capture them.

"Gundahar, this is primarily Tobias' operation, but I need your input, ruthlessness, and cunning in case we need to take them."

Gundahar grunted with a nod toward Herod.

"You two." Herod pointed to the other advisors. "Arrange for the messengers. As many as it takes. I want updates daily, more often if anything changes. Go."

Herod grabbed Tobias' arm. "Get there as soon as possible."

Tobias and Gundahar walked out of the council room together. "I'll meet you in ten minutes at the stables," Tobias said.

Gundahar gave a short nod and split off down another corridor.

18

NAZARETH

Balthazar walked along the streets of Nazareth, his eyes scanning everything they could take in. He passed by various shops and produce stands. He nodded a greeting to those who looked up from their tasks at hand. He passed the patrons examining wares, squeezing fruit, or ambling on to the next vendor. He was holding a coin in his hand, slowly turning it over and over as he walked. He smirked at the fact that the coin had Herod's face on one side. Somehow that seemed appropriate. Herod had his likeness minted on the coins in Judaea. It was no doubt an idea he pilfered from his buddy Augustus. Imitation truly is the sincerest form of flattery. More likely, he saw it as another way of stroking his own ego and trying to put himself on par with the emperor. Whatever the origin, these coins would be used to secure freedom from the man whose face adorns them. *Yes*, Balthazar thought, *that seems very fitting indeed.*

He saw three men standing along the street having a conversation. He made his way to them, hoping they might be able to assist him in his quest to locate a carpenter named Joseph.

"Pardon me, my friends, I apologize for interrupting your conversation. I was hoping you might be able to assist me with something. I am in need of a carpenter and several people suggested a man named Joseph here in Nazareth. Would any of you know where I might find this man?"

"Those are strange robes, sir. I have not seen robes like that before. Where did you get them? Are you a visitor here?" one man asked.

"Yes, my friend, I have been east for many years and am finally returning home. I believe I purchased these robes in Wusun. Now, about the carpenter Joseph?"

"My brother traveled east once. He was gone for nearly a year. He didn't bring back new robes, though," the second man said.

Balthazar stared at him blankly.

"Was it your older brother, Malcolm? He certainly should've bought new robes while he was away. He's been wearing the same robes as long as I have known you," the third man said laughing.

"Yes, it's true. Malcolm is very tight with his gold. He likes to think of it as frugal as opposed to cheap."

"Riveting story, truly," Balthazar said with a smile. "The carpenter?"

"No," Malcolm's brother shook his head. "Malcolm is no carpenter. He spent some time tending flock, but these days he has a little produce stand on the edge of town. I'm not sure he has the patience to be a carpenter. He certainly doesn't have the skill."

"I will attest to that," the third man added.

"I don't know, he may have the skillset necessary to be a carpenter," the first man said. "How can we be sure? Has anyone ever tried to teach him? Has he ever had a chance to learn? These aren't skills that just manifest on their own. One has to be shown how to create usefulness and beauty from wood. It doesn't just happen."

"I've known him all my life. He lacks basic competence. He has no hand-eye coordination. I recently saw him open a door into his own face. Don't get me wrong, he's good at running his stand, and he was good at shepherding, but I just don't believe he has the aptitude to be a carpenter."

"Gentlemen... please..." Balthazar interrupted. "I'm looking for a carpenter."

"You clearly have not been listening," the third man looked annoyed, "We've established that Malcolm is no carpenter. I must admit, I'm a little taken aback at your insistence that he is. Has your time in the east addled your brain? Have you ever met Malcolm?"

Balthazar closed his eyes, dropped his head, and sighed. This was becoming a strange day. "No, sir, I have not met Malcolm. I am looking for..."

The first man cut him off, "You're a strange man, sir. I don't understand what you're playing at, but you are being most disagreeable. Gentlemen, I suggest we move on and leave this worldly traveler to make assumptions about other people's families."

The three men regarded him with furrowed brows and disapproving stares as they began to walk away. *What just happened?* Balthazar shook his head. The men eventually returned to their conversation as they walked. Their voices grew softer as they drew off into the distance, but he could still hear them.

"I'm still not convinced. If given the chance to learn, I bet he would've been a fine carpenter."

"We'll never know now for sure. He's too old to learn a new trade."

"There are some carpenters working a couple blocks over on the left. We could ask them?"

"Yes, we could, but what's the point? Besides, I'm hungry. Let's go find some food."

Balthazar realized he was still shaking his head. *What a strange conversation.* Still, even after the odd encounter, they had provided him with a lead. It was a peculiar way to get a lead, but a lead was a lead. He headed in the direction the man suggested to his friends. He smiled as he walked and shook his head again. *People.*

Melchior and Gaspar were off on their own missions, each had tasks to accomplish that involved hiring or gaining the assistance of certain individuals. Balthazar assumed they would have success, but nothing was guaranteed. There always seemed to be curveballs, even with the best laid plans. One could never just assume things were going to go as planned. Seriously, that shit just doesn't happen. Still, the trio had been partnering for years with great success. He knew his friends were industrious and were more than capable to overcome any obstacles in their paths. As he walked, he couldn't help but wonder how their efforts were going. Were they making progress, accomplishing the things they needed to? Always a great mystery once you split up. He assumed they were wondering the same about his task.

He crossed the street and made his way to the corner. He turned left and continued down the block. At each intersection he scanned both ways, trying to locate a construction project. He walked several blocks, backtracking once or twice, but was having no luck. He was about to ask a bystander for some assistance but decided to check the next intersection instead. He scanned both directions and nearly turned around. Then, to his right, he saw what he was looking for. He continued the half block until he was there. Two men and a boy were working on the entryway to a building. They had nearly completed the framework. The boy had his back to Balthazar but appeared to be giving orders. Bold, to be sure. Balthazar raised his eyebrow at the sight. Considering his day, he was not surprised nor was he concerned. *Things just happen the way they happen. Perhaps the kid is a prodigy. Who knows?*

"Excuse me, my friend, I apologize for interrupting your duties, but I am looking for a carpenter. A specific carpenter named Joseph. He comes highly recommended."

The boy turned to look at the unannounced guest. Except, it wasn't a boy at all. The person who turned to answer his question was a full-grown man. Okay, not quite full-grown, more like two-thirds grown, but a man, nonetheless. Balthazar was surprised by his mistake since he usually didn't make them. *Perhaps I should spend more time observing and less time assuming.*

It was Asher (remember him? The cubit guy?). Asher looked annoyed, as if someone interrupted the greatest feat of cerebral magic that had ever been gifted onto the world. He had a distinct look of disdain in his eyes as he regarded Balthazar.

"What do you want? Can't you see I'm working here?"

"Indeed, I can, and you're doing a fabulous job. It all looks so complicated, but you make it look easy." Is an internal eye roll a real thing? If so, Balthazar did one here. He was fatigued by this endless game of playing down to the competition. "Again, I apologize. I am looking for a specific carpenter named Joseph. He comes highly recommended. Do you know him?"

"There's a carpenter named Joseph that works for me, but why would you want him? He's insolent and difficult. The Joseph I employ is marginally acceptable as a carpenter and even less impressive as a person. I only employ him because my work backlog far exceeds my staff availability. It could be that someone is having fun at your expense."

Balthazar sensed the smaller man had some adequacy issues. You could call it a pre-Napoleon Napoleon complex. He seemed angry and self-important, the kind of person that was difficult to be around even on a good day. "I can't be certain that your employee is the same Joseph I'm seeking. Perhaps if I spoke with him, I could get a better feel for myself. Would you be able to direct me to his location?"

Asher eyed the man skeptically. "Don't waste your time with Joseph. I have many accomplished carpenters who can assist you, all of whom are far more skilled as carpenters than Joseph. I would be willing to give you a great bargain for their services. What type of work do you need help with?"

"This Joseph, if it is indeed the man I am searching for, assisted my sister with a project. She insists I use the same man. Please, if it's not too much trouble, will you direct me to his location?"

Asher shrugged and shook his head, "Fine, whatever. You've wasted enough of my time as it is. He's doing some repair work at the synagogue about eight blocks from here. Head east until the road ends, then hang a left. You can't miss it."

Balthazar smiled a big fake toothy grin. "Thank you my lit... my friend. You've been most helpful."

If Asher heard him, he made no indication. He simply turned back to his workers and resumed micromanaging them. Balthazar headed off to find Joseph.

He eventually made it to the synagogue the small man told him about. He looked around for a bit but could not find anyone working. He asked a few people there if they had seen some workmen about. Someone let him know that they had finished early and had left for the day. The person was fairly sure they needed to come back tomorrow to wrap things up. Balthazar thanked the helpful individual and left. He would make it back tomorrow morning and try to catch the carpenters then. He could not be certain this would be the same Joseph he sought, but the way the day had unfolded, he would not be surprised if it were.

19

OVERHEARD

Maggie walked along a row of buildings near the center of Nazareth. It was nearly mid-day, and the dirt streets were teaming with people going about the business of the day. Vendors had carts scattered along the street, displaying produce or other wares. Women were returning from the well carrying buckets of water back to their homes. A man was having difficulty getting his camel to stand. The beast seemed entirely disinterested, and the man was obviously frustrated. The sound of voices carried to her ears from every direction. It was a typical day, although a touch warmer than usual.

She rounded a corner and continued her trek. Her mother had sent her to pick up fabric, which was a task she always looked forward to. She was fascinated by the weaving looms and the skill of the women who produced the cloth. She had even become friendly with a couple of them, yet still had not summoned the courage to ask them to teach her the craft. But that was fine, she was equally content to watch. Sometimes they would have elegant fabrics from Egypt or the far east. Silk was her favorite. Some would have brilliant colors and patterns, patterns that seemed impossible to create on a loom. Yet somehow, they had. It would be wonderful to take some of the exotic fabrics home, but that was not to be. Her task was to collect plain off-white linen. The same fabric her family used for just about everything. It was boring, uninspiring, and ordinary, but that was her world.

For weeks the town had been talking of the coming census. Herod and Augustus were asking that everyone report to a census station and be counted. There were proclamations posted all over town. It was made clear that this was in no way an option. Everyone had to report. Herod's soldiers were running the census stations, and they were also in charge of making people show up. Maggie was not aware of anyone who was planning to refuse. She could not understand why anyone would open themselves to punishment for something that mostly made sense. However, some people were hesitant and untrusting of the entire idea. Most had no love for Herod, which went hand in hand with the mistrust they felt. The man was an asshole.

She could see that roughly a block ahead, soldiers were assembling the census station. They had set up a large tent and were now unloading a cart. She slowed her pace and then stopped altogether to observe them. She smiled and shook her head. These morons were actually building the station next to a stable. *Wow, there is some recognition of your surroundings.* They likely had the right or permission to set up anywhere they chose. *So why did they choose to smell dung all day?* Could it be as simple as they hadn't noticed yet? It was a central location and easy to find, so from that standpoint the location made sense. *Still, they* have *to be able to smell that, don't they?*

Her curiosity was getting the best of her, and she moved closer to see if she could hear any of their conversation. Maybe one of them would say something that might make sense of such a stupid choice.

Maggie began walking toward the group of soldiers. They were engrossed in the task at hand and barely seemed to notice the people around them. Still, she thought it best to make her way around the corner from them. She would be out of sight and could get a little closer to eavesdrop. One of them looked up and smiled as she rounded the corner. She smiled back, mostly to be polite, but also because he was kind of cute. She continued for several paces even though she knew she was out of sight. She stopped and looked around. No one appeared to be paying attention to her. That was good. She walked softly back to the corner, staying just out of their field of vision. She could hear them speaking. Mostly. Young men tended to talk over one another. There seemed to be at least four of them speaking, but it was difficult to tell without seeing them.

"...that's what the man said."

"But why? Why do they need to know that?"

"It doesn't matter why, they just do. And since when do you care what your orders are?"

"I don't care. It's just... It doesn't make sense."

One of the soldiers laughed. "When have our orders ever made any sense?"

One or two others were laughing with him.

"Okay, that's fair. But why should they care about women? Or children, for that matter?"

Maggie's ears pricked up. This was not the conversation she was hoping for, but they had definitely piqued her curiosity. *Yes, tell me boys, what is it that has the small one so confused?*

"Dude, let's just get the fucking job done. I don't like this town. I doubt the people care much for us, though they'd rather have us than the Roman shitheads. It's going to take us days to talk to all these people. Let's just get this crap over with."

"Yeah, he's right. They told us everyone, so we count everyone. That means women and kids too. The quicker we get through them, the quicker we can get back to normal things."

"Yeah, yeah, I get that. But that's not the part that bothers me. It's the special forms. Why are there separate forms for pregnant women?"

Maggie eyes got wide, and she froze, heart pounding. She even stopped breathing. Separate forms? For pregnant women?

"Just shut up, maggot. Seriously. We are getting tired of the constant stream of words coming out of your mouth. They gave us forms. We talk to the people. We fill out the forms. If they or any of their neighbors are pregnant, we fill out the *other* form and send that info ahead first. We track where they live and leave someone behind to keep tabs on them. I agree with you, it's stupid, and it doesn't make sense. But those are the orders, and if you don't want to be the one who gets left behind to babysit a bunch of pregnant women, SHUT THE FUCK UP!"

"Still, it doesn't seem..."

Maggie stopped listening and walked away briskly. She was frightened to her core. The little one was right. *Why did they need to know this? What are they looking for that they needed to leave a spy?* She was almost certain she knew the answer: they were looking for Mary.

They had to be. It was the only thing that made sense. Herod must have heard the rumors started by the shepherds. They had been spreading all over Nazareth, probably all over Judaea. *But how could he possibly know she is here?* Maggie didn't believe he did. He was fishing— that's why they were logging all the pregnant women. The fact that the second forms were to be delivered right away showed the importance.

But what would Herod do with the information?

She looked behind her to make sure the soldiers were not following her and was relieved to see they were not. Maggie adjusted the bundle of fabric under her arm, then continued walking toward her mother's house. *They document every pregnant woman, get the information to Herod, then what? There must be hundreds and hundreds of them. There is no way for him to know which one is carrying the REAL messiah.* Still, it did not sit well with her. It felt like danger. Serious danger. *Would they spy on them? Have them followed? Do something worse?* She did not know, but she thought talking it through with Roger would help. Better include Mary and Joseph too, as it affected them the most. The four of them together were pretty good at dissecting things.

***

Roger and Maggie stood outside Joseph's door, hesitant to knock. It was serious déjà vu, although Mary was already on the other side of the door this time since this was now her home. Three months had passed since the wedding and the incident with the Almighty. Mary's pregnancy was beginning to show, but she still tried to hide it under her robes. Maggie thought that might be a good thing, considering what she heard from the census soldiers earlier today.

"They need to know," Maggie said.

Roger looked at her with a worried expression on his face. He turned back to the door and knocked. After several seconds, the door opened, and Mary was looking at them with a smile.

"Hey, you two. We weren't expecting you. This is a nice surprise."

Maggie frowned. "You say that now."

Mary's smile faded. "Crap... what happened?"

"First off, no one is hurt, no worries there. May we come in? We need to talk," Maggie said, "Is Joseph here? We need him for this too."

"Yes, he is. Come in, sit down. I'll get him."

Mary scurried away to another room while her guests sat on some pillows. She returned soon after with Joseph just a few seconds behind her. Mary sat on the pillows across from her friend while Joseph entered the room.

He rubbed his eyes. "What's up kids?" His voice was gravelly with sleep.

"You were asleep already?" Roger asked, smirking.

"Shut up, it was a long day."

"I know, moron, I was there too. Asher was a total knob today. Still, are you getting to the point that you need naps? Mary, you're going to have two babies to take care of." Roger grinned.

"Wow, you are such a dick. Why do I let you into my home?" Joseph was laughing.

"I need to tell you about my day. More specifically, I need to tell you about what I overheard," Maggie said, her face serious and slightly worried.

Maggie was almost never serious. The hairs on the back of Mary's neck stood on end. "Of course, Mags, what is going on?"

Joseph merely looked at her with tired eyes, hoping this was not some kind of girl drama. He hated girl drama. He glanced at Roger, trying to gauge if they were on the same wavelength. But Roger had the same serious look.

"I was in town today and saw the soldiers setting up for the census. They were building next to a stable, which seemed incredibly stupid, so I got a little closer to see if they were morons or if they just hadn't noticed yet."

"Next to a stable? Sounds like morons to me," Roger chuckled.

"I thought so too," Maggie continued, "so I snuck around the side of the tent so I could listen."

Mary's face lit up with a wry smile. "So you could listen? Or was one of them a little too cute to pass without a closer look?"

Maggie blushed a little. Roger rolled his eyes. "What, are you eleven? Were you expecting him to pass you a note? Maybe carry your books home from school?"

"Shut up, you guys. This is serious." She hoped her flushed face would return to normal before anyone noticed. "I stopped next to the tent out of sight, and I listened for a bit. It wasn't even that long. There were three of four of them setting up. They were in the middle of a conversation. One of them was a little confused about having to track women and children.

The others were giving him grief about it. Then one of them ran through their orders. Long story short, they're supposed to inquire about pregnant women. Ask if any of their neighbors or friends were pregnant. If they learn of pregnant women, they have a separate form they are to fill out and send to Herod right away. Then one of them has to stay and keep tabs on the pregnant girl."

She paused to let her last line sink in. "They are leaving someone behind to spy. If not spy, then at least to monitor.

"Mary, Herod is looking for you. What other possible reason could there be? The shepherds are selling their stories hard. They are very convincing, and almost everyone believes them. Herod must have heard them by now. This has to be about you, doesn't it?"

Mary stared blankly at her friend, trying to digest the things she had just said. Why would they possibly care about her? Some days it was easy for her to pretend none of it had happened. Some days it was easy to ignore the fact she was carrying God's child. Some days she hoped and wished it was all just a bad dream and she was a nobody-girl in Nazareth. But reality had a cruel way of asserting itself into her fantasy, jarring her back into the real world.

She thought about what Maggie had said. In fact, she considered every word. Who could possibly know? Who could possibly care? But then... Son of God... King of the Jews... if Herod had heard the stories the shepherds were spreading, he would definitely take it personally. What king wouldn't?

"It is probably just a coincidence. Let's not jump to conclusions," Joseph said with nearly no conviction whatsoever.

"Joe, stop. Think about what Mags just said. It makes perfect sense. We all know Herod must have heard the shepherds' stories. Think logically for a moment. What would you do in his place? He just heard that someone may be coming to kick his ass off his throne," Roger said.

Mary still said nothing. She looked like a scared little girl, mostly because she was a scared little girl. She was mature for her age, and she tended to play the adult well, but today she was frightened. Nothing steals self-control more than fear. Fear also had a way of erasing any maturity you may have been trying to express.

"What will he do if he finds me?" Mary asked, hoping she was wrong about the only answer she could come up with. "Will he do something to the baby? I know he's a monster, but could he really harm an infant? Would he do something so cruel?"

There was a long pause as the others stared silently back at her. She was obviously frightened, and each of them knew not to make things worse by answering. They all knew Herod would not hesitate to kill the child. He had killed his own wife. He had killed his own sons. Killing a stranger's child would mean nothing to him, especially if it eliminated a threat.

"We won't let him find you," Joseph said. His heart broke to see her this scared. He walked over and took her into his arms. Her head immediately dropped to his chest, and she began to sob openly.

Joseph stroked Mary's hair and let her cry against his chest. He looked to Maggie and Roger. "Nazareth isn't safe for us anymore, but I have no idea where to go."

Roger looked concerned. "Can we get Mary through the census line as is? No offense, Mary, but can we just say she's a little fat? It will buy us some time if we can get through without any scrutiny."

"If we just bolt, we'll be followed. Roger isn't wrong. It may work to our advantage if we can get through the line now," Joseph said.

"They're asking everyone about pregnant women they may know. Who else knows Mary is pregnant?" Maggie asked.

"Shit," Mary said, wiping the tears from her eyes. "My parents know. Joseph's folks do too, but they are far enough away that it won't matter.

Martin and Micah know. I'm sorry, I just can't think. Who else? I'm just not sure."

"How about your parents?" Maggie asked, "I know they can be a little excitable. Do you think they have been there yet?"

"I don't know," Mary said.

"Fair enough, that's something we can check." Joseph wrapped his arm around Mary. "I'm not sure anyone at the wedding would know. It's not something we advertised, and Mary is very small. I doubt anyone suspected."

Mary looked up to her husband with doe eyes. "That's so sweet."

"Oh, my God. Shut up, both of you," Maggie said. "This is no time to be adorable." Then she paused, "But Joseph... well played."

Joseph blushed.

"Seriously? Get some focus. All of you," Roger said, "We're dealing with ruthless motherfuckers. We need to blend with the masses, then get the fuck out of here, while blending with the masses."

"Where do we go?" Joseph asked.

"I... have no idea. Away from here, somewhere remote seems right. Not sure what that means, I am not much of a traveler," Roger said.

"Well, the one thing we agree on is getting the stupid census shit out of the way. We can do that tomorrow. Then we need to get out of Nazareth." Joseph looked at Maggie and Roger. "You guys have been awesome, but there's no reason you need to be part of this. Mary and I can take it from here. We really can't expect you guys to get into this kind of danger."

"Joseph!" Roger grabbed both sides of his own head. "Sometimes I am amazed at how smart you are. The way you navigate through Asher's shit while maintaining your composure, it's impressive." Roger released his head and poked a finger into Joseph's chest. "Right now, though, you're being dumb as a post. There's no way you two can get through this on your own. You just can't. I'm not rooting against you, it's just fact.

Herod has his army looking for specific shit. The two of you can pretend they aren't looking for you, but you know they are. You need friends, and your friends are right here, right now. We can run interference when needed. We can help you get out of this town, but we need to get through the frigging census first."

"Frigging?" Maggie quirked an eyebrow.

"Shut up. It was a good speech," Roger said with a sour glance toward his wife. She smirked as she nodded. She had no regrets calling him out on his choice of words.

Mary smiled weakly. The fact that her friends could still be playful was encouraging. She had never been this frightened or unsure of what to do next. Yet, her friends were setting her at ease, and she loved them for that.

"Roger is right. Let's try to maintain our shit one step at a time," Joseph said. "Let's meet back here in the morning, and we'll head to the census station together. From what Mags said earlier, the guys manning the station are not the sharpest knives in the drawer. We can do this. We just need to stick together. And please, don't do anything stupid."

20

PROGRESS

Gaspar stared at his plate. The food looked delicious, but he was exhausted. He had spent most of the last couple days locating and interviewing candidates for the positions the Wise Men needed filled. These positions would save lives and help them escape. He ate slowly as he went over the events of the day. Things were taking shape. He took the liberty of hiring several people without consulting the others. For this to work, they needed to begin immediately. He shifted in his seat, nearly spilling his wine.

"Careful with that," Melchior said as he approached the table, "You can be careless with the food, but I won't abide alcohol abuse."

Melchior sat down next to Gaspar. Before he was settled, a plate of food was placed before him. "Thank you. Excellent service as always."

"How was your day? Were you productive?"

"Yes, very. I have some excellent candidates. They understand the risks involved but are willing to play along. How about you? Any success?" Melchior asked.

"My day was productive too, even more so than yesterday. I got four to start immediately. I didn't feel we could wait." Gaspar sipped his wine. "I saw Balthazar this morning but haven't seen him since. I hope he's having success as well. Finding Joseph is key to everything."

"In your travels today, did you see the census station? We may want to take a closer look at that."

147

"I did see the census station. I agree, we should assess that, but I also saw other soldiers about as well. Not Romans, these were more of Herod's men. They didn't seem to be part of the census. My guess is they provide support, perhaps even muscle in case anything goes wrong. Herod seems to be sending more here every day. It will only make things more difficult for us. Speaking of that, any word about the ones spying on us?"

"No, nothing new there. They seem content to just hold their position and observe. There were a couple that followed me, but I lost them easy enough. I couldn't have them overhearing anything. Not yet anyway."

***

Balthazar was famished by the time he returned to camp. He made his way to the table and sat heavily into his chair. He was brought a plate of meat, cheese, and assorted vegetables. His partners had finished their meals but returned to the table when they saw him arrive. Melchior poured wine for all of them. Balthazar drank a full glass of water in several gulps before taking his wine. He asked the others about their day, and Melchior and Gaspar reported the day's events. Balthazar nodded as he listened, taking in all the information his friends could impart.

"And how was your day? Were you successful locating our carpenter?" Gaspar asked.

"I was. He showed up at the synagogue this morning as I was told he would yesterday. I watched from afar as he and two of his coworkers went about their business. Several times I nearly approached him to discuss his situation and the need for Mary and him to leave this place. Something held me back from going up to him, though. I've learned not to question these gut feelings anymore. Even more so now that we were given this mission. So I continued to observe. They completed their work, went through the completed project with someone from the synagogue, then left. I chose to follow them at a discreet distance. The trio eventually split up and went separate ways. I stayed with Joseph, deciding it would be good to know where he lives. This will give us the opportunity to speak to him together when the time is right."

"That makes sense. It will be better to approach him together. Three of us will be more convincing. When do you propose we speak to him? Herod is making things more and more difficult each day."

"We need to do it tomorrow. We just don't know what Herod's plan is or how zealous he will be in implementing it." Balthazar unwrapped his turban and removed it from his head. His black hair fell to his shoulders. "It occurred to me on my walk back to camp that we might be able to learn something at the census station. On the way to speak to Joseph tomorrow, we should stop and listen in for a bit. The lines to report have been quite long and there are a lot of people milling about afterward. We should be able to go unnoticed for a bit."

"I checked it out from a distance earlier today," Melchior said. "I didn't overhear anything, but I did watch long enough to see at any moment there are only six to eight soldiers. There also seems to be some non-military, advisors or something. These are the ones filling out the forms. I assume they are the literate ones."

Gaspar smiled. "It'll be a good opportunity to get some intel. No doubt these men are simply pawns in the game, but you never know when one will say too much. Herod's government is full of useful idiots."

21

SURVEILLANCE

Tobias was not amused. He and Gundahar had arrived at the little outpost on a hill overlooking the Wise Men's camp. Only a few clouds dotted the sky in the mid-morning sunshine. The men manning the outpost had taken over a portion of some farmer's grazing area and apparently commandeered several sheep in the process. Their idea of a covert operation was to take turns herding the sheep down the hill to observe the Wise Men's camp. Tobias shook his head and stared at the ground for several moments as he processed this "brilliant" plan. *Why are they always so stupid?*

They were so blatantly obvious in their surveillance. The Wise Men must have been onto them from the start. He did not have the time or resources to teach them all individually, but surely someone could. He considered reprimanding the men who came up with it, but the damage was done. Whatever they had to report was going to be exactly what the Wise Men had wanted them to see.

Tobias sighed and looked over at Gundahar, whose face, as always, betrayed nothing. He looked bored and disinterested. Tobias turned back to the soldier who was providing the update. "Okay, tell me what you've seen so far."

A soldier, already made uncomfortable by the arrival of these two important men and the long silence by both, answered with an unsteady voice, "The first day was simple camp set up. There was a lot of milling about, but no one left camp. We ascertain there are twenty-seven of them staying in the camp; however, over the past few days many others have come and gone. Most were delivering supplies and water. We're not certain why the others showed up. In each case, the number arriving always equaled the number leaving."

"What of the Wise Men? What have they been doing?"

"They've gone into town each day as a group but split up once they are there. We ... have had difficulty tailing them once they split up. It's as if they know they're being followed. They've been losing us in crowds or buildings. Sometimes they turn a corner, and by the time we get there, they're just gone."

Tobias closed his eyes and shook his head. "Of course, they are."

"We eventually catch up to them, but it's usually when they're returning to camp. They always return alone. Whatever they're doing, they aren't bringing anyone back to camp with them."

Tobias opened his eyes. "Well, that's something. Something worthwhile to note."

He looked off into the distance. "What are you boys up to?" He wondered aloud of the Wise Men.

Gundahar looked angry as he stepped forward to face the soldier. "Vut is your name?"

The soldier cringed a little before forcing himself to look the general in the eye. "Morton, sir. My name is Morton."

Tobias watched silently, wondering where this conversation would lead.

"Morton. You and your men are an embarrassment." Without another word, Gundahar punched the soldier in the jaw. He was unconscious before he hit the ground.

Gundahar turned to Tobias. "Tomorrow you and I vill follow ze Vise Men. Zese men are incompetent."

Tobias smiled. "Agreed, on both counts."

22

CENSUS

Mary was nervous. She and Joseph agreed they would report for the census, but she was having second thoughts. It made sense to get it out of the way early before anyone might mention her as being pregnant. That would give them time to plan a way out of Nazareth. If they could get in and out of the census as just a normal childless couple, no one would care if they left town. They would be under the radar. They would have time to work out a strategy and figure out a destination. But Mary had a bad feeling about all of it.

She went over and over the plan in her head. She could only think of a few people that knew she was pregnant. *Is it possible one of them mentioned it to someone else?* Anything was possible. If she had been reported, when she checked in, she would be followed. That would make it harder to escape town. If they did not check in at all, they would be hunted down by the soldiers. There were no easy answers here.

She ran her hand over her slightly swollen belly. This often caused an "Oh, F!" moment. It was too easy to forget her reality and think her life was normal, that she married the man she loved, and they were simply going to have a baby, just like everyone else. It was the natural order. It was what everyone did. But sooner or later, her reality would resurface. This was not simply a baby. It was the Son of God. The God. The one and only God. The great I AM. The realization would turn her into a jellyfish (not that she knew what a jellyfish was, as she had never been to the Mediterranean Sea). It would steal the strength from her muscles and render her useless. *How is any of this even possible? How can we do this? Please, God, take it away and choose someone else. I am not strong enough to bear this burden. Forgive me.* Her grandmother was the strongest woman she had ever met, perhaps God should have chosen someone like her. There must be hundreds of strong women He could choose from. A small tear formed in the corner of her eye. She was terrified. She sat on the bed and tried to catch her breath.

Joseph was staring at her from across the room. She could see the concern in his eyes. She felt guilty, as if all of this were her fault, as if it were some kind of punishment, instead of a great honor. It was hard to see the glory of the situation when a mad king was trying to hunt down an unborn child. Her child. *How crazy is that?* She tried to believe even Herod could not be so cruel as to hurt a baby, but in her heart, she knew better. What a horrible shit he was. A monster.

"Mary?" Joseph said softly. She looked up at him. "We need to go. It will be ok. Rog and Mags will be with us, just two normal couples, nothing special, just like everyone else. We check in, get out quick, then we can figure things out from there."

She smiled at him. It was a weak smile, but she tried. "I love you. Thank you for being strong, and for not running away from all this madness."

He walked to her and hugged her close. "You're not getting rid of me that easy, you shrew. I am curious though. After you give birth to God, how are you going to top it? Surely that's not the best you can do. What else ya got?"

Mary burst out laughing and hit him playfully in the chest. "You're such a jerk."

Joseph joined in the laughter.

There was a knock at the door. Joseph and Mary were still laughing as they opened the door for Roger and Maggie. Their friends seemed a little confused.

"I was expecting a more somber greeting," Roger said. "This is way better. This is good, you're loose, you're smiling. We've got this. Nothing to it."

Joseph and Mary started laughing even harder. To the point of not being able to breathe.

"Don't encourage him," Maggie said. "He already thinks he is funnier than he is. He'll get a big head."

Mary hugged Joseph again and then turned to her friends. "Thank you both. I'm probably making too much of this. I apologize, I'm being silly. We'll go to the station, check in, and come back here for some wine. Roger is right, there's nothing to it."

***

The two couples walked down the street together, making small talk and discussing inconsequential things. They were purposefully keeping things light. Each was nervous and tense, but the banter was helping them relax. They made their way down the streets, cutting through alleys, and winding their way toward the census station. As they got closer, they noticed more and more people on the street.

Ahead, toward the station, was a large gathering of people. Something wasn't quite right, there were gasps, some yelling, and people milling about. General commotion. Some of the crowd started running toward them. Mary looked to Joseph with concern in her eyes. Joseph shrugged and put his arm around her as they walked.

"Well... there is always something new and exciting happening in Nazareth. Let's see what fresh hell this is," Maggie said quietly.

Grim-faced people passed by them but said nothing. A woman was weeping with her hand over her eyes. They made their way closer, into the thick crowd of people.

"I can't believe they killed him. I just can't," another woman spoke as she approached them.

Mary grabbed the woman by the arm. "What happened? Please tell me!"

"We were in line, waiting to check in with the census people. Some of Herod's soldiers dragged a man into the street. They said they caught him trying to avoid being counted. They said he ran. They yelled to the crowd that this is what happens when you refuse to report to be counted. Then they started beating him. He pleaded for them to stop, but they didn't. They hit him well past consciousness, and still, they continued. They finally dropped him in the street. He was covered in blood, dead. They killed him."

None of the four friends spoke. Mary released the woman's arm, who continued on her way, mumbling to herself. They looked at each other with wide eyes.

"What's going on? This doesn't make sense," said Mary.

"Herod is sending a message," Joseph said. "He must think some of us won't take this seriously. Sick bastard,"

"He killed a man? To send a message?" Mary squinted and tilted her head.

"He's a sick man, not just the way Joseph means it. He isn't right in the head." Roger shook his head. "Okay, maybe exactly the way Joseph means it."

"What do we do?" Maggie asked.

"Well, we sure as hell don't run. We're here. Let's just get this over with and go home. I need that wine more than I thought," Joseph said.

Mary's sense of foreboding was getting worse. What Joseph said made sense. Getting it over with would get them home quicker, and they were already here. Clearly, this census thing was important enough to Herod that he'd kill to make it happen. Skipping it and going home was no longer an option. Her friends were silent, probably having similar inner reservations.

Although many in the crowd had dispersed, a large throng of people still congregated around the census station tent. There was an obvious line to the right populated by people waiting to check in. The remainder of the crowd was gathered in groups, some disgusted by the show of unnecessary force displayed earlier, some discussing what they had witnessed, and others just staring at Herod's guards and census personnel, waiting to see what would happen next. Inside the tent, people filed diligently to be tallied with the rest of the populace. From a distance, Mary could see they were answering questions or explaining things, some with bold gestations of their arms and hands. Joseph took her by the arm and led her to the waiting line, accompanied by Maggie and Roger. The line was fifty or sixty people deep with a mix of single people, couples, and families. More people joined the line behind them.

Mary scanned the crowd. It had been quite some time since she had seen this many people gathered for any purpose. There were a few faces she recognized, but not many. Nazareth was a big town, and she didn't often wander far from her home. When she did, it was usually toward the outskirts of the city, not to its center. *There must be hundreds of people loitering around the tent. It could even be a thousand.*

Mary noticed three men looking in her direction. They were tall, each with a beard (pretty much the norm, it was 5 BC), and each was wearing a brightly colored turban. Their clothes seemed different, as if they may be from another place, yet similar enough to fit into their surroundings. The things that made them stand out were the turbans; one red, one green, and one gold. To their left was possibly the fattest man she had ever seen. He was nearly round. He was discussing something with a non-descript man next to him while stuffing figs into his mouth.

"Missus Kimmet is in line ahead of us," Joseph said, pointing to an old woman about fifteen people ahead of them. Missus Kimmet was their neighbor. Her husband died several years ago, now she lived alone. Her children grew up and moved away, but still came to visit her now and then. Mary and Joseph made it a point to speak to her regularly. They would check in on her to make sure she had enough food or to see if she needed help with chores. She was always kind and always wore a large, pleasant smile. She seemed genuinely happy. Mary smiled and waved to her. Missus Kimmet seemed confused at first, but finally recognized them and waved back.

The line was slowly progressing. Mary could not shake the bad feeling she had. She watched the census takers in the tent, observing them as they spoke to people. There were three of them; two asking questions and one taking notes. Behind them were four guards holding pikes. Two thoughts ran through her mind simultaneously: *Pikes would be difficult to use in a crowd this size,* and *were these the guards who killed the man?* Mary did not think they were. They didn't seem to be the type to physically beat someone. To the pike soldiers' left was a very large, grizzled soldier speaking to what might be a politician. The big soldier was more likely the one. The man was nearly a giant and frightening to behold. This did little to calm her.

She clasped her hands to stop the trembling. The giant soldier seemed to be staring at her. She looked to her left and noticed the turban men seemed to be staring at her. *Now I'm becoming paranoid.* Her legs stiffened, and her heart was racing. She took Joseph's hand and squeezed it.

"You okay?" Joseph asked. "You look terrified."

"I don't want to be here."

"Me, either. It will be alright. We are almost out of here. Missus Kimmet is next to the table. It'll be our turn in a few minutes." Joseph tried to smile. It was a weak effort.

Maggie put her hand on Mary's shoulder. "Oh, honey, you're trembling. Joseph is right, we'll be out of here soon. We can do this, there's nothing to it." Maggie looked to Roger, who only shrugged. Maggie also felt that something was not right but dismissed it as Mary's nervousness.

Mary watched the census people question Missus Kimmet. She was smiling and gesturing as she answered their questions. The soldiers behind them seemed bored to tears. Mary glanced around, taking in the crowd. The fat man was still eating figs as he chatted. The turban men were no longer there. She had not seen them leave but they were gone.

She glanced back to the census table and Missus Kimmet. What she saw next froze her to the bone. From this point, everything moved in slow motion. Missus Kimmet was pointing her thin, frail arm directly at Mary. She was smiling in mid-sentence to the census takers. Each of them was staring directly at her as well. The guards behind the table were looking at her along with the others. It seemed everyone in the crowd was turning to see whom the old woman was pointing at, their eyes stopping on Mary.

No, please no! Her right hand instinctively covered her belly, and her left came to her chest. She began taking small steps backward, slowly shaking her head side to side and softly repeating "No... no... no."

23

FRENZY

Joseph's head snapped to look at Mary. She was backing up with her hands covering her belly and chest, her eyes wide with terror. He turned to locate the cause, seeing the old woman pointing at Mary, and the eyes of the crowd on her as well. They must have asked Missus Kimmet if she knew any pregnant women. Although the subject never came up between them when they spoke, Missus Kimmet was a bright, intuitive woman. He was not surprised she had pieced it together.

He reached for Mary's arm, but she recoiled from him, continuing to backpedal with her eyes fixed on their neighbor. He turned back to the table. *Fuck*.

Two of the guards saw her odd reaction and were making their way around the table. Joseph grabbed Roger's arm.

"Run interference. Block them, impede them somehow."

Roger and Maggie nodded and moved ahead to slow the guards' approach. Joseph turned back to Mary. A man in a colored turban was holding onto her arms, speaking into her ear. Two others were removing their turbans as they approached Joseph. Joseph lunged at the men with fists clenched. One of the men put both his hands up, palms out.

"Joseph, please, we don't have time to explain. We're here to help. God asked us to help. We can get you out of here. You need to come with us. Now."

Joseph drew back, confused. He was expecting a fight. He turned back to find Roger and Maggie. *Fuck! Could this day get worse?*

Roger had a guard by the shoulders, claiming he was innocent, that he was not the man they were looking for. Maggie had wrapped herself around the other in a bear hug, saying "Carl, I've missed you. Where have you been all these years?" Joseph rolled his eyes then rushed to help his friends.

"Joseph, you have to leave them. We don't have time. We need to leave now!"

Joseph ignored the man and went to free his friends. They were only ten yards away. He reached Maggie and her guard first. He threw his fist hard at the man's nose, connecting with all his strength and forward momentum. The man dropped backward with Maggie still wrapped around him, his broken nose spewing blood into the air as he fell.

Joseph spun to see Roger struggling with the other guard. The guard was trying to push him away to get to Mary. Joseph took two steps in their direction when he saw something out of the corner of his eye. He turned to see a giant of a soldier coming at him like a freight train (or something similar, since they had no idea what a freight train was). The soldier crashed into Joseph, taking them both to the ground. In one smooth motion, the soldier rolled over on top of him and held a menacing blade to his throat.

"Anyvun moves and zis vun is a dead man."

Joseph squirmed to see Mary, but she was gone, along with the three men who claimed they were there to help. He hoped they were true to their word.

24

CAPTURED

Roger, Maggie, and Joseph were seated on the ground against a wall near the census station. Three guards with pikes glared at them, hoping they would try to escape. Gundahar was seated on a stool facing them. He still had the knife in his hand, flipping it into the air and catching the handle every time. He did not speak, he merely regarded them one at a time with a stony face. He knew from experience that his face was intimidating and his silence unnerving. He had dealt with prisoners of one sort or another his entire career, and mind games were a hobby for him. He enjoyed being the most ominous thing in the room. He reveled in causing fear.

Tobias walked up to him. "What the hell was that all about?"

"Ze old voman pointed to her pregnant neighbor. Ze pregnant voman reacted... wrong. Ze guards vent to bring her for questions. Zeze sree interfered. Zat one attacked one of ze guards, broke his nose. I am going to question him, zen kill him slowly," Gundahar said in a flat tone.

Joseph's eyes got wide, but he said nothing. He continued to stare at the dirt between his legs.

Tobias regarded the three prisoners. "How did the woman interfere?"

"Ze guard said she thought he vas someone she knew, zen hugged him. Zat one attacked him vile he vas trying to deal vis ze voman."

Tobias cocked his head at an angle in thought. "What did the other man do? How is he part of this?"

162

"He thought guard vas coming for him. Probably guilty of somesing. Vas pleading he vas wrong guy."

Tobias brought his hand to his chin. "Okay, so the old woman points to her pregnant neighbor in line. The neighbor has a strange reaction. Two guards go to ask some questions. This woman intercepts one guard, this man intercepts the other, and this third guy comes in and attacks. Is that about it?"

"Yes"

"Where is the pregnant neighbor?" Tobias asked.

"She must have run off during ze scuffle."

Tobias looked coldly at the three prisoners. He slowly smiled. "I think I see what this is. This woman belongs to one of these two. The one that got away belongs to the other. So, the question is, why did they feel the need to protect her?"

Tobias walked directly in front of the three, then knelt in front of Maggie. He quickly pulled a knife and brought it to her throat. Roger lunged to protect her. One of the guards struck him hard in the forehead with the staff of his pike. Roger was out cold.

Tobias looked Maggie in the eye. She was visibly trembling. "This one is yours, then?"

Maggie nodded slowly.

Tobias stood and walked over to Joseph. He crouched before him. "So, what's the deal, tough guy? Why did you think it was necessary to risk your life to keep your woman from talking to us?"

Joseph stared at the dirt. He did not want to look this man in the eye. "She's not my woman, she's a girl from our street. She's new to Nazareth and doesn't speak our language. She'd been raped by Roman soldiers not long ago and got scared. I knew if she didn't respond to questions, it would go badly for her, but she doesn't speak our language. I overreacted. I'm sorry."

Tobias looked at Gundahar. "Sound like bullshit to you?"

Gundahar nodded.

"Sounds like bullshit to me, too," Tobias said, looking back at Joseph.

"Can I kill him now?" Gundahar asked.

"No, not yet. I'm not sure what these fucks are up to, but none of this feels right to me. Let's take them back to Jerusalem. We can get a little more persuasive with them on the trip." Tobias looked at Roger, who was beginning to stir. "If we start breaking her fingers, this one will tell us everything we want to know."

Maggie started to cry.

Tobias turned to Gundahar. "What happened to the Wise Men?"

"Ve lost zem in ze crowd during ze scuffle."

"Fuck it. I'm tired of playing hide and seek with those asshats. Let's grab them and take them back to Jerusalem as well. I don't care if they're famous or not. If they're the ones causing all this messiah nonsense, let's make them admit to it in front of Herod."

25

THE GETAWAY

Gaspar rode his horse with Mary seated in front of him. She was in a haze, barely responding to anything. She was staring at nothing, trying to make sense of the things that had just occurred. Trying to imagine what was happening to Joseph. Wondering when she would see him next, if she would see him at all. Balthazar and Melchior were each on their own horses.

Getting Mary away from the melee unnoticed was harder than they had imagined. She was inconsolable when Joseph was taken down by the giant soldier. She did not hear them as they pleaded for her to come with them before it was too late. She pushed forward, screaming and crying, trying to get to Joseph. Balthazar physically lifted her onto his shoulder, apologizing all the while, as he carried her away from the ruckus.

They had spotted Joseph and Mary moments before everything went wrong. Mary seemed spooked even before the old woman pointed to her. The Wise Men were moving in to speak with them discreetly, hoping to persuade them to come to their camp to plan Mary's departure from Nazareth. Then the old woman pointed, and everything changed. The Wise Men began removing their turbans to better blend with the crowd. Herod's men were less likely to pay attention to their clothing with such distinctive headwear to follow. Once they discarded the turbans and replaced them with common keffiyeh, their followers were less likely to be able to track them in the crowd. It was all part of the plan. But plans rarely go to plan, as it turns out. They were forced to improvise.

"It looks as though we'll need to alter our course of action," Balthazar said. "Herod's men will be coming for us, not because of Mary, but because he thinks we are plotting a coup. If he doesn't believe the shepherds, and he does not, then he'll think someone is behind it all. Unfortunately, we're the most logical suspects."

Melchior adjusted his grip on the reins. "I came to that conclusion as well. It was more than simple mistrust that caused him to have us followed."

"We'll need to get back to camp and prepare to leave immediately." Balthazar said. "We were fortunate to have put most of the pieces in place before today. We won't have much time once we get there."

"What about Joseph? And Maggie and Roger?" Mary asked. "Is your plan to just leave them with those horrible men?"

The Wise Men could not meet her gaze. It was a fair question, and they had no simple answer.

"Mary, we're not soldiers, and we don't have an army," Gaspar said. "Rescuing Joseph and your friends is beyond our power. At least, it's beyond our power at the moment. God sent us to help you, and that's our immediate priority. We have a plan to do that. Once we're safely away from Herod's men, we can come up with a plan to help them. Until then, I'm sure God will keep them safe."

"Are you? Are you sure? I've spoken with Him a couple times now, and both times He mentioned that He likes to see how things play out. He says horrible things are as much of His plan as the wonderful things. He says He can't explain it to us. Maggie called Him on it, told Him it was a cop out. So, I'm sorry, but I don't share your faith that God will keep them safe. I'm terrified and angry. If anything happens to Joseph, I won't be able to continue. Not for God, not for any…" At that moment, the baby kicked, and Mary's eyes and hands went immediately to her stomach. She had nearly forgotten her son. Her eyes filled with tears. Her hands went to her face. Fear, anger, frustration, confusion, all poured out of her as if it were water coming from a faucet. Gaspar placed his hand on her shoulder and looked to the others pleadingly.

Balthazar's eyes were glassy with welling tears. He too was frustrated that they could not do more to help Joseph and her friends. His mind was racing to come up with something, anything, that might help. But her immediate safety was more pressing. All would be lost if Mary ended up with Herod's men. There was no logic that informed this thought, only a gut feeling that he trusted more than any he could remember. They needed to get back to camp and they needed to do it now. Balthazar trotted his horse next to Mary and Gaspar.

"Mary, we're no good to you if we get caught, and you're no good to Joseph if you get caught. We need to get back to camp to implement our plan. We used this particular tactic once before. It was successful then, and I believe in all my heart that it'll be successful now."

Balthazar explained their plan to Mary. She slowly calmed and was intently listening to this stranger lay out their strategy. When he finished, she paused and furrowed her brow.

"That's your plan?" She asked, slowly shaking her head. "That's ridiculous. How can that possibly work? I thought you were supposed to be the smartest men on the planet. You'll get us all killed!"

26

THE POLLY

Several years prior, the Wise Men had to intercede in a squabble between two warring villages in Thais, a far east country on the border of the Chinese Empire. It was common for warring clans to kidnap and sometimes even murder children of their opposition. More often than not, the children were merely used as pawns in negotiations between the clans. The Wise Men stepped in to help save the daughter of one such clan. They had business dealings with this family and felt they could not deny them when asked to assist.

The Wise Men convinced the aggressor clan to meet with them in attempt to mediate hostilities between the proud families. The leader of the aggressor clan was unyielding, belligerent, and, quite frankly, such a douche that the Wise Men decided to abandon the negotiations and just steal the girl back. The plan was so successful that not a single person on either side got hurt. The Thais language was tricky for them, and they could never get the daughter's name right, so they simply called her Polly. That is how *The Polly* came to be.

The Wise Men had to modify the plan to make it work in this situation. The stakes were even higher this time. They needed to escape from King Herod's army, and Herod was backed by the Romans. Failing to pull this off would have dire consequences for everyone involved. Ideally, they needed another couple of days to plan, coordinate, rehearse the players, and prepare. That was no longer possible. Herod's men would be coming for them, and soon. Best case, they had two hours to prepare and implement their plan. There would be no rehearsing. They had to hope the people hired to assist them would be able to complete the tasks they were given.

The Wise Men and Mary rode into camp and immediately gathered everyone into the main tent. This drew the attention of Herod's spies on the hill overlooking the camp. The gathering was a change in the normal routine of the camp and needed to be reported. Thirty minutes later, it was obvious the camp was being readied for departure. The tents began coming down, wagons were being loaded, and animals were gathered. The camp was pulling up stakes to leave. Herod's spies sent a rider to inform Tobias and Gundahar of the change of status. Neither the guards nor the rider saw four people sneak away from camp on horses. The rest of the camp continued their preparations to leave.

***

The rider reached the census station as Tobias and Gundahar were preparing to take the prisoners to Jerusalem. They saw the man ride in hot and knew he must have pressing news.

The young man jumped off the horse before it had come to a full stop. He landed deftly on his feet and trotted to where the two men were standing. The rider was silently wondering how cool that looked to everyone watching.

"Sir, the Wise Men returned and are breaking camp. It appears they'll be leaving very soon."

"Fuck," Tobias said. "Ride back immediately. Have our men move in and take them. Gundahar and I will be right behind you. Don't bother with the servants, just hold the Wise Men. GO!"

The young rider was still basking in the glow of his ultra-smooth dismount and barely took in what Tobias had told him. The words eventually hit their mark. The young rider hesitated, nodded, said, "Yes, Sir," then ran back to his horse and was gone.

Tobias turned to Gundahar. "Send the three prisoners with some guards to Jerusalem. Have them held until we get back. You and I need to go back for the Wise Men. Make the arrangements with the guards, I'll go get the tallies from the census boys for the guards to take back to Herod. We leave in five minutes."

Gundahar glared briefly at Tobias. He was not accustomed to taking orders from anyone but Herod. The little man was beginning to annoy him. But given the facts of the day, he concluded that Tobias was right. Still, he was not pleased that the little man was getting comfortable ordering him around. This would have to change. Politically, they were equals. Physically, Tobias was insignificant. Gundahar had no intention of being this man's bitch. He nodded to Tobias and went to make arrangements for guards to take the three prisoners back to Jerusalem.

Tobias was back in minutes with the three census takers who were carrying stacks of parchment bundled together. He placed the bundles into a leather satchel and gave them to the four guards Gundahar had chosen to escort the prisoners to the palace.

"The larger bundle goes to the Council. The smaller bundle goes to my office. Get it right," Tobias said to the guards.

"Like I said, hold ze prisoners in ze cell until ve return. Go," Gundahar commanded.

The guards nodded in unison.

Maggie and Roger were on one horse and Joseph was on another, all three with their hands bound. The four guards, each on their own horses, led the three prisoners onto the road leading to Jerusalem.

Tobias watched for a moment as they rode away. He turned to Gundahar and said, "Let's go," as he walked toward his horse.

***

When the young rider made it back to give the order to capture the Wise Men, the caravan was already on the road pulling out. He gathered the men from the outpost and rode in pursuit. The caravan was still in sight, moving slowly. Most of the camp personnel were on horseback. The rest were in three large wagons being pulled by two oxen each. The wagons were heavily loaded with the tents and provisions.

As the soldiers approached the caravan, the camp riders on horseback scattered in different directions, riding away as fast and hard as the horses would take them. Many rode across fields, others took side roads, and a few stayed on the main road. There were too many to follow them all. Herod's men had to guess which were the Wise Men and set off after them, but the runners already had a considerable lead. The three wagons came to a stop in the road.

By the time Tobias and Gundahar made it back, everything had gone to shit. Their men were gone, and the only thing left from the caravan were the three large wagons parked in the road. They trotted to the wagons, stopping at the one in the rear. An old man had been driving this one, accompanied by a woman and a small boy. The three sat in the wagon and did not say a word.

Tobias was furious. He forced himself to regain his composure to address the servants in the wagon. He knew these were not the brains of the organization, but perhaps he could still get useful information from them.

"What happened? Where did the rest of your crew go?" Tobias asked as nicely as his temper would allow.

"They left us," the woman said. "When the soldiers approached, they bolted, in every direction. They just left us here. Who does that? Why would they leave us behind? They're such assholes."

"Did our soldiers follow them?" Tobias asked.

"Yes. Well, as many as they could. We had more riders than you had soldiers. But, yes, the soldiers left us here too."

"Why did the soldiers attack us?" The old man asked. "We've done nothing wrong."

Tobias looked at the ground and shook his head. *We underestimated them. Fuck! This is not going to go well with Herod.* Tobias knew the king's sanity was hanging by a thread. There was no telling how he would react to something like this. He wondered if he was valued enough to survive it. Or if Gundahar was. Tobias looked up and regarded the people in the wagon. Peasants. Servants. Nobody. He ignored the old man's question and rode to see who was in the other wagons. More of the same. This was not good. The wagons were packed tight with provisions. He would have them searched but knew better than to hope he would find anyone hiding there.

Gundahar approached. His normally granite expression was replaced with a scowl and angry eyes. "Ve need to find ze Vise Men. Ze two of us. Zis is unacceptable."

"Agreed. I doubt any of these moron soldiers will catch them. We can't do anything until our men report back. Their riders scattered in all directions. We don't know where to start."

Gundahar glanced at the people in the wagons. "Ve could start vis zem. See vut zey know."

"Do you seriously think the Wise Men would share their plans with the hired help? We can't waste time torturing people who know less than we do. We need to think this through. This was a little too perfect to be unplanned. They must have prepared for this days ago. From what I know of these men, they probably had several plans like this. Fuck. This is bad. They played us and made us look foolish."

Tobias hopped off of his horse and walked it back to the last wagon. "You folks need to stay until our men return. Just a formality. You can tell the other wagons the same."

The little boy in the wagon stood. He didn't say anything, he only stared. At Gundahar. The large soldier frightened grown men and women. Children were normally terrified of the old, grizzled warrior that emanated nastiness. This child did not seem to be frightened at all. If anything, he looked angry. Gundahar noticed the child glaring, dismounted his horse, and walked over to him. With the child standing on the wagon and the general on the ground, they were eye to eye. Gundahar growled at the boy. The child did not flinch, did not blink, did not say a word.

Gundahar cracked a small smile. *Vis some time, I could make zis vun a soldier.*

***

Slowly, the outpost men started returning. Each of them returned alone. Some had overtaken and stopped their prey, only to realize they had been chasing a servant, or in some cases a visitor to the camp. One of those fleeing was badly injured after falling from his horse during the chase. A nearby farmer offered to help mend the man. The rest of the soldiers were simply outrun but continued to track the runners as far as they could before returning.

Tobias sent two soldiers to search the wagons. They were to check the barrels and large parcels to ensure no one was hiding. It was a waste of time, but he wanted to cover all the bases in case he was asked. He also sent a group of soldiers to search known villages and farms for any word of Wise Men sightings. That could take some time but was necessary. He and Gundahar needed at the very least a direction in which to search for these men. It was imperative that they be the ones who brought the Wise Men to Herod. It would go a long way in smoothing over the gross mistakes and ineptitude of this debacle.

"With census activities in full swing, they'll avoid the cities and towns." Tobias was more thinking out loud than pursuing a conversation with Gundahar. "That means they could be anywhere. They're not very familiar with Galilee or Samaria, but likely have a guide to assist them. I doubt they'd go further south, closer to Herod, but then again, perhaps they would. I guess it depends on if they plan to continue their messiah hoax. Rome controls the lands to the north; I see no benefit for them to go that way. It seems to me their likely options would have them hiding out somewhere in rural Judaea or escaping east to more familiar territories."

Gundahar considered what Tobias said but made no reaction to any of it. His anger had dissipated, and he was back to looking disinterested and bored. He agreed with Tobias but did not feel the need to stroke the smaller man's ego by saying so. He stared off into the distance.

Daylight was fading, and they were going to be at least a full day behind the Wise Men before they could begin to track them. That would make things difficult. Tobias was likely right in his assessment of their escape routes, but they needed a direction or sighting to start them on the hunt.

Gundahar had been in more battles and wars than he could count. He was good at killing. It was a gift, to be sure. But as he had gotten older, the pursuit of strays or wanted men had gotten into his blood. He enjoyed the hunt, the tracking, the pursuit, the capture. These had become his new unspoken obsessions. This was a golden opportunity to do something he was truly looking forward to. He was anxious to get started, but the Wise Men had a considerable head start. It would make things more challenging, but Gundahar didn't mind.

The two men sent to search the wagons returned and reported to Tobias. They found nothing of concern nor anyone hiding amongst the provisions. In different times, they might suggest confiscating the food and wine for their own use, but since the Wise Men had escaped, there was no reason to maintain a post in this location. Lugging additional supplies back to Jerusalem would be creating more work than any of them cared to perform. They had suffered a humiliating defeat, one that would likely get them punished. Bringing back spoils seemed cocky, even from a soldier's standpoint. It would be an open invitation to Herod's wrath, and there was no reason to go down that road. Tobias dismissed the soldiers, sending them east, the one direction that had not been covered by the others.

Tobias was still working the events over in his mind. He wanted to divine the Wise Men's intent to better understand where they might be going. It was an exercise in logic and deduction. But he had to admit to himself that it was pure speculation at this point. Until they knew a direction, the Wise Men could be anywhere for reasons completely unknown to Tobias.

He walked down the gentle incline to where the wagons were still parked. When he arrived at the last wagon, he could see the old driver was napping, the woman looked bored to tears, and the small boy was standing, staring him in the eye. The kid might not even be six; the idea that he was scrutinizing Tobias was a little unsettling. *Who knows what this kid has seen in his short life? He may just hate men. It would make sense, judging by the reaction when anyone comes near the wagon.* Tobias ignored the child and walked to the front to address the woman.

"You can go. You and the other wagons. Sorry for the inconvenience."

"We can go?" She asked. "Where? Where are we supposed to go? Everyone left us here! Left us to be persecuted by the Romans! They better hope I never see them again. Bastards."

"Don't go overboard, and don't be a drama queen. We aren't Romans, and we didn't persecute you. Get a grip. Just leave before my soldiers remember how lonely they are and realize you're the only woman in the area." In his own way, that was Tobias trying to be nice.

"Ella." The old man had awakened from his nap. "Where we go is no concern of this man. He's right, we should leave."

"Listen to the old man, Ella," Tobias said. "He's right, I don't give a fuck where you go. Just go." With that, Tobias walked back up the gentle incline to the outpost.

***

The beauty of *The Polly* is its simplicity. It involves many moving parts and coordination with hired actors to set the ball in motion, but at the end of the day it is simply a method to hide in plain sight. The actual execution of the maneuver takes timing and skill, but when you take a step back, it's a simple shell game. With slight modifications from its original use, it was the perfect move to smuggle Mary out of Nazareth.

The three wagons slowly plodded down the road, barely noticed by anyone. Those who did noticed quickly put the wagons out of their mind as they attended to their own business and worries of the day. The wagons approached an intersection with a side road. The lead wagon continued down the main road. The driver in the lead raised a hand to wave to the wagons behind him but did not look back. The two trailing wagons turned left onto the side road and continued on for another hour. They came to a farmstead and pulled off the road. The resident farmer, who was in on the ruse, was already walking toward the wagons. He waved a greeting and smiled as the wagoneers dismounted and began to stretch their sore muscles.

Ella and her son walked to the side of their wagon. Ella pounded three times on the side and then stood there waiting. From somewhere inside the wagon, movement could be heard. It was the sound of muffled speech and wood sliding across wood. A click was heard and a portion of the bottom of the wagon dropped to the ground like a ramp. Gaspar slid down the ramp, somewhat awkwardly, and crawled out from beneath the wagon. Mary followed him a little more gracefully. They each stood slowly, rubbing their eyes and stretching their bodies. They had been confined in the secret compartment for several hours. Mary was initially reluctant to climb into the space but was relieved to see it was more spacious than she had expected. They had about two feet of vertical clearance, so they had to crawl to move about, but the hidden space spanned the entire length of the wagon and was adorned with blankets and pillows to aid in their comfort while hiding. It was, in effect, a more comfortable version of a Trojan horse.

Gaspar glanced to see two men climbing out from beneath the other wagon. These men would assist in their journey, primarily as security. They had weeks of travel and hiding out ahead of them. They would head west toward the Mediterranean Sea and then push south a few miles in from the coast. They would avoid larger towns and stay off the radar as much as possible.

"It's nice to breathe fresh air again. It got a little stuffy in there. Mary, are you okay? Do you need anything?" Gaspar asked.

"I could use some water."

Ella was crouching with her son, trying to coax him into taking water to Mary. He looked unsure; he was not particularly fond of strangers. He eyed her with suspicion, as if she were going to try to bite him. Slowly, he nodded to his mother and walked to Mary, holding a skin of water out to her with extended arms.

Mary crouched down to get to his level. She took the skin and thanked him. It occurred to her that she had not spent much time with children. She might be as wary of him as he was of her. *How am I going to raise one of these creatures when I know nothing about them?* She studied the boy as he returned to his mother, watching as he wrapped his arm around her thigh, half hiding behind her. The mother unconsciously ruffled the boys' hair with her hand. Mary was touched by the gentle interaction between them. Their bond was obvious, the love of a mother and her child. Mary's hand went to her belly. She was hopeful and yet terrified at the same time. *God, I hope You know what You're doing, because one of us should.*

Gaspar walked to Ella and took her hand. "Thank you. You were magnificent. You handled Herod's men brilliantly."

Ella smiled and blushed a little. The boy came from behind her leg and pushed Gaspar back a few steps, then resumed his position at her thigh. It seemed he was not going to allow that sort of fraternization. Gaspar laughed out loud and bowed to the boy. "My apologies, young master. I meant no disrespect."

"So, what happens now?" Mary asked Gaspar.

"Balthazar and Melchior snuck off earlier with a couple men, one of whom looks surprisingly like me. They'll provide random 'sightings' of the Wise Men far from our path to throw off Herod's men. We'll meet up with them later. It'll be many weeks before we see them again. We spent the last several days hiring people to assist us with this plan. Most of our caravan has been paid and released from service. They would swap garments with our new helpers who would stay at camp while our original people would leave as them. To Herod's men spying on our camp, it appeared the people visiting our camp would leave a few hours later. They had no idea we were smuggling our people out. The new ones were paid in advance. I'm impressed by how well they performed.

"Our remaining group will travel west then south. The main goal is to go unnoticed, blend in with our surroundings. We'll rejoin the others along the way. When the time is right, we'll head to Bethlehem. There may be times along the way when you'll need to hide in the wagon again. Hopefully, it doesn't come to that, but be prepared for it, nonetheless."

Mary wanted to ask questions about this plan, but had a more pressing matter to broach, "What about Joseph? How do we get him and our friends back?"

Gaspar shook his head. "I have no idea. We're travelling by wagon. We're not equipped to track soldiers on horseback. We also don't have enough people to overpower trained soldiers. The two guards we have would be no match for them."

"I can't do this without Joseph. I won't do this without Joseph. You and your friends gave yourselves the ridiculously arrogant name *Wise Men*. Earn it. Figure something out. Make another plan. Hire some help. I need to know Joseph... Joseph and my friends are okay. I need them to be with us. I can't do this without them."

Mary looked up to the sky to address God directly. "That goes for You, too," she said a little louder. "Get them back to me safely. I can't bear it otherwise. I'm not strong enough. I need them. Please. Keep them safe, and bring them back."

27

THE ROAD TO JERUSALEM

If you ride aggressively, you can make the trip from Nazareth to Jerusalem in less than eight hours, but you have to ride hard, and it may kill your horse. It appeared to Joseph that these soldiers planned to do just that. The road between the two cities was not straight and not well maintained. It was basically a dirt path strewn with large rocks. The road wound over and around large hills and mountains, and through deep valleys, with large boulders and sparse vegetation along the way. It was mostly desolate but made its way through the occasional small village. It was difficult to stay on the horse with hands bound, but Roger, Maggie, and Joseph were adept enough to do so. They had been riding for four hours. They did not speak, they only shared nervous glances and nods of encouragement.

Joseph could not stop thinking about Mary. The last time he saw her, she was with men who claimed to be there to help. *Were they there to help? Who were these men? Who sent them?* Everything had happened too quickly. *Was Mary in danger? How can I get to her?*

Throughout the ride south he had been trying to find ways to escape. The problem was there were four soldiers and only three of them, their hands were bound, and they weren't trained to fight as soldiers were. Had he been alone, he may have tried something to get away, but his friends were with him and would suffer if he did something stupid. He could see the worried expressions on their faces. Worried for themselves, worried for Mary, worried for each other.

Joseph unconsciously shook his head. This was a bad situation. He was not confident they would survive it. He wondered if God was planning to let this play out on its own. He hoped not.

The soldiers slowed their horses and pulled off the road into a shaded clearing. They dismounted and led their captive's horses over to some small trees.

"We're taking a few minutes to piss and grab some water," one of the soldiers said to Roger. Two soldiers waited with the prisoners while the others went off to take care of business. When they returned, the other two did the same.

"May I go too?" Maggie asked. Her butt and lower back were aching from the ride. She had never been on a horse this long in her life. She was not convinced she would be able to walk again if they continued. One soldier looked at the other and shrugged. They led the prisoners to some low shrubs and nodded toward them. Maggie walked to the other side and squatted.

They were given some water before being instructed to mount the horses. It was tricky with their hands bound, but they managed. Roger helped Maggie up before climbing on himself. The soldiers walked the prisoners to the edge of the road before mounting their steeds.

A small, frail, old man was standing in the road in front of them. He was dressed in rags, and his ancient sandals barely clung to his feet. He was dirty and alone. He had no horse that they could see. He must be some kind of vagrant who lived out here somewhere. Joseph noticed something about the old man's eyes: they seemed bright and alive. It could be he was crazed from exposure to the elements, but Joseph didn't think so. There was something powerful behind those eyes. It was a little unnerving.

The old man hunched over a bit and raised his arm, pointing at the three prisoners. "Those three... you should release them to me. I won't harm you if you do. You can give them to me and be on your way. Tell Herod they escaped."

The first soldier jumped down from his horse. "Ha! You make me smile, old one. I appreciate your sense of humor. We need to be on our way, please move aside. I don't wish to harm you."

"Nor I you," the elderly man said with a slight smile. "These people are not important to you. Release them to me. They're certainly not worth the beating you're about to receive if you refuse."

The smile left the soldier's face. "Crazy old fuck. Fine, let's do this your way." He unsheathed his blade and started approaching the old man.

"Need some help?" laughed one of the other soldiers.

"Shut up, moron," the soldier responded. He stopped about three feet away from the skeleton of a man. He lifted his sword and placed the tip on the old man's chin. "Get. The fuck. Away. Before you get..."

The old man moved so quickly it was difficult to see what happened. His arm came up knocking away the blade with his forearm. Two quick steps forward and a lightning-fast throat punch left the soldier unarmed on his knees, grasping at his neck, fighting for breath. The old man slowly turned to the other soldiers. "You don't have to do this. It'll end badly for you."

The soldiers dismounted in unison and attacked the old man with swords out. They approached three-wide in a V-shaped pattern. The old man stood still and watched them advance on his position. He then became a blur of movement, striking each of the soldiers in the face, ear, throat, stomach, and chin. Each soldier swayed slightly before falling face-first into the dirt. They were out cold. The old man watched them for a moment, then turned to the three prisoners. "You can dismount."

"Who... are you?" Joseph asked.

"A friend," he replied. White light began to emanate from him, and he began to change in shape and size, morphing into his natural form. In seconds he was a tall, glorious figure in white. He unfolded his wings, stretched them wide, and smiled. Maggie, Roger, and Joseph had met Gabriel when God had revealed Himself to them, but the sight of an angel was absolutely awe inspiring, even if it was not the first time. This angel seemed taller and leaner than Gabriel, though equally beautiful to behold. "I'm Michael. God thought I should step in and assist with this little predicament."

The friends just stared at him. They were speechless and star struck.

Joseph broke through the spell first. "How is Mary? Is she okay? Is she safe?"

"She's safe, though she misses you terribly. In her prayers she chews out the Boss daily for allowing these things to happen. I think it genuinely bothers Him that she is disappointed. I haven't seen that reaction from Him before."

Joseph smiled. *Yes, that's my Mary. You never have to guess what she's thinking.*

"Then maybe He shouldn't allow these things," Maggie said under her breath. Roger thumped the front of her shoulder with the back of his hand. They gave each other a stern look, his saying "keep it in your head" and hers saying "do that again, and you'll lose your hand".

Michael shook his head and smiled. "I don't spend much time with humans. You people baffle me. Anyway, you'll need to head west then south to meet up with Mary and the Wise Men."

"Wise Men?" Roger asked. "Who are they?"

"They're the men who helped Mary escape from Nazareth. As I was saying, head west then south. Go to a place called Marisa. If you have trouble finding them, seek out a young shepherd named Simon. He'll help you." Michael looked at the soldiers in the dirt. "Take three of the horses. There are some water skins in the bags of the big brown one."

"I don't know how to thank you, other than with words. Thank you for saving us," Joseph said.

Michael nodded. "You're welcome. It was my pleasure. Really. I enjoy fighting, what can I say? We all have our passions. I want you to know that all the angels are excited about the baby. This is so far outside of what we've come to expect from God. This is the biggest thing since the Creation itself. We'll all be there when the child is born. It should be quite the spectacle."

Joseph was a little confused. "Spectacle? I thought we were on the run and needed to stay out of sight. Maybe it shouldn't be a spectacle. Maybe we should keep it simple and quiet."

Michael laughed. "Yes, you probably should. However, this is a magnitude of importance that you don't quite understand. This is huge. I would expect, if I were you, that every angel in heaven will be there."

"Is that a lot? How many angels are there?" Joseph asked.

Michael's body shook with laughter, which made him seem to glow brighter. "You'll see soon enough. Be safe, my friends. Avoid towns, avoid people as much as possible. Blend in, be invisible, don't attract attention to yourselves. He may not send me back to save you a second time. Oh, one more thing, you may want to leave fairly soon. I'm not certain how long these four will be out." Michael took a couple steps before ascending into the sky and disappearing.

The trio gathered the horses and prepared to leave. They checked the saddle bags on all of the horses, searching for supplies. They found some fruit in one of the bags and a pair of knives in another. They mounted the horses and set off for Marisa.

Maggie's bottom was still hurting, but freedom had a way of quelling the pain.

28

ANGER

Fionn watched as the king's face grew red. He had seen Herod angry in the past, but this was a new level. Seeing the king angry did not bother him in the least. Over the years he grew to despise the man, but that was not uncommon. Many people dislike their employer, this was no different. Fionn and his men had been in Herod's service since the Roman Emperor gifted them to him as some sort of thank you. Fionn was disgusted by the idea that men could be given as gifts. They were not technically slaves, but it felt that way to him. This was the life of a mercenary who was very far from home.

"Where is Tobias?" Herod asked.

"Unknown, sir. He and Gundahar went after the Wise Men."

"After letting them escape! Fucking incompetence! I won't tolerate incompetence." Herod was pacing. His head was splitting from pain and he had spittle on his beard. It was a stately look, to be sure. "For their sake, they better return with the Wise Men. My patience is gone."

Fionn stood silently. He learned from years of experience that unless asked a question, it was better to stay quiet. He watched the king pace, mumbling to himself about horrible things he wanted to do to Tobias and Gundahar. On the surface, it seemed like it would be entertaining to watch, but in reality, it was not. It was boring. Fionn was over it. He had watched this scene play out far too many times before. The man was a diva. Fionn let Herod pace and spew his vitriol to the four walls of the chamber, knowing eventually the man would regain his composure and start dealing with things rationally. Well, as rationally as a madman can. Herod seemed to be slipping, his mind was not what it was, and his decision-making had been erratic of late.

Herod settled at his table and went silent, shuffling through the census summaries that had been prepared for him. The raw data was compiled by a committee who boiled down the key facts and presented them to the king in neat little tables accompanied by written paragraphs of totals, assumptions, and breakdowns of class, occupations, sex, and age groups. They also included a separate set of summaries listing the number of pregnant women in each region along with their ages, locations, anticipated due dates, and the names and supervisors of those assigned to keep track of them.

"Tell me again of the events in Nazareth," Herod said, slightly more in control of his emotions.

Fionn recanted the events in Nazareth as they were reported to him by the soldiers who were present. This was the third time the king had asked to hear it. He started with the mundane events of the morning, the killing of the captured citizen at the census station, and ended with the events leading to the capture of three prisoners and the escape of the Wise Men.

"To be clear, our soldiers went to question a woman and were attacked by three civilians?" Herod asked.

"Yes sir."

"These three civilians were captured by Gundahar?"

"Yes, sir."

"Tobias thought them of a certain value and asked that they be sent to Jerusalem?"

"Yes, sir."

186

"And somehow they never made it to Jerusalem? Our guards were overpowered by unknown assailants, and these prisoners escaped?"

"Yes, sir. The guards were severely beaten and had several broken bones, but all survived the attack. The details of their assailants are unclear. There is some discrepancy between each guard's recollection of the events. We're trying to get a clear picture of how things played out."

Herod stared blankly at his desk as he considered what the general of his Celtic Guard had said. He was having trouble making sense of it. The events of the day happened quickly enough that no one should have been aware that the prisoners were being taken to Jerusalem. Yet someone had intercepted them on the way. The reports said they were riding aggressively; it would have been impossible to overtake them from Nazareth once they learned of the intent to take the prisoners to Jerusalem. The guards would have had too long a lead. So, the assailants could not have been from Nazareth. But if not there, from where? Was it merely highwaymen attacking Herod's men randomly? That had never occurred anywhere else, and it seemed too perfect to be a coincidence. Herod needed more time to work through the possible angles. None of it was adding up.

"Keep the guards separated until you find out their stories. I don't want them collaborating. Let me know what you learn once they give their stories under duress. I may wish to ask them myself. You should mention that to them before they give their final answers. Consider it my attempt at aiding the investigation," Herod said.

"Yes, sir." Fionn nodded, then left the king alone in his chamber.

29

HIRAM AND THE ELDER

Hiram came to the temple in Jerusalem to learn, and perhaps because he had nowhere else to be. He was a portly young man with thinning hair and an impressive lack of muscle tone. Try as he might, he could not grow facial hair even if his life depended on it. His skin was uncharacteristically fair for being born in this part of the world. His appearance, his lack of self-esteem, his inability to hunt, and his abusive father, all led to his arrival at the temple. His childhood was miserable on many levels. He was teased and bullied by the neighboring children. He was always an outcast. He was beaten by his father for not being better. It made no difference what the subject matter was, he should have been better. The little girls laughed at him, and the young women they became did the same. It would be enough to crush the spirit and will of a normal kid, but Hiram would not be crushed.

Hiram knew he had a greater purpose. He wasn't sure exactly what it was, but he was sure of it, nonetheless. He was far brighter than any of the people he encountered in his youth. It took years of being away from that environment to recognize it as fact. At the time, he had no base of comparison. The people who struck blows or laughed or called names must know more, he thought, because they had so much power over him. He learned in his years away from that environment that power does not equal intelligence (Let's all reflect on that for a moment and try not to equate that sentence with anyone in the United States government... power does not equal intelligence... damn, I couldn't do it either).

Most people would be bitter or vengeful coming from that environment. Hiram didn't have time for that. He had to find his purpose. He crept away from home one night and never returned. He made his way to Jerusalem. When he saw the temple, all the tumblers of the lock in his mind fell into place. *That* was where he needed to be.

Hiram had ascended the stairs and approached the great gate of the temple tentatively. No one questioned or gave him a second look. He adjusted the bag hanging on his shoulder that contained his few meager possessions. As he approached the gate, he realized he did not know the rules. He did not know if he was allowed to be there. He scanned the random people walking about. They all seemed to have some purpose. They seemed to have a destination, somewhere they needed to be (I just mansplained destination... sorry, not sorry).

He stood to the side of the stairs and continued to watch as people entered and exited the great gate. He observed for several minutes. No one was harassed or questioned; they came and went freely. Hiram summoned his courage and continued to the gate. He walked through still tentative. He expected to be scolded, or worse, but nothing happened. No one so much as looked at him.

Inside the gate were arched covered hallways that seemed to run the entire perimeter of the temple complex. The arches were carved from wood, supported by marble columns and decorated with gold inlays. It was more opulence than Hiram had ever seen with his own eyes.

He passed beyond the cloisters and stepped out into the courtyard. He paused to take in what was before him. It was a sight unlike anything he had ever seen. The outer court was a vast expanse of stone pavers that formed a mosaic if seen from above. From Hiram's perspective, it was a sea of multi-colored stepping-stones. There were hundreds of people, some moving about while others chatted in small groups. Many of the people were dressed in odd clothing with bright colors. He assumed they were from foreign lands.

Across the courtyard he could see more steps leading to an elevated landing about fifteen feet above where he stood. It appeared to be steps to an inner courtyard. As Hiram walked toward the steps, he noticed signs along the wall on both sides of them, but they were too far away to read. He veered from the stairs and walked toward one of the signs instead.

The sign was written in both Greek and Latin. Hiram could read both, just not very well. As best he could tell, it read "No foreigner may pass within the lattice and wall around the sanctuary. Whoever is caught, the guilt for the death which will follow will be his own." Hiram read the sign several times to make sure he understood its meaning, which seemed very clear. If you entered into the inner courtyard and are not Jewish, you were going to die. *Wow, this is entirely surreal.*

He scanned the outer court once more, this time looking a little closer at the people who milled about or congregated to chat. Some were extremely tall with the darkest skin he had ever seen. They were wearing long gowns of red, yellow, white, and black. Others were smaller with long mustaches and no beards. They wore pointed hats and had wide, colorful sleeves. Still others wore local garb that Hiram recognized. And there were Romans. There were always Romans. Hiram struggled to believe that if a Roman entered the inner court, he would be killed. *Could they really do that? That would be amazing if it were true.*

Hiram turned and walked to the stairs to the inner courtyard. He began to climb, but doubt crept into his mind with every step. *What if they don't believe I'm Jewish? How do you convince someone you are? Is this a test of faith? Will they kill me as soon as I get to the top?* Hiram was concerned and confused. He knew in his heart that this was where he needed to be, that this was his place. He knew the temple was his destiny. But the sign was more than disconcerting. It was turning his legs to stone.

As he neared the top, he paused to move his bag to the other shoulder, and to catch his breath. And, if we are being honest, to stall. He slowly ascended the final few steps but stopped one step below the top. There were two guards in brown tunics on either side of the stairway. Each had a brown leather belt with a scabbard and short sword. Each held a long spear that had a shiny metal tip at least two feet long. Their backs were to the stairs as they stood silently facing the inner court. Beyond them, in the sunlight of the inner court, people milled about much as they did below.

One of the guards must have heard Hiram on the stairs. He turned and said, "Hark, someone approaches."

The other guard turned to the first. "Did you just say 'Hark'?"

The first guard faced his partner. "Yes, I did."

"No one says 'Hark'. Why would you say that? No one uses that word."

"I do."

"Well, don't."

"Why not?"

"Because no one uses that word."

"I do. It conveys exactly what I want to convey."

"Well, don't, it's stupid."

"No, it's not."

"Yes, it is. It's stupid and pretentious."

"You're stupid and pretentious."

"Are you a child?"

"Hark, I hear a stupid question."

"Oh, fuck off." The second guard turned back to face the inner court.

The first guard smiled, gloating over his victory. He, like the first guard, turned back to face the inner court, forgetting Hiram altogether.

Hiram watched the two guards cautiously, but soon realized they had lost all interest in him. They continued to stare into the inner court. Hiram scanned the people as he had below. There was none with the brightly colored clothing he saw earlier. He also noticed there were no Romans on this level. Perhaps the signs warning away foreigners were not a bluff. Perhaps they actually could kill Romans who dared enter the limits of the sanctuary. Hiram smiled. He continued scanning the people milling about, nearly forgetting why he was there in the first place.

An old man was making his way toward the gate, walking along the perimeter of the inner court. The man wore long plain robes and walked slowly, deliberately. His feet shuffled more than stepped as he made his way. Perhaps this was as fast as the old guy could manage. As he came closer to the gate, Hiram could see he was quite old indeed. He might be the oldest living person Hiram had ever seen. The man finally made it to the gate but appeared to have no intention of passing through it. He was simply walking past on his trek around the perimeter of the courtyard. The old man regarded Hiram as he passed, his eyes bright and inquisitive. He paused at the opening and smiled at Hiram.

"Hello, young man," the old man said.

Hiram was somewhat stunned at the sound of the man's voice. It wasn't the tone or timber. It was the fact that Hiram was so lost in his own thoughts, the greeting startled him. The old man smiled a little wider at Hiram's bewildered look.

"Hello, sir. It's a glorious day, don't you think?" Hiram replied, trying to maintain his proper manners.

The guards glanced back at him. One of them turned 90 degrees until he was facing the guard on the opposite side of the stairs. He continued to gaze at Hiram as the other returned to staring vacantly into the courtyard.

"Yes," the old man said. "God has given us a wonderful day."

Hiram smiled, but did not know what else to say. The old man's eyes were fixed upon him. Hiram pretended to adjust his bag, stalling until the old man moved on about his business, but the old man kept staring at him. Hiram stole a few more glances, seeing the man rooted to his spot out of the corner of his eye. The awkwardness had Hiram consider going back down to the outer courtyard.

The old man continued to watch Hiram. He brought his bony, gnarled hand to his chin and tilted his head slightly. "May I ask, young man, why do you stand glued to the top step to stare at an old man?"

Hiram froze with his eyes wide. This was uncomfortable indeed. The one person he least expected to question him was, in fact, questioning him. His face flushed a little and he stammered for his words.

"I... am resting. I..."

Hiram paused for a moment. The old man's eyes were sharp and kind. Hiram looked down at his feet as he tried to determine what to say next. He decided to tell the truth.

He looked directly into the man's kind eyes. "The truth is, good sir, that this is my first visit to the new temple and the signs below concerned me. I'm not from Jerusalem but I am from Judaea. I was concerned that no one would know where I was from and might assume me a foreigner. I was trying to determine if these two fine young men were going to kill me if I try to enter."

The old man smiled. "Tell me, why do you wish to enter?"

Hiram blushed. The reaction confused him. Why should he feel ashamed? He had done nothing wrong. He hadn't hurt anyone or broken any rules, yet the feeling of shame persisted. Would the old man chastise him for leaving his family? He didn't seem the type but what else could it be?

"I left my home. It was a horrible place with horrible people. I had to escape, so I came to Jerusalem. When I saw the Temple, I knew this is where I belong. I wish to study here, to learn, to be a part of it."

The old man continued to smile. His head tilted slightly as he considered the young man before him. "Come walk with me, young man. I would like to get to know you better. The Temple could use a little enthusiasm."

Hiram's heart lifted. He eyed the two guards cautiously as he stepped forward. The one facing the stair said, "You're good, no worries."

As Hiram started to pass him, the guard lunged at him and yelled "Raa!"

Hiram jumped, twisted in mid-air, and landed on his backside. His heart was racing, and his eyes were wide.

"Sorry," the guard laughed, "I was just messing with you. This job is so boring."

Both guards were laughing until they saw the old man scowling at them.

"Sorry sir," they said bowing.

"It was just a bit of fun."

"Perhaps I should mention this to your Captain? This sort of thing cannot be allowed to happen to new visitors. No indeed. This sort of thing must be punished," the old man said.

"Please, sir, it won't happen again."

Both guards looked around, their eyes darting back and forth to see who may have witnessed the transgression.

The old man winked at Hiram, then the corner of his mouth twitched as he faced the guards. "I was just messing with you."

The old man laughed out loud. The guards shared a nervous glance, slowly relaxing as the old man continued to laugh, relieved that he actually was messing with them.

Hiram watched the exchange with all its tension. He laughed as well when the old man delivered the punch line. He regained his feet and walked past the guards into the courtyard toward the old man.

"Thank you for welcoming me. Seriously, it's been far too long since I spoke to a friendly face. My name is Hiram. I'm at your service."

The old man grinned. "It is my absolute pleasure to meet you, Hiram. Please walk with me. I try to walk around the courtyard every day, weather permitting. It helps keep me young." He glanced back at the guards and chuckled softly.

Hiram joined the old man in the sunlight and the two began to stroll around the perimeter of the courtyard. They continued in silence for several minutes. The silence lasted long enough to become a little awkward. Hiram's stomach growled. The old man's head tilted slightly, but he did not change his gaze. His eyes remained on the pavers ahead of him.

Hiram realized it had been the better part of a day since he had eaten any food. Focusing on that would make him miserable, so he resolved to pay attention to the old man instead. Being this close removed all doubt. This was absolutely the oldest human being Hiram had ever laid eyes upon. It was amazing he could walk this far. It was amazing he could walk at all. The man must be in his nineties.

"Forgive my manners, Hiram. I did not properly introduce myself," the old man spoke as they continued along their path. "People call me the Elder, Hillel the Elder. They have been calling me that for many years now. It's not out of disrespect, just a statement of fact. As you can see, I'm old. I'm 105, to be exact. Most people don't see as many years. God has blessed me with long life. It could be because I have dedicated most of it to serving Him. But then, others have served with equal vigor and have not lasted as many summers. I try not to dwell too long on why He might want me to continue in His service. God is full of mystery, to be sure.

"I came to the old temple when I was a young man. I was 40 and to me that's young. I was a woodworker who wanted something more. I wanted to study the Torah and learn. I wanted to, how did you put it? To be part of it. In those days, there was a fee charged to students if they were to be admitted to study. I couldn't always afford the fee, so sometimes I would climb to the top of the building and listen in from the roof." The old man's eyes sparkled as he spoke. "Eventually they tired of chasing me off, and they let me attend whether I could pay the fee or not. Soon after I convinced them to drop the fee for everyone."

Hillel and Hiram continued speaking as they made their way around the perimeter of the courtyard. Hillel was curious to find out about Hiram. He wanted to learn about his childhood, his parents, his family, and even his town. Hiram told the man everything without a shred of trepidation.

Hiram was drawn to the sage and thoughtful man. His was an intense intelligence wrapped in a kind and sympathetic demeanor.

Hillel was impressed at the young man's openness and honesty. He could see that Hiram was smart and curious, two of the traits Hillel valued most. He was also measured, fair, and clear in his responses.

"My grandmother was the last person I can remember who was kind to me. She died several years ago. She was so wise and taught me much. My decision to leave was easier with her absence," Hiram said.

"What did she teach you?" Hillel asked.

"I told her once that I wanted to study the Torah, really study it, not just go to synagogue. She said 'What is hateful to you, do not do to your fellow. This is the whole Torah. The rest is explanation. Go and learn.'" Hiram smiled.

Hillel raised his eyebrows. "She said that? Did she hear that from someone else? Had she ever been to Jerusalem?"

"Yes, she said it often. I'm not certain if she had ever been here before. Not that I'm aware of, anyway. She was just clever and had a way with words," Hiram answered.

Hillel chuckled to himself. "I agree, she did have a way with words, a woman after my own heart. It's as if I said it myself. What other sayings did she have?"

Hiram considered the question. "There were many. *'Do not judge your fellow until you are in his place'*, *'A name gained is a name lost'*, *'Where there are no men, strive to be a man'*, and others as well.

Hillel stopped walking. He chuckled to himself and shook his head. "She seems very wise indeed. I'm impressed with her wisdom. I'm not sure I could say any of that better myself."

Hiram smiled but did not reply. He was not entirely sure why the Elder considered it to be funny.

"Would you care to join me for lunch?" Hillel asked. "I would enjoy speaking with you more. I'd also like to ask you to work with me. I could use an assistant, and I can think of none better than you, my new friend. I can give you a place to stay and food to eat. You won't make much money, however."

Hiram agreed immediately. He could not have been more pleased.

30

A SIMPLE MISTAKE

Two years had passed since the sunny day Hiram met Hillel the Elder for the first time. He was now a man in full. He was studying under Hillel, the greatest and smartest president the Sanhedrin had ever known. He was grateful he hadn't known who the Elder was when they originally met. It would likely have been a train wreck of stammering and babbling. He had not known then that the Sanhedrin was the supreme religious body of the entire land of Israel. Now he got to be a fly on the wall in the Hall of Hewn Stones where Hillel and his friend and most challenging intellectual rival, Shammai, would debate the laws and customs of the day.

The Sanhedrin met daily in the Hall, unless it was a festival or the sabbath. The group was made up of sixty-nine general members sitting in a semi-circle, with the two leaders, Hillel and Shammai, facing them. The Sanhedrin's responsibilities were more than just religious, as they were also tasked with political and legal aspects of Israel as well. Their meetings could be as quick as an hour or as long as twelve hours, depending on the topics of the day. The daily meetings would range from addressing prominent families, declaring public fasting days, appointing judges to Jewish courts throughout the land, and even regulating the calendar. In fact, their power was so great, they were the only body in the land that could bring legal proceedings against the king himself if they chose. A fact that annoyed Herod greatly, and the Sanhedrin knew it.

Hillel had appointed Hiram as one of the official scribes of the Sanhedrin, which required him to attend every meeting. In the off hours, the Elder tasked him with research projects and transcribing ancient scrolls. It was everything Hiram could have hoped for. He was needed and respected, and quickly became one of Hillel's greatest assets. Hiram was becoming a walking encyclopedia of Sanhedrin history and knowledge. He rarely forgot a date or a detail.

He enjoyed the research, pouring over scrolls, making notes, finding tidbits of knowledge that had been long forgotten. Hours passed like minutes, but it was more than the work, it was also the place. The libraries in new temple had a distinct odor. It was a damp and slightly musty smell, but it had hints of fragrance from the flowers brought in by the other students at the request of the Rabbis to brighten up the rooms and hallways. It was like being on the edge of a bog, without the annoyance of insects and other things that bite.

The lighting was poor, coming from candles or oil lamps. There were reading rooms available along the perimeter with windows that let in natural light. Hiram wasn't interested in natural light. He preferred the low light from the lamps and candles.

The dim light and distinct odor felt like home to him. No, that is not quite right. He hated home but loved it here. Home made him think of pain and shame. Here he felt alive and useful. Here they requested his assistance and valued his input. Here he contributed on an equal level with everyone else. So, scratch the 'felt like home' bit. This felt more like *belonging*, a feeling he never had at "home". It was a feeling he had longed for all his life.

Hiram often wondered how long they would refer to it as the new temple. It had been in use for many years now, but everyone still referred to it as new. *I suppose it makes sense since it replaced the original which had been here for hundreds of years.* Still the thought intrigued him. He imagined they might always call it the new temple. The former temple had a long and important history, and many had not trusted Herod would rebuild it. The people threatened to rebel should he not rebuild it as he had promised. The thought gave Hiram a grim smile. It was valiant for them to claim they would have fought; however, they would have all died in the process. Herod's army was nearly as cruel as Herod himself. Nearly.

In hindsight, it was a pointless threat. Herod tried to use building the new temple to ingratiate himself to the people. He was determined to make it more splendid and impressive than any of the skeptical Jews had expected. He succeeded in that. Ingratiating himself? Well, not so much.

Hiram had spent the last few days pouring through some of the oldest scrolls in Jerusalem. One turned to dust in his hands as he tried to unroll it. He hoped that it was one of the scrolls that went over mundane procedures of the Sanhedrin and not some fabulous insight from one of the great minds that once ran the organization. Hillel told him that age had consequence and years of neglect had a price. It was nice for Hiram to hear that sometimes mistakes happen, and no one was at fault. His childhood had been filled with just the opposite.

There were multiple theories in the new temple about the timing involved in the prophesies of a coming messiah. One was that the earth would last a total of six thousand years and that a messiah was going to rule for the final one thousand. This would put the messiah's arrival at just about any day now, according to the Jewish calendar. Another theory stated that there would be seventy generations from Enoch until the day of judgement. The common understanding of the day stated there would be seventy weeks of years, meaning seventy (the weeks of years) times seven (days, or in this case years in a week of years) equaling four hundred ninety years (in weeks of years). All of the theories had different timing references and none of the timing made sense to Hiram. He had a problem with the math. It seemed off to him somehow. So he poured through the old scrolls and redid the calculations. The idea that the scribes and historians from yesteryear could have made a mistake didn't cross his mind. He was face to face with an error of some kind, but he assumed it must be his error. His progress slowed to a crawl. Hiram reread all the data, recalculated, and rethought all of the results presented in the ancient literature. He came up with a definite conclusion: the historical information was wrong, or, at the very least, was misleading.

Still, Hiram was convinced the error must be his, so he redid the math yet another time but came to the same conclusion. In his heart, Hiram knew he was correct, the numbers were the numbers. He decided this was important enough to alert the president of the Sanhedrin.

Hiram walked down the long hallway to speak to the Elder. It was late afternoon. The Sanhedrin had adjourned earlier so he knew Hillel would be in his study working. He had never appeared before Hillel to contest historic proclamations from the ancient scrolls. He wondered if Hillel would laugh and point out the obvious error in Hiram's logic. Hiram was nearly afraid to knock on the door. He gathered his courage and knocked anyway, thinking it had been a fabulous couple of years. He had wonderful memories to reminisce on should this betrayal of the past cause him to lose his position.

"Hiram, my boy, what can I do for you this glorious afternoon?"

Hillel, it seemed to Hiram, never had a bad day. Ever. No matter the consequences of the day or the level of evil involved, Hillel never seemed to be negatively affected by the results. He appeared to be immune to whatever nastiness happened in the world. He always managed to find the bright side.

"Well, sir, you see... um... I found something that doesn't make sense." Hiram shifted nervously. "While digging through some of the older scrolls, I may have found a mistake. I'm probably reading it wrong, but it seems incorrect to me. I thought I should discuss it with you. It may be nothing at all. Or maybe I'm reading it wrong," Hiram said with definitely-maybe-oh-it's-probably-nothing conviction.

Hillel smiled. "Hiram, it may shock you to learn this, but mistakes happen, even in the scrolls. It's not the first time something was discovered that required correction. Just because the wisdom comes from hundreds of years ago doesn't automatically make it correct. The idea could have been flawed from the start, or it may have been transcribed incorrectly. There are any number of reasons things could be incorrect.

"Once we found a series of scrolls that were absolute gibberish, filled with unrelated sentences, wild conjecture, and bold prophesies. It was a mystery for many years. Then one of our historians found reference to a scribe that was removed from service. It seems he was caught on multiple occasions nearly incapacitated from drinking wine while working. They were certain they found and removed all of his compromised projects, but apparently a few slipped through. We had a good laugh over that.

"So, sit here and show me what you've found. You've piqued my curiosity." Hillel gestured to the chair next to him. Hiram pulled the chair back and sat, spilling his armload of scrolls and notes all over the table.

"I was reading through *The Book of the Watchers* about Enoch and his visions of heaven. I also looked at the *Book of Similitudes*. It got me thinking about the current rumors of a coming messiah, the one that the shepherds are spreading. As you know, there are countless prophesies of a messiah written throughout our literature. The most referenced and defendable prophecy refers to one coming in the seventy-seventh generation since Adam. That's when I decided to review the generational lineage.

"I may be splitting hairs here, but as I was reviewing this, it occurred to me that we, collectively, have been referencing the wrong generation number. It's probably a matter of semantics, but we currently refer to Enoch as being from the sixth generation. More specifically, that means he is the sixth generation since Adam." Hiram looked hopefully at Hillel.

"And...?" Hillel said, prodding the young man to make his point. The old man was not following him yet.

"Ok, let me see... We know Enoch was the sixth generation since Adam, Abraham was the twentieth generation since Adam, David was the thirty-fourth since Adam. What generation are we in now?"

"We are in the seventy-seventh generation," Hillel answered, still unsure where Hiram was going with his line of logic.

"Exactly!" Hiram stood. "We are in the seventy-seventh generation counting Adam's generation, but it is the seventy-sixth generation *since* Adam. Adam was the first generation. This new prophecy is still valid. The Sanhedrin was too quick to brush it aside. We are in the seventy-sixth generation *since* Adam, and if a messiah is born today, it would be the seventy-seventh generation since Adam, as predicted."

Hillel folded his hands before his face and rested his chin on them. He considered the implications of what his assistant was saying. The Sanhedrin, and all of the other bodies through the years that have been tasked with recording history, have been very good at assigning specific events to historical prophecies *after* they have taken place. *We never seem to make a compelling argument for a prophecy before the fact.* But then, many prophecies do not manifest as predicted. *It would be foolish for the Sanhedrin to try to predict which prophecies may come true and which may not. We're not fortune tellers.*

This current one was different on many levels. Rational people were claiming to be visited by the heavenly host. They claimed God was going to have a human son. One passage along these lines read; "Messiah would be born of a woman." It also mentioned something about being born of a virgin. *Did the shepherds mention that too?* Hillel could not remember.

Hiram was right, Hillel had dismissed this prophecy a little too quickly. This was significant in that it predicted the messiah would be heir to King David's throne. The very throne Herod occupied now. *How would the king feel if the Sanhedrin gave this any credence?* The thought made Hillel smile. His position required that he be cordial with the king, but personally he wanted nothing to do with the man. Herod was a murderous pig with an enormous ego.

"You aren't wrong, young Hiram. The Sanhedrin was too quick to dismiss this prophecy. You're also correct that we misuse our generational terms, and it causes confusion. We'll address that in the Hall of Hewn Stones.

"You understand that we, the Sanhedrin, can't make any claims for or against this prophecy. We can, however, make it clear to all that the timing for it fits with our understanding of the generations. If this is to happen, it'll be soon." Hillel smiled. "What do you think Herod will do when we tell him?"

Hiram's eyes got wide, and he laughed out loud.

31

SIMON (REMEMBER SIMON?)

Do you remember the shepherd kid from the beginning of the book? Well, he told his story exactly as the angel had instructed him. He told everyone who would listen. The story never changed, he always told it the same, just as it happened. Okay, if we are being honest, he did leave out the part about him wetting himself a little, but can you blame him? It was embarrassing enough trying to convince people that an angel of the Lord had spoken to him. The smaller details could be left out. He didn't see the harm and didn't think the angel would mind.

The problem he ran into was that, although most people believed him, some just did not. He never tried to convince them, that wasn't part of his task. He was tasked with spreading the news. It was up to them to believe or not. Since most of them did, he just shrugged off the rest. And through it all he kept that smile on his face.

It was a little harder to maintain that smile when the Jacob twins kept following him around all day. The twins were a pair of not-so-bright hooligans from his village near Marisa. They were a couple years younger than Simon, but the young men stood and inch or two taller. Their lack of intelligence was only outdone by their immature cruelty and bullying. They were, at the very least, smart enough to reel in their nastiness around adults. So, complaints to parents usually went unanswered.

Simon sat on top of a hill watching his sheep. The Jacob twins stood about ten yards away, staring malevolently at the young shepherd.

"You're a liar, Simon."

"Yeah, you lie to everyone. Do you expect people to believe you literally spoke to an angel? And that God is going to have a baby? That's so stupid, why would God need a baby? You really expect people to believe that garbage?"

"Just the people smarter than you two," Simon said without looking at them.

"Screw you. You must be starved for attention. Making up stories so people will pay attention to you. It's pathetic. You're a loser, Simon. A fucking lying loser."

"Yeah, you should be punished for lying so much. If your father wasn't so stupid to believe you, he would be beating you for even suggesting it."

Simon ignored the jibes and scanned his flock. He could sense the ugliness growing with these two. The fact that they were on the edge of violence made him uneasy. However, he had picked up a rock nearly the size of his palm when he sat. If he landed a couple punches with this in his hand, the fight would end quickly.

"Which one of those sheep is your girlfriend?"

The other Jacob laughed out loud. "Shoot, I bet even they ignore your sorry ass."

"You've got to have something better to do today, don't you?" Simon asked. "Surely there are some little old ladies that need to be pushed or dogs that need to be kicked?"

"We'll do what we want when we want, freak. If we want to stand here watching you make up more lies, we will. Where are your little angel friends? Are you going to call them to make us go away? Do you need them to protect you?"

Simon rolled his eyes. "Sometimes it's a shame that humans don't eat their young."

"What's that supposed to mean, liar?"

"It means you two are morons."

Simon stood. He had always been taught to turn the other cheek. He did not believe this encounter would end that way though. These two would not be happy until he was bleeding. He was fairly certain he could take either one individually, but both at once would be too much for him. They may have been younger, but they were also bigger, and there were two of them. He was glad he had picked up the rock. It might help even the score if it got to that point. On the other hand, they might take it from him and use it as he was going to. You could never be quite sure how these things were going to play out.

The Jacob twins tensed when Simon stood. They eyed him suspiciously.

"Calm down, little rabbits, I'm just standing to stretch my legs," Simon said dismissively. He noticed that all his sheep were lying down.

"We don't like you."

"No shit? I thought we were best buds. Now I'm sad." Simon rolled his eyes.

"You'll never be our friend, freak."

Out of nowhere, a trumpet sounded, followed by several more. Then harps and a chorus. The sound was so abrupt and loud, the twins fell over backwards in fright. "What the fuck!" they yelled.

"That's my line," Simon said, and then smiled. He saw a light growing brighter just above the hill to his left.

Terrified, the twins began crawling backwards like a couple crabs. Simon shook his head. *I almost feel bad for you two. I would too, if you weren't such shit heads.*

The floating glow began to take the shape of a man. The twins started crying. They had never been so frightened. This was the point where

Simon tried to run away when it happened to him the first time. The twins had already given up. One was in the fetal position, and the other soiled himself a little from the smell of it. Both were crying hysterically.

The glowing light took the form of the angel Simon had met previously. The angel nodded to Simon.

"Simon."

"Roman," Simon replied smiling.

The angel laughed and pointed at him. "That's funny. Well played."

The angel looked at the Jacob twins. "These two bothering you?"

"Yes, they are."

"Stop crying, little shit heads," the angel said, winking to Simon as he did so. He walked over to the boys and crouched down. "Whoa, little man. Did you just poo yourself? Simon, this one just pushed out a nugget."

Simon laughed.

The angel stood up, hands on his hips like a disapproving parent. "Stand up, boys, and stop crying. I'm not going to hurt you. At least not yet."

The twins stood, wiping the tears from their eyes. They looked at the angel, then to Simon, then back to the angel. They were still too frightened to speak.

"Boys, were you harassing my friend, Simon?" the angel asked.

The twins slowly nodded.

"You were teasing him because you didn't believe that an angel of the Lord, specifically *me*, came to speak to Simon?"

The twins nodded again.

"Do you believe him now?"

The twins nodded.

"Excellent, then I won't have to hurt you after all. Truth is, I never was going to. I was going to let Simon do it. Trust me, it's better this way. Simon is way tougher than he looks. You boys would have had your asses handed to you." The angel winked at Simon again. Simon appreciated the instant street cred he just received, even though they both knew it wasn't true.

"Boys, I believe you owe my friend an apology. Then you need to go home and tell everyone that Simon has been telling the truth the whole time, and that you met me too."

The twins nodded. "We're sorry, Simon. We should have believed you." They spoke in unison.

"It's like they share a brain... creepy," Simon said quietly to the angel.

"Fine, we're done here. You two can go. Do as I ask. Don't make me come find you." The angel made a shooing gesture with his hands.

The twins looked at each other and then back at the angel. "Yes, sir. Thank you, sir." And then they ran off.

"Thanks for helping me with those two. I think it was going to get ugly," Simon said.

"It looks like it might have, but I didn't come to help you with them, the timing was just a coincidence. I came because we need to ask another favor. God likes you, so He wants it to be you."

Simon's shoulders slumped a little. "You were going to let that play out?"

"Hey, nothing happened, it all worked out. And now you have a couple unlikely supporters as you talk to people." The angel smiled a full-on used-car-salesman smile. "The main reason I am here, as I said, is to ask for your assistance. This is big. God is sending the mother of His baby this way, along with her husband and some friends."

"Her... husband? She's not married to God?" Simon's forehead scrunched into a knot. Remember, he was only 15. But now that I think about it, it *is* a little confusing.

"Wow, er... yeah... it's kind of complicated. God is God. He can't marry a human. But He needs a human to have a human baby. It's funny,

I've never thought of this in your terms before. I guess it is a little odd. But believe me, it is odd for us as well. God has never done anything like this before.

"As I was saying, Mary, Joseph, and their friends are all headed this way, but they aren't together. You need to make sure they find each other. Then, God would like for you to escort them to Bethlehem. You asked me last time if you were going to get to meet God's son. It turns out you are. Congrats, little man, you must indeed be special to the Boss. This is a great honor."

Simon could not contain his joy. He jumped and danced and laughed out loud. He held his arms up like Rocky at the top of the stairs. The angel let him have his moment. He liked Simon. The truth is, all the angels did. He was a quality kid.

"People come through Marisa all the time. How am I to know which ones I'm supposed to unite?" Simon asked.

"I'm not exactly sure, Simon, but I have a good feeling you'll figure it out. You and I will see each other one more time, but we won't get to speak. So, let me thank you now. We appreciate all the help you've given us and all the help you are yet to give. Take care of yourself, young man. Enjoy every minute." The angel smiled and shook Simon's hand.

Simon's eyes teared up, this time not in fear, only gratitude and happiness.

32

DESPAIR

Nazareth was six weeks behind them as the small group moved down the coast. The country they traveled was mostly hills and rocks and grazing pasture. They avoided cities and towns, moving through open fields and deserted trails. When they found a good location, they would camp there for several days. The logic was to let those hunting them get ahead of their position, leaving no trail to follow. Their pursuers would need to stop in the population centers to ask for sightings of their group. They would find none. When the group needed additional provisions, one or two of the crew would take horses to a town to get them. Two men buying supplies would raise no suspicion at all. They were effectively moving down the coast without drawing attention from anyone.

Mary could tell Gaspar was worried about her. He would watch her with a concerned expression and speak to her gently. Mary had mostly stopped speaking and was barely eating. The few times she joined the group, her cheeks were usually stained with tears. Mostly she stayed by herself lost in her own thoughts. She missed Joseph terribly. She had no idea if he was safe, or even alive for that matter. The uncertainty was tearing her apart inside. She knew she had to eat for the baby's sake, but she struggled to get any food down. Nothing was good, nothing was satisfying, nothing appealed to her. She needed to be with her husband. She could think of nothing else.

It was dusk and the group was gathered around the fire making small talk. They had just finished a meal and were relaxing. The small caravan would be moving on in the morning. Most of the provisions and non-essentials were packed away, ready for an early departure. The rest would be collected and stowed in the morning. Mary was standing several yards away from the group. Ella was seated in a chair with her boy, Aaron, in her lap. He was struggling to stay awake.

Over the past few weeks, when Mary could bring herself to speak, it was usually with Ella. It was small talk at first, but when you are forced to spend a lot of time with people and there is nothing else to do, you find things to talk about. Both women opened up over time, revealing histories and fears, and even secrets.

When Mary asked if there was a reason the boy did not speak, Ella's eyes glassed over with tears. She wasn't prepared to talk about it then, but several days later, Ella told Mary the story. Aaron's father was confronted by three Roman soldiers on his way to meet his wife and son. She never got a straight answer when she asked after the fact, but there was an argument. They wanted information, and he had had no answers for them. Ella and Aaron saw them in a heated discussion. Aaron broke free of his mother's hand and ran to see his father, just as one of the soldiers tried to strike his father. Aaron's father grabbed the soldier's fist before it could land and pushed it to the side. It was purely a self-preservation move, but the soldiers took it to be aggressive. Two of them cut his father down in the street, letting him fall as the little boy approached. He was dead before the boy could touch his cheek.

Aaron begged his father to answer, to stand, to smile, to speak, but it was too late for that. Ella was screaming hysterically as she ran to her husband. One of the soldiers backhanded her in the face, knocking her to the ground. As Ella tried to regain her feet, she saw Aaron change. She saw pure rage grow in his eyes, some kind of madness.

The boy launched himself at the soldiers with no fear (not that five-year-old boys have any fear in the first place). He threw an overhead punch, connecting with one soldier's crotch, doubling him over. He then ran and jumped, stepping on the crotch soldier's back, hurling himself at another soldier and twisting his hands into the man's hair and pulling him to the ground. The third soldier kicked the boy in the head, leaving him unconscious in the dirt as he laughed at his friends for getting taken down by a toddler. Aaron hasn't spoken since. Ella wasn't sure if it was the shock of his father or the kick, but she was sure the boy remembered what happened. Even months later, the child's eyes would glow with rage any time he saw a soldier.

Mary was in tears upon hearing the story. It sounded outrageous, pointlessly cruel, and totally unnecessary. It was an absolute injustice, cold-blooded murder. And the poor boy witnessed it all. As had Ella. Mary could not imagine watching Joseph get murdered. She was sure she would be unable to function at all. She would just curl up into a ball and wish for death. Ella assured her she would uncurl from that ball and do whatever it took to keep her child safe.

Mary thought of that story as she watched Ella and Aaron in the chair. It had been a few weeks since she heard it, but it haunted her as much as the uncertainty of Joseph's situation. She was frustrated that God would allow any of this to happen. It was unfair. Cruel. Sadistic. And Mary was supposed to bring another uncaring God into the world? She was angry, afraid, and confused. She was losing her grip, losing her will to continue. This was all too much.

Mary started walking away from camp. Gaspar noticed, but it was common for Mary to need some alone time. He had asked her multiple times to stay close to camp, just in case. She had always agreed and never wandered too far. But this time was a little different. This time, she just kept walking, not really paying attention, just lost in her despair. She wasn't even sure how long she had been gone. Daylight was fading, but she did not care.

"You are angry with Me."

The voice startled Mary. She looked up to see God sitting on an out-cropping of rock, with Gabriel standing at his side.

"Is he your bodyguard?" she asked, nodding toward the angel.

"No. I introduced you to Gabe, you know he is My herald," God replied.

"Is he? He never says anything. It's getting kind of creepy."

God looked at Gabriel. "She's not wrong. How long do you plan to keep this up?"

Gabriel shrugged.

God looked back to Mary. "You are angry."

"Of course, I'm angry!" Tears streaked her face, and she trembled. "What have You done with my husband? Is he alive? Will I see him again? Why are You torturing me? Why should I help You when You are such a bastard? I can't believe You let Aaron watch his father die. What kind of sadistic shit is that? He's a little boy. Why would You do that? I thought I knew You. Who are You?"

"You would be surprised how often I get that question." God looked off into the distance. "Every time bad things happen, people rail at Me, curse Me, question Me, demean Me. But I understand it. From your point of view, it looks cruel and uncaring.

"How many people do you think are in the world this very moment?"

"Excuse me?" Mary replied, confused.

"How many people do you think are alive on the planet at this moment?"

"I don't know, I have no idea."

"It's around 300 million, give or take. Please child, come here and take My hand. I would like to show you something."

Mary hesitated but went to Him. He was God after all. She reached out her hand and He took it.

"Close your eyes. I am going to show you something."

She closed her eyes reluctantly.

"Very good. I need to suspend time as you know it for a few seconds. Now..."

In a flash she was looking at hundreds of thousands of eyes. They flashed by impossibly fast and yet it seemed she saw each pair individually. Eyes in every shape, color, and size raced by her own eyes. Old eyes, young eyes, every age in between. Kind eyes, evil eyes, crying eyes, laughing eyes, tortured eyes. It was nearly too much for her to handle. It was over as quickly as it started. She felt dizzy and a little nauseous.

"You have just looked into the eyes of every person alive today. My point in showing you this is to try to explain My magnitude in terms you will understand. You saw all the eyes alive in the world today. I see all the eyes that have ever lived before them and all that will ever come after them. I see them all the time at the same time. I know everything about every one of them. I know their names, families, hopes, and dreams. I know the things that happen today that will shape the way things will happen thousands of years from now.

"I ask that you consider this. Perhaps, with the things I know... perhaps, there might be a reason for things to happen the way they do. Perhaps good things need to come of bad things. Perhaps bad things need to come from good things. Perhaps some things mean nothing at all, while others mean everything. I ask that you have a little faith in Me."

Mary felt very small. Her eyes were damp and fixated on her feet. Her voice was barely audible. "Please forgive me. I have been insolent and disrespectful. I have obviously forgotten that I am in Your presence. I should not question or doubt You. And I speak to You far too cavalierly."

"You, I'll allow it from. You make Me smile. I like to smile. And you've had a rough go of things these last several weeks." God ran His fingers through her hair and winked at her.

"You may not be aware, but external stimulus actually transfers directly to a woman's baby. The music you hear, the food you eat, the kindness you display, the cruelty you witness, all get transferred to the unborn baby in various ways. Showing you the eyes of the world was not solely for your benefit. It's not uncommon for Me to accomplish multiple things with a single act.

"I would like to show both of you something else. I need for the child to experience this. For you, consider it an apology from Me, because you are about to see something no other living human has ever seen. I'm going to give you a very brief glimpse of heaven."

Mary froze. Heaven? Actually *see* heaven? Her mind could not comprehend what God had just said. She was suddenly frightened. "Are You sure that's a good idea? I am... I..."

"Yes, I'm sure. Nearly every second of every day, I am sure. About everything." God grinned. "I only added the 'nearly' because there may come a day sometime when I am not quite sure, but I sincerely doubt it. It hasn't happened yet, but never say never, eh?" God smiled and winked at her while holding out his hand. "Please take My hand again. You need not be afraid; you're going to like this."

Mary took it without hesitation.

You may have heard the expression 'it's like trying to describe color to a blind man.' That seems like a simple task compared with describing Marys' experience, but let's give it a shot anyway. Mary was instantly enveloped in bright white light, so impossibly bright that one would assume you've just cooked your retinas. That was not the case, however. She could see everything without squinting at all. She saw a combination of the best of all five senses, and perhaps some senses never before experienced. It was a feeling of home and peace and warmth and joy. It was beauty and color and elegance and grace. She could see a musical experience of ocean and nature and calm and melody. It smelled and tasted like every wonderful memory. But the very best part was that every person she had loved and lost was greeting her with smiles and open arms. It was overwhelming love and happiness.

And then it was gone. It took Mary several minutes to move as the feelings slowly left her, dissolving away into nothing. But the memory of her experience did not fade, not even a little. She slowly sat on the ground, wrapped her arms around herself, and wept tears of joy and understanding. She got it now. She understood why her baby needed to come into the world. She was no longer afraid.

God hopped off the outcropping and crouched down next to Mary. He reached over and mussed her hair. "I appreciate you, kiddo, I really do. Stick with Me on this. Continue to have faith. We've got this." He stood and walked over to Gabriel.

Mary quickly ran to Him and wrapped her arms in a bear hug around His chest. She didn't speak. She didn't need to. He kissed her on the head. She released Him and watched as God and Gabriel disappeared. Before they were gone, the angel gave a little wave. It made her laugh. She felt whole, reenergized, and ready to continue her journey. She stood silently for a moment before returning to camp.

It was nearly dark, but there was still enough light that she found her way back without incident. As she approached, she saw her group in exactly the same positions as when she left. Aaron had lost his battle and was sound asleep on Ella's lap. The sight filled her with love. *I can't wait to meet you little one*, she thought as her hand caressed her belly.

Gaspar waved to her as he watched her approach. She saw his expression change from cordial to confused. "Are you... okay?" he asked.

"Yes, I'm great. Why do you ask?"

"You seem to be... glowing." Gaspar hesitated. "It's probably my eyes playing tricks on me from staring at the fire."

Mary grinned. "Is there any food left? I'm starving."

33

FAILURE

You should kill them.

"I'm considering it." Herod walked to the window and gazed down to the sunlit streets below.

You killed me easy enough, and I didn't do anything compared to what those two buffoons let happen.

"Yes, Miriam, as you remind me almost daily. And you're not wrong, they screwed up badly. They let the Wise Men get away. It was careless and sloppy."

Yet they still live, and I'm trapped as your personal ghost. You know I hate you, right?

"Oh, it's fairly obvious that you hate me. But for good reason. I was wrong to kill you. I was young and brash."

Are you seriously going to make excuses? You were young and brash, so killing your wife is perfectly acceptable?

"Actually, for a king, it is. A king doesn't need a reason."

Hmph! That's a stupid rule. I can't wait until you're dead too.

Herod could picture her sitting cross-legged on the floor with her shoulders slumped, pouting. It was a sight he witnessed more times than he could count. His gaze drifted to the horizon, not really seeing anything, just staring. His head hurt nearly constantly these days, his guts were a twisted fiery cauldron, and this only made things worse.

Gundahar and Tobias had returned a couple days prior with their tails between their legs. Neither could look Herod in the eye. He was furious. These were two of his best, neither had ever disappointed him before now, which was the only reason they were still breathing. His men were toyed with and made to look foolish. But then, that was part of the Wise Men's mystique, always a step or two ahead of their opposition.

His "two best" had tracked the Wise Men for several weeks. They even split up to cover more ground, following up on reports of sightings. Some of the sightings made no sense, causing them to backtrack or veer off on some illogical tangent. But when tracking unpredictable men, logic sometimes flies out the window. The sightings seemed legitimate, with corroboration between multiple witnesses. Yet none led to anything viable.

At least each of them owned their failure when they faced him. This was another reason Herod was willing to give them another shot, combined with the fact that he was not exactly surrounded by capable, intelligent men. It would be nearly impossible to replace them, especially Tobias. He had a gift for finding secrets and obtaining information. It was true that Gundahr was one of the best soldiers Herod had ever seen, but he was not as young as he once was. Finding a replacement for him would not be as difficult. But Gundahar had a ruthlessness that appealed to Herod, as well as uncommon intelligence. No, these men were still useful to him.

You're really not going to kill them?

"No, I'm not," Herod replied, annoyed by her tone.

You are spineless. People will laugh at your weakness.

"Not if they want to live. Enough, Miriam, you are giving me a headache, and I need to concentrate."

Hahaha... you think you can just dismiss me now? You can't get rid of me. You can't do anything. You have no leverage. How do you make me leave? It's not like you can kill me again.

Herod grabbed a vase off a shelf and hurled it at the wall. Shards scattered across the floor.

A servant ran into the room, responding to the sound.

"GET OUT!"

The servant left as quickly as he had come in.

Herod paced the room, hoping Miriam would leave him in peace for a while. Her constant nagging and belittling were making him crazy. He settled into a padded chair. He had much to consider. The Wise Men were still out there, somewhere, and he was determined to find them. He had sent search parties in all directions. Even if he did not find them right away, keeping them on the run would likely prevent them from completing their messiah scheme. He was not about to let them accomplish some sort of coup.

The thought of catching them made him smile. He had endless ideas on how to make them suffer for planting these ideas into the heads of his people. It would be a slow painful death for each of them.

34

MY PEOPLE

Simon sat staring off into the distance. The sheep were grazing quietly as they always had and always would. Being a shepherd was a fairly low-stress occupation on most days. The incident with the twins was a rarity, and thanks to the angel, would never be repeated. The majority of his time, even when rounding up the occasional wayward lamb, was spent in his own head. He was the only human for miles in every direction. It gave one ample opportunity to get lost in thought.

Since his encounters with the angel, his thoughts were consumed with bigger things than he had ever considered before. God liked him. That thought never grew old and was the source of a perpetual grin he carried every day since. He was determined to do whatever he could to stay in His good graces. Simon was determined to follow through on the second request for assistance. Yet, he was troubled about how he was supposed to locate the people that God wanted him to help.

The mid-day sun was warm and felt good on his head. He glanced at his flock, making sure none had strayed too far away, then he laid back onto the grass and closed his eyes. He was not tired; he simply wanted the sun on his face while he thought about this dilemma. *How do you find someone you've never met when you have no idea where they are or what they look like? I'm not even certain how many people I am to look for.* The angel had told him he would figure it out, but Simon had no idea how he was going to do that.

His spot on the hill was surprisingly comfortable and the sun was very relaxing. The only sounds were a slight breeze and grazing livestock. Simon might end up napping after all. He considered various possibilities for beginning his search. He could go into town and wait there as most people passing through came that way. He could stay out here in the hills because they offered a great view for miles in all directions. He could even travel to adjacent towns and ask around there. He may have to do a combination of all those things. He was not entirely sure.

It was the warm smelly breath on his face that startled him out of sleep. He was too frightened to open his eyes, not knowing who or what was close enough to him that he could feel the warm breath. *Oh geez, definitely a what, by the smell of it.* His heart froze and he remained completely still as his mind raced to come up with possibilities. Lions and leopards were rare, but they were certainly a possibility. Wolves were known to pass through on occasion as well. Yet somehow that did not compute. A predator would have alarmed the sheep. The sound of their panic would have awakened him.

Simon slowly cracked one eye open, just enough to make out the shape of a horse standing above him. *Oh no, Romans.* His heart sank. He would almost prefer the lions or leopards. At least they would just be following their instincts in killing him, instead of being giant asshats about it.

"Are you alive, there, young man? I saw you jump a little when the horse sniffed you. It's a little late to play dead."

Simon opened his eyes and slowly sat up with his arms raised. There were three people on horses, two men and one woman. He was relieved to see that they did not appear to be soldiers, Roman or otherwise. Still, they were strangers, and he was in a vulnerable position. He regarded each of them carefully. They seemed like normal, everyday people. *Wait, are these my people? Is this the woman who is going to have God's baby? But how does one broach that subject with strangers?* Simon decided to remain silent for the moment until he could get a better take on his current situation.

"You can put your arms down, son. We aren't here to hurt you or take anything. We just need some information. We are looking for a shepherd named Simon. Do you know him?"

Simon's eyes lit up and he smiled broadly. "You *are* my people. The angel said you would come!"

"You know Michael?" Joseph asked.

"Who is Michael?" Simon replied.

"He... never mind."

Simon looked at the woman. "That's crazy, I would never even know you're pregnant."

Her eyes grew wide and a little crazy, making the expression on Simon's face change to one of fear. "You think I look pregnant? What a rude little shit. Why would you say that to a total stranger? I should smack..."

The other man grabbed her shoulder. He was the first to understand, and really, how often does that happen? "This isn't Mary," he said, "this is my wife, Maggie. I am Roger, and this is Joseph, Mary's husband."

Simon processed the information slowly. It took him several seconds to remember the angel said Mary and her friends were not together. "That's right, he said you would be arriving separately."

"Who did? Michael?" Joseph asked.

"Who's Michael? I'm Simon." He turned to Maggie and Roger. "Is he okay? Head injury or something?"

Roger laughed. "Maybe, but yes, he's okay. We met an angel named Michael who told us to seek you out."

"Oh, right, that makes more sense. No... well, actually I am not sure. He never really introduced himself by name. Maybe it's the same guy... angel. Who knows? Anyway, my angel told me that I'm supposed to make sure... hold on, I want to get this right... that you all find each other. Then I am supposed to escort you to Bethlehem. Yes, that's what he said." Simon smiled.

"I'm from Bethlehem. I can get us there," Joseph said.

Simon's smile faded away. "Oh no. No sir. No. The angel said I'm supposed to escort you, so I am going to escort you. I may be young, but I take my duties very seriously. God sent the angel. That is what the angel said, and God likes me." Simon beamed.

Joseph held up his hands. "Okay, son, okay. You win. You will escort us." He raised one eyebrow. "God likes you? What an odd thing to say."

Simon smiled wide. "Maybe, but it's true. The angel said so. Anyway, it's getting late enough that I need to round up the sheep and take them home. You should all come with me. My family would love to meet you. We can set you up with a good meal and a soft bed. Then tomorrow we can figure out how to find your wife."

"Michael mentioned she is with the Wise Men. Do you know them? Are they good people? Do you trust them?" Joseph asked.

"I'm sorry, I don't know who they are."

Maggie reached over to Joseph's shoulder. "Reel it in, big guy. He's a kid and spends all his time out here. How could he know? I'm sure she's okay."

Simon watched the interaction silently. *Old people are so weird.* He turned to gather his sheep.

35

THE 77ᵀᴴ GENERATION

Herod was annoyed by the inconvenience but was also a little curious too. It was almost unheard of for Hillel the Elder to call for a meeting with the king. He was annoyed to have to meet with him at the new temple, but the old man was not as mobile these days, so Herod allowed it. Besides, it was good to get out of the palace now and then. It was another bright and beautiful day, with only a few clouds breaking up a nearly perfect sea of blue sky.

He traveled in a convoy of chariots accompanied by his Celtic Guard. He was using them more frequently since Gundahar's mishaps with the Wise Men. Perhaps it was childish to punish him this way, by removing responsibilities and relying on others, but Herod liked sending nonverbal messages. Gundahar and Tobias were fortunate to be alive as far as the king was concerned.

The more he used the Celtic Guard, the more he realized that Fionn, the Celtic general, was every bit as reliable as Gundahar and appeared to be several years younger. He was also a fierce warrior in his own right, likely equal to Gundahar. It would be fascinating to pit the two against one another, but that would be a waste of his two best men.

The convoy made its way into the outer courtyard of the temple. Hillel agreed to meet with him here since none of the kings' guard were permitted within the inner courtyard by penalty of death, king's men or not, as they were foreigners and likely pagans. This was a further annoyance to Herod who felt he and his men should have access wherever the king chose. However, a lifetime with the Jewish people gave him an understanding that their holy laws were not to be trifled with. Even kings must deal with minor annoyances.

The king and his men were led down a flight of stairs to a room along the outer wall of the courtyard. Two of the kings' guard took a post at the top of the stairs while two others stood outside the door of the meeting room. The king spied the old man sitting at a table, accompanied by a pasty, non-descript lump of a young man with an armful of scrolls.

Hillel stood, bowed slightly and said, "Welcome, my king." He glanced to the young man who looked entirely lost and nodded for him to bow as well. The lump did so, spilling most of his scrolls to the ground in the process. Herod thought this one would starve if he ever had to provide for himself. *But then, the same could be said for most of my council.*

"This is my scribe, Hiram," Hillel said to the king.

Herod did not care and ignored the introduction, motioning for Hillel to sit as he did so himself. The lump was still trying to gather his scrolls. "It's good to see you, Elder. It's been too long. As always, you and the Sanhedrin have things running smoothly."

"We do our best. I'm fortunate to be surrounded by talented people."

Herod smirked. "I'm curious why you've requested this meeting. It's uncommon for you to wish to speak to me one-on-one. Is there a problem?"

Hillel smiled, partly at the king's arrogance and partly at the news he had to share. He had no compunction ruining this man's day. "No problems to report. I thank you for making the trip, traveling even short distances is wearisome for me these days. The reason I requested to meet with you is to give you a bit of news that I thought might be of consequence to you. But forgive my manners, would you care for wine or some food?"

Herod glanced at the trays of fruit and cheese. "I appreciate your hospitality, but I'm in a bit of a rush today. There's always too much to do and not enough time to do it."

"Well then, I'll get on with it. I assume you've heard the latest prophesies coming from the shepherding community, yes?"

"We've identified the culprits responsible for spreading these lies designed to destabilize the realm. We're pursuing them to bring them to justice as we speak." Herod crossed his arms and sat back.

"Oh, wonderful. I'm pleased you have the situation under control." Hillel clasped his hands together and rested them on the table before him, pausing briefly. "We, the Sanhedrin, have reviewed the claims of the prophecy and compared them to what has been written about such things. While we are not in a position to promote or dissuade such claims, we can tell you how they stack up against the historical scrolls and knowledge that we maintain. There has been much written about the arrival of a messiah, born of a woman, who will assume the title King of the Jews. The most powerful and compelling of these has to do with his arrival occurring in the seventy-seventh generation. I could go into detail but I'm sure you know these prophesies as well as I do. The specific claims of this latest prophecy do align with much of what has been written, more or less. That in itself is not conclusive. These things never quite play out as predicted. But the intriguing part, and the reason I felt you might have some interest in this, is the timing.

"It was recently brought to my attention that we, the Sanhedrin, have been somewhat caviler in our references to time. We have mistakenly made the assumption that others understand our references as we do. We refer to our current place in time as the seventy-seventh generation, and that is correct. But if we are to compare apples to apples, the seventy-seventh generation the scrolls refer to is the seventy-seventh generation since

Adam. While we refer to the present as the seventy-seventh generation, it is in fact the seventy-sixth generation *since* Adam."

Herod looked down at the table. He understood completely. "You're saying a messiah born today would align with the seventy-seventh generation since Adam. That the timing for this latest prophecy is correct. And that, combined with the details reported from the shepherds, makes this prophecy a strong possibility."

"As I said earlier, we don't promote or dissuade anyone's belief in such matters. We're not fortune tellers. But in all my years I've never seen the details and timing align more perfectly," Hillel responded with a wry smirk.

Herod's eyes flashed red. "How much are the Wise Men paying you?"

"Paying me? Ha. You know better, young Herod, you know it in your heart. Perhaps you should take some time and reflect on what we've discussed today. Hiram, my boy, will you assist me back to my study?"

The Elder turned to the king and bowed slightly. "Good day, my king." Hiram also turned and bowed, dropping the scrolls once again.

Herod did not acknowledge them. He remained seated staring at the table as the two left. *Fuck. Fuck, fuck.* Herod stood and went to the table with the food and wine, poured himself a full cup, then drained it. His head was pounding. *Could I be wrong about the Wise Men? Could this really be happening?* He would need to digest this information, work it over in his head before making a plan of action. His initial reaction was to cover his bases and deal with the Wise Men and the baby situation equally, emphatically, and without mercy.

36

FOLLOWED

Mary was tired of traveling in the wagon. It felt like an eternity since she was in one place long enough to feel comfortable. They would spend a few days here and a week or more there as they continued the slow progression south. Her body ached and she struggled to find a comfortable position while the wagon plodded on. She was well along in her pregnancy now and knew that had more to do with her discomfort than anything else. If she was to have the baby in Bethlehem, they should probably start heading that way before long.

Gaspar was good about trying to make her comfortable. He was tuned to her needs and went out of his way to help her. The group was getting to know each other well, sensing the signs to give space when needed, or offer a hug when the situation called for it. When little Aaron became stir-crazy in the wagon, the men were quick to help by placing him on a horse and trying to teach him to ride. He remained silent, but his smile was all that was needed to see to know how he was feeling.

Some days the group barely spoke to each other at all, each lost in their own thoughts. Other days were filled with laughter, and the day would be over before they knew it. Every day brought a different recipe of ways to pass the time. On travel days, they would be moving for hours and hours. Today was a quiet day.

Mary would often watch the interactions of the other members in the group. It would help keep her mind off the cramping, discomfort, and the need to pee every hour. Her favorite part of the trip thus far, other than the magnificence God showed her, was the way Gaspar and Ella were slowly being drawn together. Their eyes met often, and they seemed to chat more frequently. Mary felt warm inside to see what she hoped was the beginning of a loving relationship, although they would likely deny any such thing at this point. Their interactions were cute but watching them also had the effect of reminding her how much she missed Joseph.

The wagons were cresting a hill when the old man called for Gaspar. "Behind us, about a mile back, there are two horses moving quickly this way. There's no chance we can outrun them."

Gaspar looked back the way they had come, scanning the rolling hills to see for himself. It took a minute before he finally saw them as well. "Damn. That's unfortunate. I suppose it was only a matter of time. Better two than a whole platoon."

Mary did not think the number would matter if they were Herod's men. She scanned the immediate area without any luck of finding a suitable hiding place. Their plan was to avoid cities and towns, preferring the rolling wilderness instead. The downside of the plan was they were totally vulnerable out in the open. There was no one to assist them. There was no one to protect them.

"Let's head down off this hill and stay low. With any luck the riders have no interest in us," Gaspar said, "Mary, I need you, Ella and Aaron to hide in the compartment. Just in case."

Mary nodded. They didn't have much time. The three of them climbed in and Gaspar secured the drop door. The wagons then made the way off the hill into a shallow valley, stopping next to a small stream. Gaspar and the guards dismounted and tied the horses to the wagons. The guards took up a defensive position while Gaspar went to the stream to fill the water jugs. It seemed a normal thing to do. Should strangers come up on them quickly, at least it would not seem provocative. If they were indeed being followed, their followers would be upon them any moment.

Mary lay in the darkness of the compartment. It was not pitch black, there were slits and gaps between boards that let a small amount of light in, but it was still dark. The darkness wasn't the problem for her though. The silence was. The men outside were not speaking, so there was no way to know what was going on. She had not been inside this compartment since they escaped Nazareth. It was far more uncomfortable for her now. She fussed with the pillows and blankets, trying to find a comfortable position. It was more difficult for her to move as her belly was considerably larger than last time. She was straining to listen for any movement or sound outside. There was still nothing to hear.

Why does time slow down when you want it to speed up? Why does it speed up when you want it to slow down? These were silly thoughts to have, and yet these were the questions in her mind as she lay there waiting. *The next time I see God, if I ever get the chance again, I'm going to ask him.* Her hand went to her belly. *Or maybe you can answer that for me.*

She heard a muffled voice call but was not sure what was said or who had said it. It sounded several yards away. Then there was an exchange of voices, a conversation, still not clear enough to make out any words. She could not determine from the sound whether it was congenial or argumentative. She was becoming frustrated by not knowing what was happening. The voices grew louder, multiple people speaking at once, the tone was higher and slightly louder. Yet she still could not make out the words. *Was it agitation? Aggression?* Her frustration grew. She was frightened, and her imagination was going to dark places. She glanced over to Ella and Aaron. Both were wide eyed and very still, also straining to listen.

The verbal exchange stopped and only silence followed. She waited for the conversation or argument to resume but it did not. The silence was worse than hearing and not knowing what was said. She realized she was holding her breath. The first time she was in this compartment, the waiting was not nearly this bad. Then they had more allies and the element of surprise. Also, they were not yet being hunted.

There were two sharp knocks on the side of the wagon, the signal that Gaspar was going to open the drop door. He waited a few seconds before opening the hidden door, in case someone was on top of it. The door dropped open, allowing more light into the chamber.

"It's okay, you can come out now," Gaspar said.

Ella crawled down the drop door ramp first, followed by Aaron and Mary. The bright daylight caused them to squint until their eyes could adjust to the light. They regained their feet next to the wagon, scanning the area reflexively. Their traveling companions were all there, along with two new men standing several feet away. The men were dirty and disheveled, both taking big drinks of water from the jugs.

"Who is this?" Mary asked, nodding to the newcomers.

"You don't recognize them? I guess that makes sense, you barely know them. It's Balthazar and Melchior. They've been searching the area for us the last few days," Gaspar said.

"Did they find Joseph? Is he okay?"

"They didn't mention it, but we only spoke briefly. Let's let them clean up a bit, and then we can sit and catch up with them on their travels. We might as well set up camp here next to the stream. Give me a hand?" Gaspar said.

Mary helped unload some of the comfort items like chairs and pillows. The guards began setting up the big tent. The old man unloaded the cooking supplies and gathered wood for a fire. Setting up camp was a routine by now. They had been traveling together for so long that everyone reflexively did their part to help.

Before long, the old man had a fire going and was preparing food for a meal. Tonight was, after all, a reunion that required celebration.

Everyone took the opportunity to bathe in the stream. They had been travelling for a long time and these opportunities would sometimes take days or weeks to present themselves. Don't make that face. It was over two thousand years ago; things were different then. Other than the aqueducts in Rome, there was no running water.

Gaspar was visibly ecstatic to have his companions back, and they were equally happy to reunite with him. There was much joking and laughing. The entire group gathered around the small fire and shared a meal. Gaspar brought out the wine. A party was well overdue; this was a day to celebrate the safe return of friends. Living in the open, always looking over your shoulder, took a toll on all involved. Even Aaron felt the stress release as the mood of the camp lifted, and he laughed along with the adults.

Gaspar raised a tankard toward Balthazar and Melchior. "Tell us of your adventures since the last time we saw you. Quite honestly, you looked like crap when you showed up. I nearly didn't recognize you. There has to be a story or two behind that."

Balthazar laughed and shared a look with Melchior. "Oh, it's more than a story or two."

Melchior smiled and nodded.

"It's hard to know where to begin." Melchior said. "There has been a lot happening. Riding, making our presence known, escaping, running, fighting, getting beaten and robbed. It hasn't been all daisies and rainbows. And we haven't had decent wine in weeks." He tipped his cup.

"That last might be the truest words you've ever spoken," Balthazar said, downing his cup as well. Ella quickly refilled it, anxious to hear the rest of the tale. "For those not fully in on the plan from the beginning,

Mel and I snuck out of camp a day early with a guide and another fellow who looked suspiciously like Gaspar here. It took a bit to find and hire that chap. He was a great choice, he played his part better than expected, except he was left-handed, but I don't think anyone noticed. Anyway, we rode off to muddy the trail for Herod's men. We set off west, then veered north, riding for several hours before stopping. We made just enough of a spectacle of ourselves to be noticed by the locals, drinking at the local inn and allowing ourselves to be overheard, but not in an obvious way. We moved on north for a while then headed east, repeating the spectacle along the way to the border.

"We were far enough ahead of Herod's men that we didn't run into any trouble, not at that point anyway. Once we got to the border, we turned south for a bit then went west, almost turning a full circle. This time we stayed south of Nazareth and tried to stay off everyone's radar for a while. Then we decided it would be fun to pop up in random parts of Judaea, just to mess with Herod and his men. We spent a few weeks showing up and being noticed in a pattern that no one could possibly follow. We made a game of it, rewarding ourselves with drinks at each stop. We had fun with it while it lasted." Balthazar paused to enjoy more wine.

Melchior smiled at the memory. "The first time we ran into real trouble was when we were near Jerusalem. Granted, it was reckless to be near Jerusalem in the first place, but there was some logic in thinking they would be searching for us further away. They were, to our credit, but it turns out they were looking close as well. It's kind of flattering, if you think about it, we were important enough to them that they were searching everywhere. I'm not sure we factored that into our plan. There's always something.

"Anyway, we were spotted by some of Herod's men near Jerusalem. We were able to get away but had to split from our guide and pseudo-Gaspar to do it. They went one way; we went the other. We never did meet up with them again after that, but we are confident they got away. They had better horses than we did, and we gave them an exit route that was sure to lose Herod's men. We had a tough time losing them, but we did eventually. When being chased, a crowd is your best friend. We led them to the city and lost them in the crowd."

Mary was hanging on every word. "Is that when you were beaten and robbed?"

"Not exactly. Once we lost Herod's men, we decided it was time to change our appearance. We trimmed our beards, cut our hair, and found some local clothes that helped us blend in. We thought that since we were in Jerusalem, we might as well see if we could gather some information. We had been weeks on the road at this point and weren't able to find out what was happening in the world, specifically with Herod. In Jerusalem, gossip is the currency of the land. Finding answers was easy. We spent a week there mingling with the locals and divining all we could.

"It turns out, Herod thinks we, the Wise Men, are responsible for creating and spreading the rumors of the coming messiah, the very rumors the shepherds are spreading. He thinks we're the only ones wealthy enough and savvy enough to pull something like this off, that we bribed the shepherds and all the locals that believe them. It's really quite fascinating. He thinks we're starting a coup to unseat him. We've never had political aspirations, and anyone who knows us would attest to that, yet Herod is convinced we're responsible. That is why he's so desperately trying to capture us. Quite honestly, we couldn't afford the pay cut. What we do is quite lucrative."

"That's fantastic." Gaspar grinned. "If Herod thinks we're responsible for the rumors, thinks that the rumors are merely a ruse to unseat him, he won't be searching for pregnant women. Mary and her baby will be safe."

"That's what we thought as well. It's good news, as long as no one tells him otherwise. We'll happily be the target of his aggression if it means

Mary and Joseph... and God... can have their baby in peace," Balthazar said.

"Speaking of Joseph, were you able to find him? Free him? Did you see him? Is he okay?" Mary asked.

Balthazar shrugged. "I'm sorry, Mary, but no, we didn't see him. It wasn't part of our plan. To be honest, I'm not sure we could've freed him if we wanted to. There were only four of us, and he was with Herod's soldiers. With time, we might've been able to come up with something, but time was something we never had on our side after we left you."

"It's okay, I understand, but I had to ask." Mary realized her question was a bit of a buzz kill. She was so twisted up inside worrying about Joseph that she could not help herself. She was confident God would make sure Joseph would be safe, but even after the glory God had shown her, even after the miracles He put before her eyes, she still had doubts. She missed her husband terribly and wanted desperately to see him.

Ella saw the light fade in Mary's eyes and decided to change the subject. "So then, is this when the robbery happened?"

"The robbery happened on the way to Marisa. We had camped in a hidden valley, not much different than this one. We needed supplies, so I offered to ride into the nearest town. I was only about fifteen minutes out when I came upon a couple men on the trail. They were standing next to their horses facing me as I approached. They didn't seem threatening or dangerous. I asked if they needed help. One of them produced a large khopesh, you know, the curved Egyptian sword? That's when I knew I was in trouble. The other stepped out to intercept my horse as I slowed. Anyway, I ended up giving them what they thought was all of my money. The bigger one with the sword punched me in the side of the head, knocking me to the ground. I was fortunate they were content with that and left me with my ears ringing."

"That's horrible," Mary said, realizing how lucky her group had been to not run into any thugs.

"It definitely could've been worse."

"Yes, they might have damaged that pretty face of yours, and then where would you be? It's your only redeeming quality," Melchior said.

37

IN THE DISTANCE

Joseph gazed across the fields. The early sunlight cut through the mist, energizing the hazy green of morning into a bright emerald field of swaying, sparkling stars of shiny dew on each blade of grass. A breeze blew his hair out of his eyes as he carried supplies to the horses. Simon's family had been more than gracious the night before. They had prepared a fabulous meal, the best meal Joseph could remember having in months. Simon's parents were warm and welcoming, treating each of their party as long-lost friends. If Simon was correct, that God did in fact "like him" as he claimed, it was a direct consequence of being raised by two such wonderful people. Joseph smiled to himself as he placed the items into the saddle bags.

They would be heading northeast from Simon's homestead. It was time to make their way to Bethlehem. God was clear that the baby would be born there. Joseph knew the time was growing near, that Mary was getting close to her birthing date. He could feel it in his bones. He stepped away from the horses and scanned the horizon as he always did anytime he got a free moment, hoping against hope that he might see Mary and these Wise Men off in the distance riding this way. It was part of his daily ritual and was a reflex at this point. The horizon, as was the case every other morning, was empty. There were no riders approaching. There was nothing at all.

Then a curious thing happened. He spotted something in the distance, far away on the horizon. He was barely certain he saw anything at all. He strained his eyes, trying to ascertain what it could be. It was so very far away. Was it horses he saw in the distance? Maybe a wagon? He couldn't be sure. Joseph convinced himself he was seeing things, that hope was causing him to see something that was not there at all. He almost turned back to get more supplies for the trip, not believing his own eyes, but then he saw a flash of light, like a reflection off glass. That was enough to keep his gaze to the distance.

Roger and Maggie saw Joseph standing perfectly still, staring off into the distance. It was a sight they had witnessed almost every day since Mary was separated from the group. Normally it was thirty seconds or so, and then he was back to his normal chores. Today he just stood there, staring. It was enough of a change in behavior that they stopped what they were doing and walked up next to him.

"What's going on, big guy?" Roger asked.

"Can you see that?" Joseph pointed. "It might be a wagon, maybe some livestock, it's definitely something. There, beyond the big hill with the tree, just this side of the horizon."

Roger strained to see, more out of politeness than actual anticipation of seeing something real. He looked to the area Joseph suggested, not really seeing anything other than landscape. He saw rolling hills covered in green, with specks of brown that were likely rock outcroppings or boulders. It was hard to tell exactly what Joseph was hoping he would see, until he saw movement. Roger stiffened, training his eyes on where he saw motion. It was far away, but he was convinced he saw something move. It was too far to tell what it was that moved.

"Yes, I saw movement. I'm not sure what it was though. It could be anything or anyone. It could even be Herod's men hunting for us. How much are you willing to gamble?" Roger asked.

"We have horses. Whoever is in the distance appears to have a wagon. They don't look to be able to track us down quickly, but you're correct, they're too far off to know for sure. Let's watch for a bit. If they look like soldiers, we can bolt for Bethlehem," Joseph said.

Roger nodded, his eyes still on the horizon.

"What's going on?" Simon asked. He led his donkey to where his traveling companions had gathered. The donkey was loaded with as many supplies as Simon could load and still be able to ride.

"Where's your horse? Don't you have a horse?" Maggie asked.

"I don't have a horse, just my donkey. But he can keep up."

"He can keep up? With horses? A donkey? I don't think so, kid." Maggie smirked and shook her head.

"It's fine, we can try it for a while and see what kind of pace it can keep. We won't be riding hard anyway," Roger said.

Simon stroked the donkey's neck. "So, what's going on? What are you staring at?"

"We see something way off in the distance. Might be a wagon, we're not sure. We're waiting until it gets a little closer," Joseph said.

"Why not ride your horse far enough out to get a closer look?" Simon asked. "Wouldn't that be quicker?"

Joseph and Roger looked at each other without saying anything. The kid was right. Why hadn't they thought of that? Both of them looked down at their feet, slightly embarrassed. Maggie shook her head and smiled.

"We... ah, we're heading out to do that now," Joseph said.

Maggie laughed out loud. "Of course, you are. That was the plan all along."

"Shut up," Roger said softly as he playfully pushed her shoulder.

He and Joseph got on their horses and trotted in the direction of the wagon. They did not want to push the beasts too hard since they were loaded down with supplies and still had a long trip ahead. They rode a decent pace for ten minutes or so before slowing and walking the horses up a small hill. Joseph scanned the horizon looking for the wagon but was having no luck. He dismounted and climbed the rest of the way up the hill on foot. Rolling hills and boulders, shrubs and stunted trees, dirt and grass, but no sign of the wagon.

Roger followed him up the hill. "There," he said, pointing.

Joseph followed the trajectory of his finger and strained to see. Yes, there it was, a wagon and several horses carrying people that were too far away to see clearly. One, maybe two women, and a child. One of the women moved her arm in a familiar way.

"It's Mary!" Joseph ran back to his horse and fumbled with the straps of the saddle bags.

"Are you sure?" Roger squinted with a grimace. "They're very far away still. If you're wrong this could end very badly."

"I can tell by the way she moves. It's her."

"I'll take your bags back. If it's them, bring them back to the others. If it isn't, get the hell out of there before you get caught or worse."

The bags dropped from Joseph's horse. "Thanks."

Joseph jumped on his horse and dug his heels in. He was off at a full run. The horse was going faster than Joseph normally cared to go, but he had to see his wife. He was not an accomplished rider and had no business running a horse at this pace. He was fortunate to still be on the horse at all, but I am convinced that had more to do with the horse than the rider.

38

REUNION

Aaron was used to the bumps and creaking of the wagon, sitting in the back, spending hours finding new ways to spend his time as they traveled across the country. He had long since grown bored of looking at the beautiful scenery. It had become part of the daily travel routine. His mother would still engage him when something particularly new or beautiful or different would appear, but even she knew he was bored to see these wonders. He had moved on to other things to occupy his time. Today it was the two small wooden horses that Gaspar had carved for him. The name formed in Aaron's mind as 'Gapsbar'. Even at five years old it was difficult to pretend they were horses. They looked more like dogs, but Gapsbar said they were horses.

Aaron moved them along the rail of the wagon, one chasing the other. His imagination would play out countless scenarios between the two horse-dogs. Villains, outlaws, races, family rides, kings, Sanhedrin, and sometimes just horses, would find their way along the wagon railing. Almost everything, except soldiers. Aaron hated soldiers, and soldiers were not allowed to enter his imagination kingdom. *Soldiers killed Daddy.* Soldiers were the epitome of everything evil to the boy. He was never afraid when he saw one in person. Fear never occurred to him, only rage. He had complete disdain for them, even though he had no idea what "disdain" meant.

One of the horse-dogs slipped out of his fingers and slid toward the front of the wagon. Gapsbar heard the sound and turned to see what happened. He reached back and scooped the horse up, extending it to Aaron. "Here you go, little man."

Aaron accepted it and nodded his appreciation. He was determined to never speak again. He had also been determined never to smile again, but Mommy would sometimes tickle him, and he was helpless against such an attack. He had to abandon his desire to never smile but tried his best to only share them with her since she was the only one who deserved smiles. Although sometimes the Mary-lady would make him smile. He was a little conflicted when it came to Gapsbar. Aaron had little trust in men, yet Gapsbar and the other men in the group were nice to him. They were even teaching him how to ride a horse, and that was the best fun ever. He reminded himself that they were not soldiers, so they might be okay. Mommy seemed to like and trust Gapsbar, which was another source of his confusion. *Is it okay for Mommy to be nice to a man who isn't Daddy?* Aaron wasn't sure and didn't know who to consult in the matter. These are big issues for someone just out of toddlerhood. It was nice to see Mommy smile more, though.

One of the horse-men in front of the wagon yelled something, causing the wagon to stop. Aaron stood to see what the problem was. The horse-man was pointing into the distance, then turning to say words to Gapsbar, Mommy, and the Mary-lady. It was difficult to hear what he said, he was too far ahead of the wagon. He and the other horse-men drew their swords. That was never a good thing. Gapsbar stood to look where the man was pointing. Then the Mary-lady did too.

"There's a rider coming fast." Gapsbar pointed to where the horse-man was still pointing. The Mary-lady's eyes followed the pointing, stopping when she could see the rider approaching. Even though he was standing in the wagon, Aaron could not see what the others were watching. That was frustrating him, so he climbed onto some boxes for a better look. In the distance, he, too, saw the rider approaching quickly.

The man in front spoke again. "There's only one. Clearly, he's seen us. Should we ride to intercept him?"

Gapsbar looked to the rider then back to the horse-man. "Yes, go now."

"No!" the Mary-lady shouted. "No, it's Joseph! I know it is."

She climbed down out of the wagon and started toward the rider. Aaron saw tears running down her face, which was odd since she was always talking about how much she missed the Joseph-man. If it really was him, she should be happy. Adults could be confusing at times. Aaron liked the Mary-lady, even though she had a baby trapped inside of her. It made her look very odd, like a stick that swallowed a melon. She was the same size as Mommy, except for the fat belly. Mommy said he came from her belly just like that, but he didn't believe her. He would remember something that crazy.

"Mary, no, the rider's too far away, you can't be sure," Gapsbar called to the Mary-lady. She ignored him and was doing something that resembled running, but not quite. It was more of a fast-walking waddle. She was headed directly for the approaching rider.

Gapsbar jumped down off the wagon to follow, but Mommy jumped down after him and grabbed his arm. "No, wait." He hesitated, staring after the Mary-lady.

The rider could see the Mary-lady coming toward him as he pushed his horse even faster. When it looked like he was going to run her down with the horse, he suddenly slowed, then jumped off. He landed in a full stride run, exactly how every rider of the wooden horse-dogs would dismount from this day forward. The man she thought was Joseph tackled her and started kissing her. The Mary lady was crying. Aaron looked to the adults, but all they were doing was staring at the two of them.

Aaron decided he would handle it, since no one else was moving to help the Mary-lady. He jumped down out of the wagon and ran toward the couple. Aaron would never sit back and watch bad things happen ever again. His eyes focused solely on the man, running as fast as his little feet would carry him. Once he was upon the man, he grabbed the man's hair in one hand, pulled it straight up so he was no longer hurting the Mary-lady, and punched him as hard as he could in the face.

"What the fuck!" Joseph yelled, rubbing his jaw with his hand, more out of surprise than pain, "Who is this little shit?"

Aaron punched him again.

***

The adults watched the reunion with tears in their eyes. Aaron didn't understand why they were sad. Mommy thanked him for protecting the Mary-lady. She then explained that Joseph was the Mary-lady's husband, and it was okay to let them have this moment. They had been apart a long time and needed to be together now. That made sense to Aaron. If Mommy had been gone for a long time, he would want to spend all his time with her.

A little more than an hour later, two men and a woman rode up to the group. One of the men, who looked more like a boy, was riding a donkey. The other two waved to the Mary-lady as they stopped to dismount their horses. She let out a small scream as she saw them, then waddle-ran to greet them. She had nearly contained her tears from her reunion with Joseph, but all bets were off now, the tears flowed freely once again. The longing, the worry, and the uncertainty were over. She hugged her friends tightly.

39

THE RIDDLE REVEALED

Working on your resume? Since you'll be out of a job soon, I thought you might look into another line of work. With a new King of the Jews coming, maybe you can be a puppeteer? Or a street vendor? Oh, better yet, you can be the poor slob who has to clean the public bath. Herod could hear Miriam's derisive cackle as though she were right in front of him.

"Shut up, Miriam." Herod's right eye was nearly shut from the throbbing in his head.

Oh, you're right of course. Deposed kings don't take on new careers. They get assassinated. I can't wait to watch you die. I hope it's slow and painful. Do you suppose they'll torture you first? I sincerely hope they do, you fucking monster. Remember when you burned those kids alive for taking down the golden eagle? That seems like a fitting way for you to die. Oh, but there are so many other options.

"The more you talk, the happier I am that I killed you when I did." Herod rubbed his right eye, trying to get it open. The pain was like an ice pick behind his right ear. Each morning when he awoke, it was never a question of whether there would be pain, only how it would manifest itself that day. Some days it would concentrate more on his guts, today it was his head. Some days it was both. The worse the pain, the more often he was haunted by Miriam.

You're going to die. There's a messiah coming, coming for your throne, and there's nothing you can do about it. Her cackling laughter echoed in his head.

"How certain are you about that? How certain are you that there's nothing I can do? Don't be so sure, bitch. This is *my* kingdom, and I'll be damned if some infant is going to dethrone me."

Herod had called for a meeting with his small council. He stood from his chair, gave his eye one last rub, then left his study for the meeting. Walking seemed to ease the pain a bit and cleared his head a little. His steps echoed down the empty stone hallway. The result of his meeting with the Elder had caught him off guard. It seemed the window for the prophesized biblical messiah was indeed upon them. He had spent far too much time and energy hunting for the Wise Men for spreading rumors when he should have been focused on the prophecy itself.

Herod entered the council chamber and assumed his normal position at the head of the table. He scanned the room before speaking, making eye contact with each person seated at the table. Tobias, Gundahar, and Fionn were there along with the political advisors. The generals and Tobias never flinched when he stared them in the eye, which was part of the reason he respected them. The others were weak and avoided his gaze, but more heads were often needed when looking for ideas. The advisors had value when it came to the mundane day-to-day operations of the realm. They occasionally came up with useful ideas.

"Tell me of the star to the south. What do we know?" Herod asked.

The newest and youngest of the advisors stood to speak. "It appears to be getting brighter or moving closer, like a comet. It's difficult to know which for sure. We've been observing it nightly when cloud cover allows for that. It's actually visible in the daylight now, although barely. The shepherds claim it's part of the message from God, that those who wish to witness the birth of His child need only follow the star."

"Have we? Have we followed the star?" Herod asked with a blank expression.

The young advisor raised his eyebrows. "Well... no. Why would we follow the star?"

Herod stared at the man. The walk to the meeting helped alleviate his headache, but this man's stupidity brought it back in spades. "Oh, I don't know, how about TO SEE IF WE CAN LEARN ANYTHING!" Herod brough his hand to his forehead. *I'm surrounded by fucking morons.*

The young man sat down quickly and avoided eye contact with anyone.

Herod tried to remain calm. "What do we know? Give me facts."

A bald man with a slight overbite stood. "The shepherds report that the child is to be born in the City of David. This has been consistent throughout each report we've heard. I think it makes sense to abandon any searches or reconnaissance in Nazareth. What you seek is here in Jerusalem."

"Better. Continue."

"The census teams identified the pregnant women in Jerusalem and have them under surveillance." Overbite said. "We need only wait until the crowds begin to congregate. The very invitation to witness the birth will lead us to whomever they claim to be this messiah."

"Fionn, Gundahar, have your men ready," Herod said.

The generals both nodded. Gundahar glared at Fionn. *His name before mine? Herod is still angry. But zis one needs to learn I am still number vun.*

"I have a question." A small, meek man in the back half raised his hand before standing. "I'm not sure I understand. If God is going to have a baby, shouldn't we be happy about that? Why are we threatened by this prophecy? It seems to me this is a good thing if it's real."

"A good thing? A new King of the Jews is a good thing? Hmmm? How can I explain this so you'll be sure to understand?" Herod paced to the back wall pretending to look pensive. He lifted a small marble statue off a shelf and returned to the table, cradling the statue like a baby. "First, I'm not entirely convinced that God is going to have a baby, human or otherwise. The Sanhedrin believe the timing fits the prophecy narrative, but they don't specifically support the prophecy. Second, prophesies are never fulfilled as prophesized, there's always something just different enough that you can never be sure the prophecy is real. Under normal circumstances I would ignore this one completely. These aren't normal circumstances, however. The combination of events, the shepherds, the star, the Sanhedrin, all combine to make me believe something is happening." Herod lightly touched the face of the statue with his finger, as if caressing an infant.

"All of you at this table are here because of me. I've chosen you as generals or advisors. I've made each of you rich and comfortable. Your posh lives are the result of my good graces. So, if a baby is born in Jerusalem who makes a claim for my throne by birthright or by divine proclamation, and if this child is somehow successful..." Herod grabbed the head of the small statue and hurled it at the small man with great force. The statue struck him in the forehead with a dull crunch, killing him instantly. "... You are all fucked! If anything happens to me, you will all be killed as well. Welcome to the fucking team."

Gundahar laughed. "Nice shot."

The small man's body fell backward and hit the floor. His head sounded like a melon dropped on the stone floor. The advisors all stared at the table afraid to move.

Herod turned away from the table. No one dared speak. He paced to the back of the room and then returned to the head of the table. "A good thing my ass. Perhaps the rest of you will keep your questions to your fucking selves."

Tobias stood slowly. Herod eyed him cautiously, he was not in the mood for Tobias's jokes.

"Something isn't right. Something about the prophecy has been eating at me."

"Go on."

"Why do they say 'City of David'? Why not 'Jerusalem'?"

"Who the fuck knows?" Herod lifted his palms. "Why did they bring 'tidings of comfort and joy'? Prophesies are full of cryptic shit. It's never as simple as it seems."

"Exactly. It's never as simple as it seems. Was King David born in Jerusalem?" Tobias asked.

"No, sir," another advisor offered. "He was born in Bethlehem."

"Fuck," Herod said.

Everyone went silent, just staring at each other for what felt like minutes.

"We didn't track them in Bethlehem, the pregnant women. Son of a..." Herod turned quickly. "Fionn, get your men to Bethlehem. Start going door to door. Find all pregnant women and newborns, mark their homes so we know. Go."

Fionn stood quickly and left.

"Tobias, Gundahar, stay here. The rest of you get out. Take the corpse with you."

40

NO ROOM AT THE INN

Mary could not take riding in the wagon any longer, the pain in her lower back was too much. She tried the horses and even tried a camel, but the only relief she found came from riding Simon's donkey. Joseph walked alongside the donkey with his hand on Mary's shoulder or back, afraid to let her out of his sight.

Their reunion had lasted several hours, with the two of them fawning over each other like lovestruck teenagers. While Mary and Joseph pinched themselves to make sure it was real, other introductions were made. Simon insisted he get to know everyone by name as he had been instructed by the angel to lead this expedition to Bethlehem.

The group was not going to make it to their destination until long after sunset. They had three more hours to travel at this pace and daylight was already fading. Joseph explained to Simon that he grew up in Bethlehem and had family and friends there. Once Simon got them to the city, Joseph could help lead them to his parents' home. It was going to be a major inconvenience for them as this was a large group. Joseph hoped they would understand. The baby was restless and Mary was convinced He was coming soon. With Mary on his donkey, Simon led the caravan on one of the horses, heading directly toward the star that was pointing the way. It was much brighter now, easily visible even though the sun had not fully set.

The Wise Men and Ella laughed and told stories as they rode in the wagon. Aaron smiled and listened, not wanting to miss a thing. Roger and Maggie, who rode next to Mary and Joseph, filled Mary in on their adventures of being kidnapped and then freed.

Simon headed the caravan, content to ride alone. He was drawn to the star leading them to Bethlehem, the star that changed everything in his world. It was a marker placed by God, a road sign for those who wished to welcome His son. His mind was in a hundred places as they rode. He lost track of time. He was not sure how long they had been riding, only that it was much darker now.

Simon tilted his head, listening. He held his left fist in the air and came to a stop. The rest of the caravan halted. Joseph walked Mary and the donkey up to Simon to see what caused him to stop.

"Do you hear what I hear?" Simon asked.

The couple strained to listen. "Is that music?" Mary asked.

"Yes, I hear it too. It's far away but I hear it," Simon replied.

"Do you see what I see?" Joseph asked, pointing toward the star. It was growing brighter as they watched, considerably brighter. Light from the star was extending toward the ground, like the tail of a kite pointing the way.

"Whoa!" Simon exclaimed. "It's changing even as we watch."

"Do you know what I know?" Mary asked.

Simon and Joseph both looked at her curiously.

"If we don't get to Bethlehem soon, I'm having this baby on a donkey. I don't want that, you don't want that, and I'm pretty sure God doesn't want that. We need to go. This is happening. Tonight."

***

It was fully dark when they saw the lights of Bethlehem in the distance. They rode the last few miles in silence, passing the occasional farmhouse or shack along the road as they approached the city. Joseph bade the group to stop, joining Simon at the head of the caravan.

"I think it wise that Roger and I ride ahead to make sure things are safe. Bethlehem is very close to Jerusalem and there's no telling what Herod is up to these days."

"I would like to join you," Balthazar said. "An extra set of eyes can't hurt."

Joseph nodded. The three of them rode off toward the city. The brightness of the star made their silhouettes visible for miles.

The men returned less than an hour after they left. They covered the few miles in minutes on the horses. They slowed as they approached the small caravan, dismounting as they stopped.

"This isn't good." Joseph shook his head.

Balthazar nodded in agreement. "The place is crawling with Herod's soldiers. I'm glad Joseph suggested checking first, we nearly rode into a shit storm."

"I'm not certain what's going on. The soldiers seem to be searching door to door, looking for something or someone. There's no way we can make it into the city to my parents' place. There're just too many of them," Joseph said.

"I don't have much time, Joe. This baby is coming soon, soldiers or no soldiers." Mary placed her hands on the sides of her belly.

"My uncle has a farm not far from here. We rode by it on the way back just to check it out. It may be a bit awkward, but I think he'll take us in. He and my dad don't really get along so well, but as far as I know he's okay with me. There's no way he'll take all of us though."

"Don't worry about the group." Balthazar said. "Take Mary to your uncle's place. She needs shelter to have the baby. We can stay somewhere nearby. I can get the rest of us close to where you'll be."

"Thank you all. Roj and Mags, please come with us. We need the help, and my uncle has met you, it won't seem strange to him."

Roger raised his eyebrows and laughed. "Joe, look at the star. Everything is going to seem strange to them tonight."

"Fair." Joseph turned to Mary on the donkey. "Let's go."

***

The small group approached the farm silently. There was a main house, a barn, and several pens with oxen, pigs, and sheep. Joseph could smell the livestock as they approached, and crinkled his nose out of reflex. He was never comfortable around large animals, and their odor was the reason he went into carpentry in the first place. His father had always assumed it was to be more like him, but the truth was Joseph's aversion to farm animals. The group made their way to the main house and tied their rides to the hitching post.

Joseph paused before knocking on the door. It was late and his uncle was a man with a short fuse. He tapped lightly on the door. A dog started barking inside the home. The muffled sound of a put-out, annoyed, grumpy, old cuss could be heard from within. Footsteps thumping along the wooden floor could be heard approaching the door as the barking grew louder. The door swung open, and the older man was about to complain and rail at the late-night visitors, but he stopped with a confused look on his face.

"Joe? Joseph? What are you doing here? I thought you were Herod's men. They've been terrorizing the neighborhood all night." The uncle glanced over Joseph and his party, stopping on Mary. His eyes grew wide. "No. No, sir, no. I'm sorry, son, I know you are kin, but no. Herod's men are looking for pregnant women. They're marking the doors of homes with pregnant women. They've never done it before, and I have no idea why they're doing it now. Fuck, boy, are they looking for you? And her?"

Joseph stared directly into his uncle's eyes. "Yes. I think they are looking for us."

"Well, fuck me sideways. What the hell did you do?" The uncle started pacing in the doorway, working things over in his head. The dog lost interest in the newcomers, watching his owner pace back and forth. This was a fun new game, and made his tail wag furiously.

Mary touched Joseph's shoulder.

Joseph said, "Wait," quietly under his breath.

"Fuck, son. You put me in a bad place."

"There were too many soldiers. We couldn't make it to my folk's place."

The uncle sighed. "Those bastards are just about everywhere. It isn't safe for you to be inside the house. I know it's not proper nor polite, but you can hide in the barn. The soldiers won't search there. I'm sorry, son, it's the best I can do." He had a pleading look on his face, and Joseph knew it was not just his own safety he was concerned about.

"That would be perfect. Thank you. Um... Mary is likely giving birth tonight. Can I sneak in the back and get some water and supplies? It'll likely be a long night."

"Of course, you can. We always help family. We'll help you with anything you need. We'll keep an eye out for the soldiers."

"I'm sorry to bring this to your home. Things are going to get strange. You noticed the star, right?"

"Yes, I did. The damn thing is directly above the house. What do you suppose that is all about?"

41

A BARN

The barn was a working barn, with pens running down the length of one wall. A large ox was in the first pen near the main door. There were also sheep and some chickens. It smelled like a barn. Mary could not believe that this, of all places, would be the place her son, God's Son, would be born. She shook her head and had to fight back the tears. She envisioned something much grander for the occasion of His birth. She was embarrassed and ashamed. It felt like failure.

Getting Mary comfortable was the first order of business. Roger and Joseph fashioned a bed of straw and hay, covering it with several blankets. It was better than they had hoped considering their location but was not a proper bed. It would have to do. Mary settled into her new bed, making a point not to complain or look disappointed. Joseph went to the main house to get additional supplies. Roger went to find the caravan to let them know where Mary was. Maggie sat on the dirt next to Mary's bed and held her hand. It had been a long time since the two of them were alone together.

"I don't mean to sound ungrateful, but this isn't what I imagined when I learned I was going to have God's baby," Mary said.

"I don't think any of us would have imagined this. What a strange ride it's been only to end up in a dirty little barn on the edge of a town we barely know," Maggie said.

"Don't forget we have an insane king looking for us. It really helps round out the picture, don't you think?"

"It does add that special something. Anyone can have God's baby. But going into labor while being hunted by a psychopath, that definitely adds to the magic." Maggie smiled.

"Well, fuck. Excuse my language, but really? Mags, how am I supposed to do this? Here? I just want to cry."

"I don't know, Mare. Nothing has gone right, yet somehow it all seems to be working. Maybe it'll be special after all. Who can say?"

"I love your optimism. Thank you for sticking with me. I couldn't do this without you."

***

Joseph returned with his uncle, both men with arms full of blankets, water, and other miscellaneous items that seemed useful to Joseph. His uncle only shook his head and humored the young man who had obviously never been near childbirth before.

Roger returned soon after with Simon.

"Things are getting very strange out there." Simon's eyes were wide.

"What's going on? Soldiers?" Joseph asked.

"No, that's not it. It's people," Simon said. "Hundreds of them, maybe thousands. Shepherds, farmers, men, women, kids, they all keep showing up. They're all outside the barn, just waiting, with more coming every minute. You can see them in the distance walking this way."

"Okay, this is getting awkward," Mary said, "No pressure, just pop out a baby for an audience. Dance, monkey, dance."

Maggie laughed. "'Dance, monkey, dance?' I'm so stealing that."

"Um," Roger stammered. "That's not all."

"What?" Mary asked as her shoulders dropped.

"Angels. They're gathering in the sky. Hundreds of them. Big ones, small ones, some I would never guess were angels at all. Between the angels and the star, it is so bright out there it's nearly like daytime."

And that's when Mary's water broke.

42

WRATH

Herod stood with his hands resting on the parapet overlooking the palace grounds, his eyes fixed on the southern sky. Something was happening, the sky was unnaturally bright, the tail of the star nearly reaching the ground somewhere near Bethlehem. He was angry, but that was his only mood these days. He had sent his Celtic Guard to Bethlehem earlier in the day. This development, the bright sky at night, changed everything. Something was happening in Bethlehem. Tonight. This would not do.

"I've never seen anything like this," Tobias said.

"I doubt anyone has. This may, in fact, be an act of God," Herod said.

"Do you believe that?"

"I don't know what to believe anymore. Whatever is happening there, I'm going to stop it. God or no God, there will be no new 'King of the Jews' coming from Bethlehem."

"How do you stop an act of God?" Tobias asked.

Herod faced Tobias. "By unleashing hell."

Tobias stared back at the king but did not speak. He had questioned the man's sanity for a long while now, and that last comment sent chills down his spine. He was genuinely frightened by his king's lost grip on reality. This could get very unpleasant.

"Gundahar, take your men to Bethlehem immediately. Kill every child under five. Kill every pregnant woman. Kill anyone who tries to stop you. Go, now."

Gundahar stared back at the king, pausing for nearly a minute, as if considering what he had just heard. He nodded, then turned and left.

"Sir, that's too much," Tobias said. "The people will rise against you. You can't. That's..." His mind raced but he could not find the right words to express his outrage and disgust.

"I can't? What the fuck do you mean 'I can't'? *I just did.* The order's been given. Grow some balls, or get the fuck out of my sight." Herod turned and walked back into the palace.

43

JOY TO THE WORLD

God created angels, a lot of them. They have existed with God for eons upon eons. There are many kinds, and they have different roles as part of the Heavenly Host. Angels, Archangels, Virtues, Powers, Principality, Domination, Thrones, Cherubim, and Seraphim all fall under the umbrella term "angel". They are God's support staff, his family, and his friends. They are not equal to God, but they are a lot closer than humans. Angels and God have a long history together, so when God informed them that He was going to have a Son, the angels insisted they be present. They would not miss such a monumental occasion, the first of its kind. In their long history together, there had never been anything like this.

Angels are creatures of light. When they choose to be seen by humans, they are typically quite bright. Happiness amplifies this effect. In moments of great love and happiness, angels will "leak" light, like sweat off the brow of an athlete or water through a sprinkler head. Light separates from them in tiny points of brilliant white, drifting toward the earth like tiny flower petals in a breeze. It is an impressive sight when one angel leaks light. This night, every angel was gathered above the barn in Bethlehem, every angel was joyous and excited, and millions of tiny points of light drifted to the ground like lightly falling snow. The people gathered outside the barn held out their hands to catch the droplets of light. It was the most beautiful sight any of them ever beheld.

Inside the barn, Mary was in labor. Joseph, Maggie, and Roger were helping as best they could, having never assisted in delivering a baby before. Maggie at least had conversations with her mother about the topic and what the process was, making her the nurse in charge. You might expect delivering the Son of God would be a painless experience, but if that is what you expect, you haven't been paying attention. The rewarding road is never the easy road. Mary called out in pain as she worked through the progressively more frequent contractions. With every indication of discomfort, Joseph cringed in his helplessness. He was frightened by the entire process and prayed that God would spare her anymore pain. The baby crowned, Mary screamed, and things moved quickly.

The animals in the barn were agitated by all the commotion. A small lamb squeezed out of the stall it shared with his mother and trotted unsteadily to the stall with the large ox near the barn door. The lamb somehow found his way under the gate to the ox stall but could not find a way to get back out.

Gabriel drifted down to the barn and placed both his palms on the door, knowing the Glory that was about to grace the earth. He heard Mary's cries, he heard Maggie say "Here He comes", and he heard a very tiny first breath.

At that moment many things happened at once. The angels, all of them, burst into song with glorious music emanating from every direction. At no point in history had all of them joined together as one in song. The hundreds of people gathered outside the barn were overcome by the beauty and wept openly. The sky lit up with bright light as the angels leaked so many pinpoints of sparkle it resembled a blizzard in sunlight. Across the globe, every person on every continent paused briefly with a feeling of warmth and contentment very much like love, most not understanding the significance.

Gabriel opened the barn door as Joseph and Roger dragged a feeding trough closer to Mary's makeshift bed. The Baby was wrapped in rags from the uncle's house and was laying quietly on His mother's breast. Maggie dabbed at the Child's eyes and face with a wet towel to help finish cleaning Him off. The men emptied the manger and gathered new clean straw to line it before placing several blankets as a bed. Joseph looked over at Gabriel and noticed the angel had tears running down his face.

"It's so bright out there, is it morning already?" Joseph asked Gabriel.

Gabriel shook his head. "God is light, He is here." Raising both arms with his palms up, indicating everywhere.

"Did you just speak?" Maggie asked with a smile.

"Yes, I did. Oh, stop grinning at me like that. I have to go give a speech. It's what I do." He smiled and winked at her.

Gabriel turned to the people and angels outside the barn, raising his palms to the sky, his voice booming, "Glory to God in the Highest. The Christ Child is born. Jesus, the Son of God is before you. He is your salvation. Come meet the King of Kings. His reign will last forever."

The people approached the open barn door, creating a large semicircle around the opening. Jesus was in the manger, mostly oblivious to His surroundings. Mary was leaning against the side of the manger with her hand on her Son's head, unable to take her eyes off Him. Joseph knelt beside her, smiling with tear-stained eyes. The music from the Heavenly Host reverberated across Bethlehem. The angels were gathered above the people, above the barn, with tears of joy as they sang. Something caught Mary's eye. She spotted a kindly old man smiling at her with His hand over His heart. He mouthed the words "thank you", winked at her, and was gone.

Balthazar walked slowly toward the manger, carrying a small chest. His eyes were nearly as wide as his smile. He knelt before the Baby and placed the small chest at the foot of the manger. "Please accept this small gift as a token of my love and loyalty."

Melchior was behind Balthazar with a burlap bag about the size of a large melon. Gaspar stood behind Mel with a larger chest and Simon was behind him with a jug of wine the Wise Men had given him as a thank you for leading them to Bethlehem. Simon asked if he could give it to the new Messiah and His family. They were not offended by his plan to regift, it was probably better than letting a fifteen-year-old have wine anyway. Other people joined the line, one after another, all eager to offer some gift of thanks to this new miracle.

Simon glanced up to the sky to watch the angels drift back and forth as they floated above the crowd. One of the angels stopped above him. It was Simon's angel, the one who had visited him in Marisa. The angel waved down to him, and Simon smiled brightly as he waved back. He never learned the angel's name. Simon regretted not asking because he considered the angel his friend. After all, the angel had most definitely changed his life.

One by one, the people approached the baby in the manger, leaving a gift if they had one. Each of them lingering too long, unable to pull their eyes away from the glorious Child. Mary and Joseph were humbled at the generosity of total strangers.

***

Gaspar was standing next to Ella as they watched the line of people wait patiently to pay respects to the new king. The sky was still snowing drops of light from the angels, who continued to sing glorious songs of worship and praise. The music that drifted down was unlike anything the people had ever heard. Gaspar noticed that Aaron was pulling his mother's dress, as if trying to get to the line of people cued to see the baby Jesus. Gaspar had an idea.

Gaspar walked to Balthazar and Melchior. "Please, come with me, I need your help." The two men nodded and followed Gaspar as he cut through the crowd and made his way to where they had left the wagon. He grabbed a wooden bucket and looked around, searching for something else.

"What are you looking for? What do you need?" Melchior asked.

"I need a bit of leather skin and some cord or thick string. I also need two sticks of equal size and weight, about a cubit long," Gaspar said.

Balthazar looked at Melchior and shrugged. "I have a bit of leather skin and I'm sure I can find a couple sticks."

"I have some cord in with my stuff. It's not a lot, but it should suffice if I'm right about what you're doing," Melchior said.

"Yes, we're making a drum for Aaron. Trust me, he needs this."

"Say no more, we're on it."

The men gathered the supplies. Two of them stretched the skin over the top of the bucket, pulled it tight and then toward the bottom. Gaspar wrapped the cord several times around the skin covered bucket, pulling the cord as tight as he possibly could. He tied it off, and the Wise Men took a step back. Melchior pulled out a knife and trimmed the skin and cord, completing the drum.

Balthazar picked up the sticks Gaspar had asked for. "May I?"

"Yes, please," Gaspar said.

Balthazar crouched next to the drum and began to beat it with the sticks. Bum da bum da bum bum bum bum. The sound was perfect.

"This is going to be cool." Gaspar wrapped the drum with the rest of the cord, making a small strap that could go over the head of the young boy. He fashioned a knot to adjust the length of the strap to make it just right. "Awesome. Let's get back."

The three men made their way back through the crowd outside the barn. Gaspar caught Ella's eye, winked at her, then approached Aaron slowly, kneeling before him. "Hey Aaron, looks to me like you want to give the new messiah a gift but aren't sure what to do."

Aaron looked a Gapsbar and nodded.

Gaspar produced the drum and held it before the boy. Aaron smiled ear to ear, taking it immediately. Gaspar passed him the sticks as well. Aaron instinctively pulled the strap over his head and positioned the drum directly in front of him. Adjustments were made to the length, then he took the sticks and tested the drum. Bum da bum da bum da bum. He was a natural.

Gaspar stood and turned to Ella. "Would you like to escort him through the line? I think he has a gift for the new king."

Ella smiled. "You are incredible. Thank you for this. Thank you for everything." She hugged him tightly.

Ella knelt before her son. "Would you like to play your drum for the new King?"

Aaron smiled and nodded.

Ella led the boy to the line, and they waited patiently for their moment with the new Messiah. Time seemed to go quickly as they stared at the Babe. He was engulfed in light and seemed far too content for a newborn, especially one that was lying in a manger in a smelly barn. The people in front of them each said a few words and then presented a gift, pausing too long afterward. Eventually they would leave and the next would approach.

Ella was unsure what to say when the person in front of them finished and finally left to the side. She held Aaron's hand and stared at a tiny baby in the manger. *How could someone so small be so very important to the world? How could this tiny soul be the actual Son of God?* She looked to the people, her new friends and traveling companions, the parents next to the Child. They looked at her with patience and understanding. She took a step forward.

"We don't have much, we would love to be able to give you something, anything. My son just received this drum as a gift. Aaron would like to play it for you, for Him. Would that be alright?" Ella asked.

Mary, who to this point had been unable to take her eyes off her son, looked up at Ella and then to Aaron. She smiled a very pleasant smile, then nodded.

Ella knelt next to Aaron and whispered, "It's your stage. Kill it." She walked off to the side, leaving Aaron before the Lord alone.

The ox next to the barn door, who had been docile the entire time until now, was being pestered by horseflies. The biting was more than it could stand, especially on its backside. The ox began whipping its tail in a semicircle, swatting it against its own behind, trying to drive the horseflies away. Whap... whap... whap...whap...

The small lamb that was still trapped in the ox stall was frightened by the whap of the ox's tail and tried to escape the stall by jumping up and hitting the lower board of the stall gate with his two front feet. Pa pa... pa pa... pa pa... pa pa...

The combination of sounds was a very rhythmic whap, pa pa... whap, pa pa... whap, pa pa... whap, pa pa...

Aaron adjusted his drum slightly, looked up at the Baby and His parents, then looked back at his drum. The ox and lamb continued in the barn, whap, pa pa... whap, pa pa... whap, pa pa..., and Aaron began to play.

Throughout our history, there have been amazing percussionists. Drummers whose skills remove all doubt of their God-given ability to deliver precise rhythms and pounding beats. Everyone has their favorites, from Buddy Rich to Bill Buford to John Bonham to Neil Peart. Elvin Jones, Keith Moon, Levon Helm, Sheila E, Dave Grohl, Carter Beauford, and Evelyn Glennie, all amazing examples of incredible skill on the skins. There are hundreds of others, many with names we don't recognize, like the kids killing it on plastic buckets on the street corners or the college drum corps that amaze and entertain fans at competitions. Stomp and Blue Man Group brought originality and fun to the stage using household items and plastic pipes, never sacrificing the intense percussive precision of those talented performers.

Aaron, however, had nothing in common with any of the legends listed above. He played for a couple minutes, but it seemed longer for everyone listening. He played without rhythm, he played without tempo, he played without skill. In fact, it sounded every bit like someone just handed a drum to a five-year-old who had never seen a drum before and asked him to play it.

"That was truly cringe-worthy," Melchior whispered to Gaspar.

"Not exactly how I pictured it," Gaspar whispered back.

Aaron slowly looked up from his drum and dropped his hands to his side, still clutching the sticks in a death grip.

Mary smiled brightly. "Thank you, young man. Your gift was very special, and I'm so very impressed that you were brave enough to stand here and play in front of all these people."

Aaron approached the Baby, who smiled when He saw the drummer boy. It was likely just gas, as He was a newborn and not in command of His facial muscles just yet, but let's not split hairs. To Aaron it was a smile, and that was all that mattered.

"Nailed it," Aaron said as he turned back to his mother. Ella's jaw dropped. She ran to him and hugged him tightly as tears slipped down her cheeks.

44

WHAT CHILD IS THIS?

As Herod had commanded, Fionn and his Celtic Guard marched through the streets of Bethlehem, knocking on doors, searching homes, and marking the fronts of homes with newborns or pregnant women. They had been at it for hours. The unnatural bright light to their south was unsettling to his soldiers, who grumbled about it loud enough for him to overhear. The light seemed to be getting brighter, as if the sun was cresting the horizon, yet it was just after midnight. Strange things were afoot and Fionn glimpsed fear in the eyes of his men, something he never witnessed from them in battle.

Though they had originally come from nearly a thousand leagues northwest of Judaea, the Celtic Guard had lived there long enough to begin to adopt the customs of the Judaean people. Many had converted to Judaism and worshiped alongside the locals. All of them were familiar with the prophesies of the shepherds. Many of them believed it to be true. Fionn held on to his pagan beliefs, though he was not one to care who or what others worshiped. He had come to appreciate the Jewish people much more than the peoples of Rome or Egypt. At least their God made sense in the abstract, even if He did not have a name.

When the music and angel chorus began, all the soldiers froze in place, glancing left and right and to the sky. Fionn was annoyed as much as he was disturbed by the strangeness of this night. Their task would likely take them until morning to complete, longer with these odd happenings slowing their progress. Yet this new development was a cause for concern. The music and singing meant something was happening that needed to be investigated. He gathered his men and instructed them to follow. It was time to determine the source of this disturbance.

They marched south through the empty streets of Bethlehem, the homes dark and still. The residents were asleep this late at night, only troublemakers would be out at this hour. Yet it sounded as though there was a party in the distance as they followed the sound of the music. Though difficult to hear, and unfamiliar, it had a soothing effect that irritated Fionn.

Without warning the music stopped, making the night feel empty. Then came the sound of drumming, soft in the distance. It was too erratic to be normal drumming and did not fit with the music that played before. It was as if someone was purposefully playing poorly. The drumming went silent soon after, and the music and chorus began again. There was something troubling about all of it.

The Celtic Guard came to the end of a row of buildings on the south end of town. Fionn raised his left fist, stopping his marching force as they rounded the buildings. He squinted and tilted his head, trying to make sense of what he was seeing. He could see hundreds of people gathered outside of a barn, and what appeared to be angels floating and milling about in the sky above the gathering. The bright star was blasting down on the scene like a spotlight, and the angels seemed to be nearly as bright as the star.

Some of Fionn's soldiers dropped to their knees in prayer. They had all heard the prophesies and some may have believed before, but not like at this moment. It's got to be hard to be a sceptic with hundreds of angels in the sky before you. Fionn coaxed his men up and began moving slowly toward the crowd.

"Keep your swords sheathed, this is a peaceful gathering," he said to his men.

They moved toward the barn and the spectacle, unsure what they were approaching, yet each of them could feel in their hearts there was no danger here. Those at the back of the crowd began to pull away from the approaching soldiers, creating an opening straight to the barn door and the people gathered at its opening. Fionn stopped his men again, finally seeing the Baby in the manger. *It looks as though I've been praying to the wrong gods all my life.* He stood staring at the Child, unable to take his eyes off Him.

Aaron saw the soldiers standing in awe. These soldiers were different, their hair and beards were reddish brown, and their skin was pink from the sun, not dark brown or olive like the ones Aaron was familiar with. The big one in front had hair to his shoulders and strange clothes. He was obviously not a Roman.

Aaron walked directly into the empty semicircle surrounding the barn door and headed for Fionn. There was no hate or anger in his eyes as with other soldiers, only curiosity. He approached the giant general fearlessly, pausing right in front of him. Fionn looked down at the boy. Aaron reached out and took his hand, walking him to the barn door. He led the big foreigner directly to the foot of the manger, then dropped his hand and went back to his mother.

Fionn stared down at the tiny Baby, struggling to understand the conflicting emotions within him. He slowly sank to one knee, his eyes locked in the gaze of the Child. He wrestled with his feelings, trying to define this new unfamiliar one that was beginning to overwhelm him. He had vague memories of it, memories that had been long suppressed out of necessity, his vocation such as it is, and time. He was a paid killer for kings and queens, a slave with benefits as long as his skill and tactical knowledge pleased his rulers. He had lived a hard, violent life, one that required a hard, violent mindset. He had no regrets. He had done well for himself, advancing to a general's rank and commanding his own men. He never once asked himself about the internal cost of his lifestyle or the things he left behind. His eyes began to burn as tears filled them, the vague memories becoming clearer. Love. As foreign a concept to him minutes ago as speaking fluent Chinese. It was love, filling him with warmth and joy. This was more than a mere baby in front of him, it was Love.

The music slowed to a stop. Cries of anguish and pain could be heard faintly in the distance north of them. Fionn stood to look back the way he had come, as did the crowd gathered around the barn. The screams of terror continued, growing louder as each minute passed.

Simon and the Wise Men approached the manger.

"We need to go, this is about to get ugly," Gaspar said to Mary and Joseph.

"The wagon is not far, you should leave here," Balthazar said.

"Leave?" Mary asked, "Where would we go? We just got here."

Joseph stood, keeping his hand on Mary's head. "They're right, Mare. Herod will be coming. It sounds like he might be here already, or soon will be."

"Whoever is coming, your child is safe while I still stand," Fionn said, "but your man is right, Herod is coming. I will hold them back as long as I can."

45

FLIGHT

The angels went silent, looking to the north beyond the buildings. One by one, they descended to the manger, each kissing the Christ Child on the forehead before vanishing entirely. The sky went slowly darker as the angels departed. The star was still bright, with its tail illuminating the barn like a spotlight, yet that too started to fade.

Gundahar led the Germanic Guard around the row of buildings, stopping to take in the odd sight before them. Even from this distance, Fionn could see blood on their swords. *You Germanic fuck-stick, what have you done?* He knew whatever atrocities they had committed came directly from Herod, but he also knew Gundahar would not question anything. He would simply follow orders. He was the perfect tool, always effective and absolutely no push-back whatsoever.

Fionn walked to his Celtic Guard. "My friends, I can't ask you take the stand I am about to take. It will make you wanted men, fugitives to Herod the Great, outlaws. However, our associates are here to kill the Child of the real God, and I, for one, have no intention of letting that happen. Stand with me only if you feel it right in your heart. There is no shame in leaving, not for this fight. It's been my honor to lead you."

Each soldier drew his sword. Not one hesitated, not one left.

Fionn raised his sword and touched the pommel to his forehead. "Thank you, my brothers. I'm unworthy of this loyalty, but I thank you for it. Let's kill these fucks."

The Celtic Guard unleashed a fierce battle cry.

***

"Simon, get some people to help carry the gifts to the wagon," Joseph shouted. Simon ran to the crowd. All it took for assistance was to ask, everyone was there for the new King. Joseph lifted the Baby out of the manger and handed Him to Mary. Then he lifted her with the Baby and headed for the wagon. Maggie grabbed Mary and Joseph's things and Roger picked up as many of the gifts as he could carry. Simon and the volunteers each grabbed gifts as well and headed for the wagon. The Wise Men followed suit and helped the others.

They loaded the wagon quickly and Joseph made sure his wife and child had a comfortable space to ride. "Where do we go?" Joseph asked.

"We'll get you to Egypt, you'll be safe there. Gaius Turranius, the Prefect of Egypt, owes us a favor. Even if Herod does try to find you there, Turranius will help us," Balthazar said.

"The Prefect of Egypt owes you a favor? Who are you people?" Simon asked.

"Yes, he does. A big one. And we are of no consequence. Not at the moment. We should go." Balthazar went to his horse.

The smaller caravan pulled out, consisting of one heavily laden wagon and several horses. Simon rode one of the horses with his donkey on a lead line tied to his saddle. Simon, the Wise Men, Ella and Aaron, Maggie and Roger, and the Holy family, all set off for Egypt.

"We have no protection, no bodyguards or real fighters," Melchior said.

Balthazar frowned. "We don't have time to find anyone. We'll have to take our chances."

***

Gundahar could see the Celtic Guard in the distance. They had not received the latest orders and did not know to kill the children around them. He could see at least one small boy and one baby from this distance. Hopefully the Gemanic Guard's approach would not spook the people who seemed comfortable around the Celtic Guard. Gundahar called for his troops to march forward, but not in a threatening way. This was not a military advance. As they marched, the Celtic Guard let out a battle cry, causing Gundahar to halt his men. He regarded them cautiously. The Celts went silent soon after and began walking toward them. The cry must have been a celebratory thing, maybe cultural, meaningless for sure. Who the fuck knew or cared? Gundahar moved his men forward to meet the Celts.

"Vat is all of zis?" Gundahar asked Fionn, waiving his arm toward the barn and the light.

"The new King of the Jews was born here," Fionn replied, looking back toward the barn. "Did you see the angels before they left?"

"I saw... somezing, zere was moofment in ze sky. Angels, you say? Are you a shepherd now?"

"No, I'm not. But they were right, I saw Him with my own eyes."

"Good for you, I don't give a fuck. Our orders changed. Ve kill all children. Not all of zem, but little vons, especially babies. Our king commands it."

"Does he? Interesting. I'm guessing that's what you kids were doing on the way here? Killing babies?" Fionn asked.

"Crazy king says kill babies, ve kill babies. Vat we do is not hard, ve get orders, obey orders, get paid vell. You suddenly develop a conscience? I've seen you do horrible sings over ze years, why ze attitude now?"

"Because I saw the Child Herod is looking for and know in my heart that He is the King of Kings."

"Vat ze fuck does zat mean?"

"It means I'm not going to let you touch Him. Not now, not ever."

Gundahar's eyes narrowed. "Ve have orders, orders from Herod. Vat ze fuck do you sink you're doing? Vy do you care?"

Fionn raised his sword and touched the pommel to his forehead. "I never cared much for you or your men, but I respect you all as soldiers. You, Gundahar, are one of the best I've seen. It seems a shame to kill you."

Gundahar laughed. It was the first time Fionn had ever seen him show any emotion other than indifference or anger. "Is zis how you choose to die, orange man? Perhaps you should step aside and let ze real men do zeir verk."

And then it began. Swords were drawn, soldiers squared off, and blood began to flow. How does it play out when the best meets the best? How would LeBron James do against Michael Jordan in a one-on-one game if they were both the same age? How would the late seventies Pittsburgh Steelers do against the early nineties Dallas Cowboys if they all trained in the same decade (and took the same steroids)? Do you remember the epic Super Bowl LII between the Philadelphia Eagles and the New England Patriots? The underdog led most of the game, but you knew the favorite would come back in the end. Or would they? However, this was not a sporting event, this was life or death between two fine-tuned killing machines.

The battle waged for nearly an hour, both sides gaining a brief advantage before the other overpowered them, a sine wave fluctuating back and forth. Only one angel remained above the fray. Michael observed in silence. He wanted to assist Fionn, but was forbade to do so, which is why he merely watched. He longed for a chance to take out Gundahar and his men, but it seemed that was not meant to be.

These were two of the finest fighting forces in the land, both well-trained, both well-conditioned, and both completely loyal to their leaders. The crowd had long since dispersed as the battle pressed on, skill on skill. The bright star faded and disappeared entirely as the sun crept toward the horizon, replacing one bright light with another.

The small caravan was over an hour into their journey to Egypt. The battle before the barn in Bethlehem pressed on, nearly at a stalemate. Slowly, ever so slowly, the Germanic Guard took the advantage. Just as slowly, they leaned in on the Celts in an attempt to wipe them out entirely.

Fionn felt the tide shift and knew at that moment his men were about to lose.

"Brothers," Fionn called to them. "Go home. Go back to our homeland and tell them of the things we witnessed this day. Not the battle, the Child!"

With that, Fionn lunged at Gundahar, slicing him across the midsection. Gundahar winced in pain, clutching his side, blood flowing freely through his fingers. Gundahar glanced up at Fionn quickly, and just as quickly buried a dagger into his throat. Fionn collapsed to the ground, clutching his neck as he bled out.

Michael, above the fray, put his head in his hands and turned away. *If only I had been allowed to help.*

The Celtic Guard, the ones that remained, watched Fionn hit the ground. They fought back their urge to retaliate and fled the battleground as he had commanded. There was no shame or regret. They were following the orders of the only leader that mattered to them. Fionn told them to return home, and each of them wanted that more than they had ever admitted to themselves.

The Germanic Guard went in pursuit of the Celts, until Gundahar called them back.

"Fuck zem. Ve need to follow ze vagon. Ve need to follow ze Baby."

"Vat about ze vounded?" a soldier asked.

Gundahar surveilled the battlefield. There were dead and wounded splayed across the ground in all directions. It had been a costly battle for both sides. Only a third or less of his men remained standing.

"Fuck zem too, ve have no time." He began to run, and his men joined him, following the small caravan. Even though they were exhausted from the battle. Even though they were leaving their friends dead or dying on the battlefield. They ran.

***

It was full morning with the sun free of the horizon, blasting the wasteland between Bethlehem and Marisa. The small caravan moved slowly forward. No one spoke, they only shared occasional glances over their shoulders, searching the distance for the followers sure to come.

As they made it to Marisa, the small caravan slowed to a stop. It was time for Simon to say goodbye, whether he wanted to or not. Simon had played his part, a significant part at that. And God liked him. And he got to meet God's son.

Simon rode slowly to the front of the small group and dismounted from the horse and unleashed his donkey. "I can't thank you all enough. This has been beyond wonderous, I have no words for my gratitude. Thank you, all of you."

Joseph helped Mary off the wagon. She was still weak but wanted to thank Simon and say goodbye properly.

"Be good, young man. Thank you." Mary hugged him tightly and kissed his cheek.

He blushed and smiled. "You're welcome. I'm honored I could be part of all of this. Goodbye, friends. Please stop by if you ever travel through these parts again." Simon waved, then climbed onto his donkey and headed toward his home.

"He's a good kid," Roger said.

Joseph and the Wise Men nodded.

"We should get going." Joseph helped Mary back into the wagon. "The big red guy may have stopped the other soldiers, but we can't count on that. Sooner or later, someone will be coming after us."

They pushed on for another hour when they saw a lone man ahead of them standing directly in their path. They approached cautiously, not knowing what to expect. As they got closer, Roger, Maggie, and Joseph recognized the scrawny old man, and it brought a smile to each of their faces. They slowed the wagon and horses, stopping just short of the old man.

"It's good to see you again," Roger said.

"Likewise," Michael replied.

"Are you here for us?" Roger asked.

"Not exactly. I'm here to help you get to your destination. You're being followed. What's left of the Germanic Guard is on foot chasing you. The funny part is they're gaining on you. You people ride slow."

"We can't ride too fast with a newborn and new mother. Should we be worried?"

"No. I'll handle it. It's what I do. You folks have a nice, safe trip."

"Thank you. I hope we meet again."

"We will."

They waved as they pulled away. The tension of looking over their shoulders expecting the worst melted away. They began to laugh and talk openly about how scared they had been. The trip to Egypt was uneventful from that point forward, and for that they were grateful.

***

The Germanic Guard stopped briefly for water and a bit of rest only twice. Otherwise, they ran. It was easy to track the wagon and Gundahar knew that they would catch up eventually. His men did not complain. They kept up with him the entire way, with none falling back or requesting a break. The ground was uneven and difficult to traverse in sandals, but still they continued.

Gundahar saw a small person ahead in the distance directly in their path, and soon the others saw him too. They continued running toward the solitary figure and saw he was a frail old man dressed in rags. They slowed as they approached, not out of fear, more out of curiosity. Gundahar examined the old-timer closely, noting his skin-and-bone appearance. He looked like he was at death's doorway, but something about his eyes did not seem right. They appeared sharp and bright, like he knew something they did not.

The Germanic Guard was never heard from again.

46

ROYAL WARNING

Herod sat in his study waiting, with Tobias at his side. They each had a cup of wine but had not taken a drink as that would be rude. Their guest was overdue but would be there shortly. Herod received word that Augustus was sending an envoy. There was no mention of the purpose of the visit, only that one was coming. He then received word that a full complement of Roman soldiers was marching toward the palace. Herod considered it overkill, arriving with a large show of force. It was unnecessary and uninspired. Octavian should know better.

"Any idea what this is about?" Tobias asked.

"No." Herod was in a mood. Tobias left it at that.

After several uncomfortable minutes, a servant tentatively entered the room. "I beg your pardon, Your Majesty. Lucius Magonus brings word from Augustus."

Lucius Magonus stepped forward and bowed. "It's a pleasure to see you again, Herod the Great."

Herod stood. "Lucius, I'm pleased Octavian sent you. It's nice to see you again, my boy. And how is our exalted Emperor?"

"It's still Augustus. Augustus is well, and the Empire thrives. He sends greetings."

"It's a pity he couldn't make the trip himself. It would be nice to see my old friend again. It's been far too long. Please sit, join us. Tobias, pour the man some wine. We must have a toast to our brilliant leader." Herod trudged through the tired pageantry of social graces. He had played this game far too long. The expected niceties made his stomach queasy; it was all so phony. Yet this was the dance that was expected.

Lucius accepted the cup and raised it in the air. "To Augustus, long may he reign."

"Long may he reign," they repeated and had a drink. The three men sat.

"I'm surprised and pleased to see you, but also curious as to what brought you all this way. How can I be of service?" Herod asked.

"Augustus has heard troubling news from Judaea. One of the things he likes best, about you and Judaea, is that he never hears troubling news from or about you. That has recently changed. There was public outrage, outrage that made its way all the way to Rome. Is it true that your men slaughtered women and children in Bethlehem last month?"

Herod looked down at the table. "Sadly, it's true."

Lucius Magonus looked confused. "You admit this? This was something you ordered?"

"My men slaughtered children and several women in Bethlehem. But no, it was not something I ordered. My Germanic Guard went rogue. They went to Bethlehem in the middle of the night, killing children. God only knows why. My Celtic Guard tried to stop them. By the time it was over, the Celtic Guard were all dead, and whatever remained of the Germanic Guard deserted. It was a tragedy on many levels. These two generals were my friends. I can only assume that something drove Gundahar mad. Nothing else makes sense. A tragedy, indeed."

Lucius paused to take in the king's story. "Your general went mad and took his troops to Bethlehem where they killed only women and children. That's the story you want me to take back to Augustus?"

"That's the truth of the matter. He went mad, or someone pushed him too far. I can't begin to guess what would cause such an action."

"So, it had nothing to do with rumors of a messiah being born in Bethlehem and you trying to kill it before said messiah could dethrone you?"

"There are always rumors of a messiah in Judaea. I have dealt with those rumors my entire career. I got over them long before you were born."

Lucius Magonus stared blankly at the king. Herod could tell he was processing what Herod had just said versus what was reported to Octavian and could not get the two ends to meet. Herod merely stared back at the young emissary, waiting for him to decide. Nothing is more useful in a negotiation than silence.

Lucius shook his head. "I'll return to Rome and tell Augustus exactly what you've told me, about your rogue general. Is there anything else you would like to add before I leave?"

"There is nothing more to add," Herod said.

Lucius downed the rest of his wine, bowed to Herod, and left. Tobias and the king sat silently for several minutes.

"Do you think he bought that?" Tobias asked.

"No, I don't. He's a sharp kid. But my story is what he'll report to Octavian."

"It was serious overkill to bring all those soldiers for a five-minute meeting," Tobias said.

"That was a message, a very clear warning. The emperor is not pleased. The next time he feels the need to send soldiers to Judaea, there won't be a messenger with them."

"So, you just got your hand slapped."

"I just got my one and only warning."

47

EGYPT

Just east of Alexandria on the shore of the Mediterranean Sea, a young woman sat on the beach watching her husband and child play in the sand. The sun was shining, and a gentle breeze blew her long, black hair off her shoulders. She closed her eyes and tilted her head back to feel the warmth of the sun on her face. The sound of the waves on the shore soothed her soul.

It had been a year since they escaped Bethlehem and made their way to Egypt. Roger and Maggie had stayed with them for a while, but ultimately had to return to Nazareth. The Wise Men checked in from time to time, giving them news of the happenings in Judaea. Gaspar and Ella got married on that very beach just last month. It was fun seeing them so happy together, and their wedding reception was one of the craziest parties Joseph and Mary had every experienced. The alcohol flowed like a fountain. Mary was introduced to her very first hangover.

Mary looked down to the water's edge where Joseph and Jesus were playing in the sand. They were digging a trench from the water to a small pool they dug out that would fill with water each time a wave came in. Jesus was unsteady on his feet but had learned to walk. The sand proved tricky for him, however, and He found Himself on His butt after every six or seven steps.

They had purchased a small home a few blocks from the beach. Though she missed Nazareth terribly, their new home was nice. It was comfortable and off the beaten path. They used false names while they were here and blended in as much as possible. They hadn't made many friends in Egypt, mainly because they felt it was a temporary situation, but also because they needed to stay hidden in case Herod was still searching for them.

They longed to hear of Herod's death so they could return to Judaea, to Nazareth. Each time they received news about home it included a report of how crazy and feeble the king was becoming. Last year they all speculated that Herod was sick; this year it was obvious to everyone. His health was failing.

Joseph was expanding the little pond while Jesus giggled and splashed in the water. The pond was about a foot deep and was continually fed from the waves, keeping a constant water elevation. Jesus picked up a shell that He found hilarious, holding it above His head as He laughed.

"Mary! Mary!" a voice called from behind her. She turned to see the Wise Men, Ella, and Aaron walking toward them in the sand. She quickly got up and ran to them.

"Hey! I didn't think we'd see you for a while. How are you?" she asked.

"All is good in our world. How are you guys?" Gaspar asked. "How's the Baby?"

"He's walking now. He was close when we saw you last month, but He's all over it now. I can barely keep up. Come, let's go down to Joseph and Jesus." Mary led them down the beach to her family. Aaron ran ahead, laughing, to play with Jesus.

"That's quite a lagoon you two are making," Balthazar said.

Joseph was a little startled by Balthazar's voice. He had been focused on the task at hand and hadn't heard their approach above the sound of the surf. He smiled and stood.

"Balthazar, Mel, and the happy couple, it's so good to see you all. I didn't expect to see you so soon; it's only been a month," Joseph said.

"We couldn't bear to be away too long, we missed you so." Melchior blew Joseph a kiss and winked.

"Smartass."

"I'm curious." Balthazar stroked his beard. "I hope you don't take this as rude, but how has it been raising the Son of God? Anything strange? Has He started parting puddles like Moses?"

Mary laughed. "Nothing like that. He's a good kid. He rarely cries, He smiles all the time, He's super curious about everything and likes to see things up close. He's great. So far it's been easy."

"Must be nice. Aaron was a little monster," Ella said.

"Seriously, what brings you guys?" Joseph asked.

"Good news brings us. Really good news. We couldn't wait to tell you. Herod is dead. You can go home to Nazareth," Balthazar said.

Mary chirped out a little cry, placed her hands over her face and began jumping up and down. Joseph smiled wide as a small tear crept out of the corner of his eye.

"Joseph, we get to go home! Can we go today? I miss my family so much."

Joseph shook his head. "Me too. Today is a little soon, we have to make some preparations. But tomorrow or the next day for sure."

"So how did the evil bastard die? Did someone finally kill him, one of his family perhaps? That would be poetic justice."

"No, nothing so dramatic. His sickness finally overtook him. There were a couple weeks where no one saw him, rumors that he was bedridden in terrible pain surrounded by his doctors. Soon after, they announced he was dead," Melchior said. "They had an opulent, kingly funeral, and I have no doubt they're hard at work creating statues to honor the man."

"I'm glad he's dead," Ella said.

Gaspar shrugged. "Me too, but the next one might be just as bad."

"Who is king now?" Mary asked.

"No one. The kingdom was divided between Herod's three sons. Augustus didn't grant them the title of king, so each is to rule his own territory as governor, I guess."

"Which one rules Nazareth?" Joseph asked.

"Antipas rules Galilee. I don't know much about him," Gaspar said. "Yet."

"I don't care about any of that right now. I just want to go home," Mary said.

Joseph heard the boys playing off to his right.

"How do You do that? How does He do that?" Aaron was asking.

Joseph turned to see. His mouth gaped, and his skin went pale. He reached out and grabbed Mary's shoulder. "I think we spoke too soon. I think things are about to get very difficult with this one."

Mary turned to see Jesus standing bent over with His hands on His knees, giggling uncontrollably. He was standing in the middle of the lagoon that He and Joseph had created. He was not standing in the water. He was standing on top of it.

"How does He do that?" Aaron asked again.

Mary's eyes grew wide, and she brought her hand to her mouth. "Oh, Jesus Christ!"

ACKNOWLEDGMENTS

I am eternally grateful to my wife, Sheila, who accepts (or perhaps tolerates) my writing obsession with patience and grace. I fully expected to be buried in a shallow grave in the pollinator garden while she helped the search party look for me elsewhere. Instead, she offered support and priceless advice. Thank you, Sheila. I love you.

I would like to thank my editor, Krystyl A Garrett, for helping make this the best book it could be. Her suggestions were both insightful and necessary. She's done more to improve my writing than any MFA program. I'm glad she didn't charge per correction. The bill would look like the national debt.

Thanks to Scotty's Midwest Writers for accepting me into their circle of wonderful misfits. It was a nice welcome to a strange new world.

Special thanks to Holly Miller (former Senior Editor of the Saturday Evening Post) whose reaction to the first chapter helped me believe I was onto something special.

Big thanks to Pastor Steve for convincing me that the majority of faithful people would recognize that a humorous story can also be respectful.

Thanks to my friend Ted Blahnik for providing me with a better understanding of Albert Einstein.

And finally, thank you. Yes, I mean you. You know who you are.

(This is to cover my ass in case I forgot anyone. I'm sure I did.)

DJ O'Toole is an American writer living in Indianapolis, Indiana. His short stories have won awards from Writer's Digest Magazine and the Midwest Writers Workshop. He is the best writer you've never heard of... (if you ignore talent, grasp of the English language, story arcs, character development, sentence structure, and imagination). He is currently wanted in twenty-eight states for adverb abuse. And yes, as appalling as it is to put in print, he dangles his participles.

Made in the USA
Columbia, SC
06 December 2021

50195583R00183